LEADING RESEARCH UNIVERSITIES
IN A COMPETITIVE WORLD

LEADING RESEARCH UNIVERSITIES IN A COMPETITIVE WORLD

ROBERT LACROIX and *LOUIS MAHEU*

Translated by Paul Klassen

McGill-Queen's University Press
Montreal & Kingston • London • Ithaca

KH

ISBN 978-0-7735-4477-2 (cloth)
ISBN 978-0-7735-8483-9 (ePDF)
ISBN 978-0-7735-8484-6 (ePUB)

Legal deposit first quarter 2015
Bibliothèque nationale du Québec

Printed in Canada on acid-free paper that is 100% ancient forest free
(100% post-consumer recycled), processed chlorine free

McGill-Queen's University Press acknowledges the support of the Canada
Council for the Arts for our publishing program. We also acknowledge the
financial support of the Government of Canada through the Canada Book
Fund for our publishing activities.

Library and Archives Canada Cataloguing in Publication

Lacroix, Robert, 1940–
    [Grandes universités de recherche. English]
    Leading research universities in a competitive world/Robert Lacroix &
Louis Maheu; translated by Paul Klassen.

    Translation of: Les grandes universités de recherche.
    Includes bibliographical references and index.
    Issued in print and electronic formats.
    ISBN 978-0-7735-4477-2 (bound). – ISBN 978-0-7735-8483-9 (ePDF). –
    ISBN 978-0-7735-8484-6 (ePUB)

    1. Universities and colleges – Ratings and rankings. 2. Universities and
colleges – Research. 3. Universities and colleges – Finance. 4. Education
and globalization. I. Maheu, Louis, author II. Klassen, Paul, translator
III. Title. IV. Title: Grandes universités de recherche. English

LB2331.62.L3213 2015   378.007   C2014-905955-8
                                           C2014-905956-6

This book was typeset by Interscript in 10.5/13 Sabon.

3/2/16

CONTENTS

Tables   vii

Acknowledgments   xi

Preface   xiii

1 The Emergence of the Research University   3

2 University Rankings   12

3 The International Distribution   36

4 The University System in the United States   48

5 The University System in the United Kingdom   85

6 The University System in Canada   118

7 The University System in France   158

8 A Broader Analytical Framework   196

9 Conclusion: The Future of Research Universities   219

Notes   245

References   259

Index   269

TABLES

2.1   Frequency of universities in ARWU and THES,
       2003–2010   26
2.2   Differentials in university rankings for each year in ARWU
       and THES   27
3.1   Distribution of world-class universities by country,
       2012   37
3.2   Macroeconomic indicators   42
3.3   Country performance relative to the United States   44
4.1   Funding of university-based research by source and
       category of university, Group of 37, United States, 2008–
       2009, in thousands of US$ 62
4.2   Funding of university-based research by source and
       category of university, Group of 200, United States, 2008–
       2009, in thousands of US$ 63
4.3   External research funds per professor and graduate student,
       United States, 2008–2009   64
4.4   External research funds per PhD graduate, United States,
       2008–2009   65
4.5   Funding of operating expenditures by source and category
       of public university, United States, 2008–2009, in thousands
       of US$ 66
4.6   Funding of operating expenditures by source and category
       of university, Group of 37, United States, 2008–2009, in
       thousands of US$ 67
4.7   Tuition fees paid in the various states of the US, 2009   69
4.8   Full-time university students by level of studies and
       category of university, Group of 37 and Group of 200,
       United States, 2009   72

A-4.1   Operating cost per full-time student, in US$, United States, 2009, public universities   84

A-4.2   Operating cost per student, in US$, United States, 2008–2009, private universities   84

5.1   Funding of university-based research by source and category of university, United Kingdom, 2009–2010, in thousands of US$ 101

5.2   Sources of operating funds, United Kingdom, 2009–2010, in thousands of US$ 104

5.3   Distribution of students, full-time equivalent, by level of studies and category of university, United Kingdom, 2009–2010   107

5.4   Research spending per professor and postgraduate student, United Kingdom, 2009–2010, full-time equivalent, in US$ 112

6.1   Sources of university R&D funding, Canada 2009, millions of CAN$ 133

6.2   External research funds by source and category of university, Canada 2007–2008, in thousands of CAN$ 135

6.3   External research funds by source, region, and annual mean, Canada 2000–2008, in thousands of CAN$ 137

6.4   Operating expenditures by category of university, Canada, 2007–2008, in thousands of CAN$ 138

6.5   Funding of operating expenditures by source and university, 2007–2008, in thousands of CAN$ 139

6.6   Funding of operating expenditures by source and region, Canada–Quebec, 2007–2008, in thousands of CAN$ 140

6.7   Distribution of full-time equivalent students, by level of studies and category of university, Canada, 2007–2008   142

6.8   Distribution of full-time equivalent students, by region and level of studies, Canada–Quebec, 2007–2008   143

6.9   Operating costs per student, by group and by province, Canada, 2007–2008   145

6.10   Research income from external sources, by professor and by full-time equivalent student, in CAN$, Canada, 2007–2008   146

A-6.1   External research funds by source, Group of Six, Canada, 2007–2008, in thousands of CAN$ 154

A-6.2   Operating expenditures, Group of Six, Canada, 2007–2008,
         in thousands of CAN$ 155
A-6.3   Funding of operating expenditures by source, Group of Six,
         Canada, 2007–2008, in thousands of CAN$ 156
A-6.4   Research income from external sources, by professor and
         by full-time equivalent student, in CAN$, Canada, Group
         of Six, 2007–2008   157
7.1   Funding of operating expenditures by source and category
         of university, France, 2009, in thousands of US$ 179
7.2   Distribution of full- and part-time students by level of studies
         and category of university, France, 2009–2010   181

ACKNOWLEDGMENTS

Preparation of this book benefited from assistance provided by the Centre for Interuniversity Research and Analysis on Organizations (CIRANO). Claude Montmarquette, president and chief executive officer of CIRANO, believed in this project and provided us with both intellectual and material support. His comments and suggestions also contributed to improving our manuscript.

We received support from various colleagues in the form of interviews and the provision of information on the university systems in which they are active. Some of them also agreed to read and comment on earlier versions of this manuscript. We wish to particularly acknowledge the support of Bernard Belloc, former president of the Université de Toulouse 1 and former adviser to the French president; Marcel Boyer of CIRANO; Marcel Fournier of the Université de Montréal; Howard Green, who served at Staffordshire University and on the Council for Graduate Education of the United Kingdom; Ian Haines, formerly of the London Metropolitan University and executive secretary of UK Deans of Science; and Neil MacFarlane of Oxford University.

We also benefited from the suggestions and comments of colleagues who evaluated our manuscript at the request of the publishers. Their input made a real contribution to its quality. The outstanding translation work of Paul Klassen will make our book accessible to an English-speaking readership with an interest in the future of university systems and research universities. And Gillian Scobie added a very professional edit to this version of our manuscript.

Ji Jia and Julien Tousignant, research assistants at CIRANO, provided us with ongoing help in the collection of data and information on various national university systems, while Nathalie Bannier for-matted several versions of the manuscript.

Ryan Van Huijstee, managing editor at MQUP, showed a great deal of interest in our manuscript and made significant contributions in the form of suggestions, comments, and thoughtful input. Finally, this version of our manuscript benefited from thorough indexing by Vicki Low.

Finally, we are very grateful to Ginette and Céline. Understanding the time and investment that completing this book required, they both gracefully provided us with sustained and appreciated support throughout its writing.

We wish to express our profound gratitude to these individuals, and we assume full responsibility for any remaining flaws or merit in this work.

Robert Lacroix
Louis Maheu

PREFACE

During thirty-five years or more spent in academia working as professors, researchers, and managers, we have had the opportunity to forge close ties with colleagues and institutions in many countries. Participating in projects evaluating different university systems has given us an intimate familiarity with the academic milieus of various geopolitical entities. This cumulative experience has strengthened our conviction that universities everywhere have a major impact on their environment, be it through scientific advancement, knowledge transfers, or the training of a highly skilled labour force.

With the proliferation of knowledge, academia has seen the rise of a particular type of institution with an even more pronounced impact on society: the research university. Owing to its high research intensity and advanced training in research, the research university plays a role that is both more direct and more central, not only in scientific advancement, but also in the broader economy and the society in which it is rooted. The research university is thus a distinct form of academic institution.

Like many other observers, we have been struck by the fact that research universities not only engaged on a path of sustained development, but also acquired greater visibility. The international reputation of some of the leading research institutions is not a new thing, of course, but we observe that those institutions are receiving more attention and publicity, especially in the case of some US universities. This phenomenon, which we explore below, is not surprising.[1] Many other countries have shown great vigour in this domain, though some have outperformed others. It appears that national systems differ in their ability to promote and sustain the emergence of world-class institutions, among other things.

Some voices denounce the impact of globalization – and the associated international rankings – of universities, concerned that it could inexorably result in ever-increasing uniformity. We will be looking at this issue against the backdrop of how research universities are embedded in their milieus. That is the purpose of our book: to obtain a clearer picture of the elements that shape the prospects of research universities in a variety of national settings. There is every reason to believe that such an examination will not bear out the belief that these institutions are being irresistibly driven toward uniformity. To this end, we have to begin by defining a methodological approach that is both rigorous and relevant.

Our work is divided into nine chapters. The first is a retrospective of general trends that have appeared in university systems over the course of the past century. We focus on a very specific strand. We seek to illustrate how research, and more particularly the discovery of new knowledge, emerged and progressively became the domain of universities. We note here that, while all universities profess a deep respect for knowledge and the spirit of research, their missions and the core functions they assume are not all the same.

Our second chapter deals with traditions that have evolved, especially in the United States, to evaluate the activities of universities and to rank them. We will see that these exercises were particularly targeted at research universities from the beginning. When China set its sights on integrating into the knowledge economy, it had to choose what kinds of universities it wanted to foster. Accordingly, Jiao Tong University created an international comparison, the Academic Ranking of World Universities (ARWU), which sent shock waves throughout many industrialized countries following its release in 2003. These types of rankings are generally national in scope, but their extension to the international sphere quickly became inevitable. The ARWU ranking system was followed the next year by that of the *Times Higher Education Supplement* (THES), which is still being issued, though with some major changes. Many other, more targeted, international rankings have been devised since then.

We are not uncritical boosters of university rankings, even international ones, being too well acquainted with their limitations and flaws. The results of these rankings must be used with care and discernment and require the utmost in acumen. The two rankings we use (ARWU and THES) will primarily allow us to establish university samples distributed across various countries, which we can use to delve more deeply into our research questions. The results of these two rankings, like those of many others, corroborate the hegemony of the large US research universities. Similarly, they bear out the vigour of the industrialized countries, where the some 400 institutions identified as world-class research universities are largely distributed. These ranking exercises also attest to a very skewed international distribution.

Chapter 3 documents the socio-economic factors that contribute to the strong concentration of world-class universities in the United States, as well as the much weaker concentrations in Canada and Australia. However, this framework and the elements it models do not adequately explain other significant features, such as the excellence of universities in the United Kingdom, for example, or the underperformance of those in the French system.

Using these international rankings as a starting point, we then delve deeper into our research issues. In the case of a smaller group of countries, we use data on either all, or a sample, including the lion's share of universities in their systems (depending on the availability of data) to obtain a greater understanding of the historic development of these institutions. In short, the pool of universities used in each system studied will be significantly larger than that used for the rankings. Reconstituted and extended samples thus underpin an analysis of the specific characteristics of complex university systems.

The second part of this book (chapters 4, 5, 6, and 7) presents a comparative examination of the organizational structures that frame the development of research universities in the United States, the United Kingdom, Canada, and France.

The last two chapters contain an expanded analytical framework and a discussion of the challenges confronting major research universities. In chapter 8 we go beyond an understanding of US domination and the inequalities in the international distribution of world-class universities to examine the key factors and dynamics that characterize the functioning of the observed university systems and modulate the quality of their performance.

While research universities are facing many challenges, in chapter 9 we only focus on the ones that seem most important and might be relevant to a majority of industrialized countries. Thus, focusing principally on US and Canadian universities, we address issues such as the tension between teaching and research, the trend toward privatization, and the more or less sweeping cuts to, combined with greater targeting of, government funding. Finally, we share some observations on the state of education at the level of university degree programs in these two countries, as well as some of the main challenges confronting their PhDs in the current global environment.

A number of university systems are currently experiencing a profound upheaval as they strive to improve the quality and performance of their member institutions, in particular research universities. We trust that the fruit of the research presented in this book will help to define policies that will facilitate this transformation.

Robert Lacroix
Louis Maheu

LEADING RESEARCH UNIVERSITIES
IN A COMPETITIVE WORLD

1

THE EMERGENCE OF THE RESEARCH
UNIVERSITY

Research universities are a recent phenomenon. For many centuries, until the time of the industrial revolution, universities played only a limited role in training the workforce and developing production techniques. Few in number, and attended by a minuscule proportion of the population, they were places that provided training to practitioners of the liberal professions and to clerks, in government and the church, and that safeguarded and transmitted the legacy of learning.

Research, as an experimental procedure conducted in a spirit of discovery, first appeared in German universities in the nineteenth century, notably guided by the ideas of Humboldt. However, this did not occur without some dispute and wrangling, because integrating research and teaching under the same roof was not a self-evident proposition. Even today, universities who have succeeded in this are very rare and represent only a fraction of institutions in the higher education system. We will return to this issue frequently.

William Clark[1] documents how young professionals in German universities of the second half of the nineteenth century slowly abandoned encyclopedic reference texts in their courses and seminars in favour of information gathered in the field, maps and graphs, catalogues, and lists of specialized data. These professors increasingly based their teaching on recent or ongoing scientific advances. At the same time, a movement requiring that students' work be modelled on the scientific research conducted by their teachers was growing. Students were thus challenged to perform academic work that was related as closely as possible to the work that formed the basis for the teaching they received. This required initiating students into the methodological skills, greater analytical and theoretical knowledge and tools, as well as expert tips and tricks, needed to facilitate data collection, experimentation, and analysis.

Against this backdrop, many German post-secondary institutions and universities strove to stand out as modern universities by combining teaching and research, which in turn benefited a growing academic labour market. It is noteworthy that this drive to train and hire individuals who placed a high value on generating new knowledge by means of the experimental process also corresponded, at least for a while, to a period of great expansion of knowledge in several disciplines. Many of these new scientific processes were sufficiently documented and mastered from the theoretical and conceptual perspective to be easily transferred into course materials suitable for higher education.[2]

The upshot was that integrating teaching and research was, for a time, a key vector of the functioning of prestigious German universities. Soon however, as Ben-David emphasizes, real difficulties became apparent. The system of chairs that were occupied by a single distinguished professor was not conducive to an effective deployment of the new scientific disciplines, in particular those that primarily attracted the interest of younger professors and the new class of research professionals. Moreover, some of these disciplines had not yet attained a sufficient level of new knowledge formalization to make them suitable for translation into a course syllabus; they were more in the nature of an on-the-job apprenticeship in the new techniques and analytical frameworks. In general, the need for new types of knowledge did not extend beyond the demands of the academic milieu. Finally, some rapidly expanding scientific disciplines, such as physics, splintered into many sub-specialities that ran up against resistant academic structures. Furthermore, in this discipline in particular, very expensive equipment was required for exploration and experimentation activities.

In short, by the end of the nineteenth century the innovative philosophy of combining and integrating teaching and research, as promoted by the Humboldtian vision, was facing many hurdles. As a result, some research universities ended up delegating experimental research activities to in-house institutes under the aegis of individual professors – thus keeping them separate from their core operations. Institutes for basic research, parallel to the university system but lacking a teaching mission, were subsequently founded and financed from the same government funds.

Thus, in an ironic turn of events, the cradle of the research university movement gradually grew some distance from that model of a modern university. Then, paradoxically, at the beginning of the twentieth century, the ideal of combining and integrating teaching and research once again gave rise to the development of the modern research university, but this time in North America. Thanks to their strong commitment to basic research, to contextualized and applied research, and to training researchers, some institutions in the US national higher education system have asserted themselves as prestigious research universities.

The socio-economic backdrop against which US research universities experienced their rapid growth brings us forward to a much more recent stage in the evolution of scientific knowledge and the trends shaping the rise of a highly skilled labour force. Increasingly throughout the twentieth century, and especially during the second half, firms in the manufacturing sector have come to understand that maintaining the momentum of the industrial revolution requires a systematic use of knowledge. Specialized labour became an essential input into growth and, as a consequence, the crucial role of the institutions responsible for its training manifested itself.

In many countries, lively debates sprang up regarding the contribution of contemporary universities to knowledge that is useful and that can be applied to improving welfare. In Great Britain, for example, the debate opposed proponents of a university that imparts core knowledge and the basic habitus of the educated mind, on one side, to advocates of extending professional training to the specific service of industry, on the other. Newer institutions, such as the "Red-Brick Universities," proved more receptive to this latter vision. These were founded in the early years of the twentieth century in the main industrial cities of Britain, offering an education that emphasized natural and applied sciences and engineering.

A similar movement was born in the United States starting in the second half of the nineteenth century and progressing in fits and starts throughout the twentieth. The states of the union were endowed with federal lands that they could sell for funds to devote to founding institutions; these Land-Grant Colleges, most of which became Land-Grant Universities, were the forerunners of the public university system. These institutions, which later also received earmarked subsidies from the federal government, were particularly mandated to pursue practical instruction, especially in agriculture and mechanics. It should be noted that these institutions notably distinguished themselves from private universities by their mission of providing instruction that was responsive to the surrounding civil society's requirements for training and specialized knowledge. We know that today, in highly industrialized countries, more than 70 per cent of newly created jobs require post-secondary education, a large portion of which is from universities.

The twentieth century was also a period during which the experimental approach had a pronounced impact on new scientific knowledge and technologies. This knowledge has percolated through several levels of higher education systems, in particular within North America. Further along we will specify, for example, how and why the institutional structure of US research universities has fostered the proliferation of scientific discoveries in the academic milieu. Also, this knowledge, as well as the research professionals who mastered it, soon became more accessible to organizations and firms, and thus contributed to socio-economic development. Competition driven by new products and techniques flourished, becoming even more intense after the Second World War. Accordingly, a growing number of firms took on a new function, research and development (R&D) – which was specifically tasked not only with improving existing products and techniques, but also with discovering new ones. Even firms with no in-house R&D department sought to innovate by assimilating new products created by their suppliers and partners.

Overall, the acquisition of new knowledge and the application of existing knowledge were increasingly used by firms as a preferred means of improving their competitive positions. The design of goods and new techniques, as well as their production and distribution, has become increasingly sophisticated. Industry's demand for a skilled, or even highly skilled, labour force thus experienced strong and sustained growth. Universities were increasingly harnessed to meet not only their own needs, but also the need for a labour force whose principal vocation was in manufacturing and industry.

RESEARCH UNIVERSITIES AS A REFERENCE STANDARD

Since its appearance in Germany and its subsequent consolidation with new structural forms in the United States, the research university has become a point of reference and a standard with strong ideological overtones. In most societies today any university that takes itself seriously claims to be a research university. Indeed, the very term suggests an academic institution that assigns great value to the spirit of discovery as constituting the very basis of research activity. It also implies that these academic institutions strive to infuse their education with materials and programs imbued with the latest findings of scientific research. This term also accounts for ongoing efforts by academic institutions to ensure that a spirit of discovery, and the promotion of research and its spinoffs, combined with a critical capacity to assess its theoretical and methodological foundations, shape the culture of its students.

Assuming this label, and referring to this standard, thus shows, first and foremost, the quality and the seriousness of the university mission and the programs universities offer. It is not surprising, then, that most, if not all, of the institutions in a given national academic system will attempt to pass themselves off as research universities.

More rigorous differentiations between academic institutions must, nonetheless, be made. The specific mission and offerings of institutions constituting a national university system are not all totally equivalent.

This observation is all the more evident when we provide more concrete, precise, and comparable measures of the distinct contributions made by the assorted academic institutions. They differ, in fact, in many ways: their academic programs; their coverage of subjects and disciplines; their effective research practices; the specific expertise of their faculty members; and the relative weight they give to instruction at the graduate level, in particular doctoral and postdoctoral – all of which constitute the scope of their educational mission.

It has been possible to make these distinctions for a number of years now, because responsible agencies in various countries have provided the relevant classifications. The idea of the research university, in this context of institutional classification, thus assumes a much more precise meaning. Rather than invoking a reference point or standard, it differentiates between academic institutions on the basis of their specific missions and unique outputs.

THE RESEARCH UNIVERSITY
AS AN INSTITUTIONAL TYPE

During the post-Second World War period a number of US institutions stood out for their intensive research efforts and an equally pronounced growth in training in advanced research. The Carnegie Foundation contributed a great deal to popularizing the term "research-intensive university," based on classifications, regularly updated from 1970 until today, that were applied to the vast network of US universities.

The traditional classification by the Carnegie Foundation uses the dominant educational programs in a given academic institution to identify its specific mission. It classifies institutions that focus on undergraduate education, such as liberal arts colleges, separately, on the basis of this fundamental approach, differentiating them from institutions that, in addition to teaching at the undergraduate level, also include master's degree programs, such as in certain disciplines of the arts and sciences, or professional master's programs.

The Foundation also has a classification that accounts for the characteristics of so-called research universities. The main criteria on which the Carnegie Foundation characterizes and classifies US research universities have been accepted and refined over many years. Since the category of research university proposed by the Foundation has acquired widespread exposure, it is worth taking a closer look at it.

According to the Foundation's methodology, research universities are institutions that offer a broad and rich array of undergraduate studies. These form the base of their diversified pyramid of teaching programs. These institutions are further characterized by the fact that the peak of their pyramid reflects the weight they assign to teaching at the upper graduate levels, in particular those centred on research, in a number of different disciplines. Moreover, to be considered a research university, the institution must award a certain, by no means inconsequential, minimum number of PhDs in any given year. Of course, the greater the difference between this threshold and the actual number of PhDs awarded, the more firmly that university is entrenched in the elite group of institutions characterized as research universities.

The other criterion for being called a research university is that the institution must carry on a large amount of basic research. The intensity of this effort will be measured by the magnitude of research grants received by its professorial-research staff from funding agencies that base their allocation decisions on the peer review process. Also, to be considered a research-intensive university, the classification requires that, over a given number of years, an institution receive a minimum, by no means inconsequential, amount of such subsidies. Here again, the greater the excess of the research subsidies received over the threshold, the stronger the institution's attachment to an elite group of research-intensive universities.

At the end of the twentieth century, drawing from a sample of over 4,000 US universities, including some with and some without a faculty of medicine, the Carnegie Foundation counted only a few hundred universities (approximately 300, in fact) that met the afore-mentioned criteria for research-intensive universities.[3] We observe that, according to this classification, fewer than ten per cent of US institutions can be considered research-intensive universities using the Carnegie Foundation's criteria.

In the United States, being a research-intensive university thus involves more than simply asserting the claim, or trying to effect that status by alluding to the reference point or standard of a research university. To legitimately claim to belong to this class of institution, or to be classified as such by external agencies that base their ratings on concrete criteria, a university must adhere to specific parameters and standards every year that objectively distinguish it from other academic institutions. In chapter 4, we will look in more detail at two essential characteristics of the US university system – the differentia-tion of institutions on the basis of their primary mission and the con-centration of the mission of research university in so few institutions.

We note that these two iron laws of the development of the US university system are also true, up to a point, of higher education systems in other countries we have selected. We will examine those in detail below.

WORLD-CLASS UNIVERSITIES

In recent years international attention has been focused on universi-ties with such strong reputations that they can be called world-class. This is largely based on their exceptional performance in research, teaching, and the global reach of their graduates. Moreover, it is quite clear that this recognition refers not only to the results of comparative assessments, but also to a hierarchical ranking of uni-versities. In the same vein, such recognition stems from a focus on benchmarking exercises which, now at the international level, add to academic institutions' assessments and rankings. These are increas-ingly common in a number of countries.

In chapter 2 we will look in greater detail at these national and international ranking exercises. There we will develop more detailed, critical, and comparative assessments and distinctions for the methodologies and criteria that have been deployed in various international efforts to rank universities in the past ten years.

For the moment, we will simply identify the primary characteristic shared by all the institutions that stand out internationally for purposes of selecting, from a relatively large pool of candidates, the top 200 or 400 in the world. The vast majority, even the totality, of these institutions are research-intensive universities. Of course, not all institutions with the status of a research university in any given country will belong to this elite international club, but all those that do qualify are research universities.

However, it must be emphasized that a national university system cannot fulfill its mission of teaching, research, dissemination, and networking with the surrounding community by putting all its eggs in the research-university basket, even if the latter are world-class. On the contrary, other ingredients are essential if it is to fulfill its multiple vocations. As we see from the US example, high-quality institutions are needed to provide undergraduate education in key disciplines in the arts and sciences, humanities, biomedical sciences, and professional training. What is required are institutions that are solidly anchored in each nation's different regions, capable of contributing instruction and research practices that foster local potential while generating visibility and a significant return on a national and, in some cases, international scale.

Ensuring vigour and dynamism in a national system of universities requires bringing together a diversity of institutions able to make high-quality contributions in their specific areas of excellence. We will return to this subject at the end of this book. However, there is another characteristic that is increasingly essential to a high-quality national system of academic institutions: It must feature research universities that are not only successful, but that can position themselves as world-leading contenders.

This constraint is all the more binding when this national university system is located in a country that posts a high research intensity and is part of a knowledge economy. As we know, knowledge economies largely rely on their scientific accomplishments and discoveries and on technological and organizational innovation for their economic growth and the welfare of their citizens. Analysts identify explicit relationships between research intensity, as measured by the share of gross domestic product dedicated to investments in science and technology, and economies that are driven by the creation of new knowledge and the transfer of specialized know-how.

We also know that knowledge societies and economies are distinguished by a particular type of human capital. Research has established that countries on the frontier of scientific and technological innovation have a tendency to rely on highly skilled workers with a knack for creating and innovating, generating new knowledge, and imparting advanced training at the higher levels of graduate education, especially at the PhD level. Conversely, countries farther from this scientific and technological innovation frontier have a tendency to mostly rely on a labour force that has a less advanced university education but is skilled in transferring specialized know-how.[4] All of this is to say that in a national university system, research universities, indeed world-class universities, play a special and vital role.

2

UNIVERSITY RANKINGS

Since our ultimate goal is to obtain a broad overview of world-class universities and explain their international distribution, we need a reasonably accurate picture of what and where they are. In this chapter, we will take a look at university rankings to gain a better understanding of their rationale, their relevance, and their relative value. This information will provide the basis for the choice of the two international ranking systems we will subsequently use.

NATIONAL RANKINGS

Over the course of the twentieth century, and more particularly after the Second World War, the roles played by universities in the industrialized nations changed substantially. The factors driving this historical trend included an expanding demand by business for a more skilled labour force, the proliferation of major scientific discoveries, strong post-war economic growth, and favourable demographics.

In addition to training the labour force, universities were increasingly tasked with meeting the demand for innovation, and entirely new relationships arose in industrialized countries between the agents who create new knowledge (academic, governmental, and industrial). Basic research, which is highly concentrated in academia, continued to play a central role, and the work forces of countries at the forefront of scientific and technological innovation have been increasingly characterized by higher education, in particular at the master's and doctoral level.

This centrality of universities, which has now become indisputable, provides the backdrop against which the new tradition of university rankings has assumed a growing significance. The trend first appeared domestically in a few countries, then spread to the international level.

A Tradition Rooted in Academia

The first decades of the twentieth century saw the emergence of attempts to evaluate and rank doctoral programs in US universities.[1] Though specifically designed to assess these programs, they soon became ranking operations as the assigned scores gave rise to hierarchical orderings. By extension, the rankings of the best programs tended to carry over to the institutions hosting them. Also, these assessments were primarily based on the judgment of a sample of peers. Faculty members from selected universities were invited to evaluate programs in their own disciplines. The quality of a given program was inferred from the professional reputation of the faculty responsible for it. This reputation, evaluated in an increasingly rigorous manner, soon became a trademark of these evaluations. Over the years, more objective measures were introduced: research funds awarded by granting agencies, success in publishing research, and awards received.

All these changes accentuated the trends, mentioned above, from an evaluation to a ranking of programs, and then from a program ranking to a ranking of the institutions hosting them. Forces and pressure groups from within academia itself contributed to these drifts.

These trends were accentuated by the Carnegie Foundation, an organization with close links to the world of higher education. Its classification of institutions on the basis of their core teaching programs was seminal, despite the fact that the Foundation resisted treating it as a ranking operation. However, competition between academic institutions to attract the best students and professors and acquire the most resources for teaching, higher education, and research, soon resulted in the Carnegie Foundation's classification operations being diverted from their initial objective.

What began as a simple classification of institutions on the basis of their offerings and specializations soon gave rise to judgments, or to promotional and advertising campaigns. During the 2000s, the Foundation opted to make significant changes to its classification operations. The methodology it chose now allows for classification by broad program type: undergraduate, graduate, professional training, etc. A single institution might now stand out for the large number of degrees awarded in several categories or, conversely, be strong in a specific category, such as graduate programs, while posting relatively mediocre results elsewhere.

It should be noted that the tradition of classifying research universities remains strongly entrenched. In this vein, The Center,[2] originally from the University of Florida, which specializes in evaluating universities, publishes an annual assessment of these institutions on the basis of nine criteria. These are mostly objective and quantitative, such as research funding, awards and recognition received by the faculty, doctorates awarded, number of post-doctoral researchers, etc. To be included in the sample, an institution must have attained a certain threshold of federal research subsidies and be among the top twenty-five institutions in at least one of the nine criteria used.

This evaluation leads to a ranking of institutions, both private and public, as a function of the position shared by variably sized groups of research universities posting similar results for the nine performance and yield factors measured. The institutions are thus ranked in categories, with each level containing more than one university. Institutions at the same level are subsequently ordered alphabetically.

The Entrance of Mass Media

Evaluations and rankings soon outgrew their origins in the ivory towers and were taken up by the marketplace of general circulation mass media. Whether for youths seeking a good university education or employers desiring excellence in their staffing choices, information on the relative performance of universities acquired a strategic importance. In fact, university rankings reflected a double trend toward, first, mass higher education and, soon thereafter, mass graduate education, including advanced training in research.

Consumers' need for information thus became a market. Suddenly, these evaluations extended beyond graduate studies and embraced all levels of university education. Contributions to research, associated with publications in scientific journals, were not overlooked – especially in light of the fact that they, like some other elements, such as libraries, computer infrastructure, and access to financial resources, provide key indicators of the quality of an institution and its faculty members. While more or less systematic rankings of universities had been part of the US landscape for over a century, the entry, in 1981, of *U.S. News and World Report* into the field inaugurated the era of mass media.

Assessing, ranking, and classifying academic programs is thus a very new activity. From their roots in academia early in the last century, these exercises have mutated and expanded to become the domain of general-circulation mass media over the past thirty years, a short tradition, in light of the fact that universities have been around for over one thousand years.

Why did this process of evaluating and publicly ranking universities first appear in the United States? Because the US had the greatest need for this type of information. Compared with other industrialized countries, it was in the United States that recourse to a highly trained labour force with a university education and the intensive use of R&D by firms developed most rapidly. Over the course of the twentieth century the United States became the torchbearer for innovation in all sectors of the economy. This unique economic development created a strong demand for highly qualified workers and new skills. Americans understood, very rapidly and before everyone else, the key role of universities and university education in a knowledge society and economy.

Furthermore, geographical mobility was always a key part of the American way of life, and businesses came to expect it of their management. One implication of this mobility of families was the mobility of their children, who tended to receive their education from a variety of establishments. Moreover, since post-secondary education was far from free in the US, students, and their parents, wanted to be sure of a good return on the substantial investment they were making in university. For some time, this particular confluence remained unique to the United States – the first country to experience the dual move toward mass higher education and mass graduate training. It was to meet this latent demand for information that the first systematic ranking of universities by mass media appeared in the United States.

These US university rankings have been changing constantly over the past thirty years, but from the beginning they revealed a strong differentiation between universities. In its most recent ranking, *U.S. News and World Report* proposes a division into four categories.

The first category is **national universities**. This group includes 262 establishments (164 public and 98 private) that offer a full slate of undergraduate and master's programs alongside a considerable number of doctoral programs. In general, these universities finance their research with funds received from the federal government.

The second category is **national liberal arts colleges**. This includes 266 establishments, of which 28 are public. These institutions emphasize undergraduate education and must award at least 50 per cent of their degrees in disciplines in the liberal arts, such as languages and literature, biology and life sciences, philosophy, psychology, etc. The third category is **regional universities**, which includes 572 establishments, of which 254 are public. They offer the full slate of undergraduate programs and a certain number of master's programs. However, they offer few, if any, doctoral programs. The last category is **regional baccalaureate colleges**. This category includes 219 establishments, of which 76 are public. To belong to this category, at least 10 per cent of all the post-secondary degrees awarded by the institution must be bachelor's degrees.

The indicators used to assess the relative quality of an establishment deal with both inputs, the resources devoted to the educational mission, and outputs, the quality of education received. To measure an institution's quality, the indicators used by *U.S. News and World Report* can be grouped into seven broad categories: peer assessments; graduation and retention rates; faculty resources; student selectivity; financial resources; alumni giving; and graduation rate performance, which compares expectations at admission with the results obtained. The raw data are mostly from questionnaires completed by the establishments and cross-checked with publicly available information.

We note that *U.S. News and World Report* also evaluates and ranks PhD programs in over 1,500 graduate schools in US universities. This program-based ranking draws on questionnaires asking directors of departments and heads of graduate studies to evaluate programs that are identical to their own, but given elsewhere.

National rankings of this sort subsequently appeared in a variety of countries. Most of these rankings draw principally on the US example, though they are not always able to devote the same level of resources to them.

These rankings, both in the mass media and from academic sources, have been, and still are, criticized by the universities themselves (especially those that fare poorly) and by faculty associations. The main fault found with them is that they are simplistic in light of the complexity of the world of university education and each establishment's unique mission. Many critics maintain that any attempt to capture the quality of an institution that instructs students in hundreds of programs as different as the humanities and medical chemistry, from the bachelor's to the doctoral level, with a weighted aggregation of a handful of global indicators, is quite simply impossible.

These criticisms are not baseless, even though existing rankings are not, in general, widely incompatible with the subjective perceptions of those in the know. If that were not the case, it would be hard to imagine how they could have lasted for nearly a century, taken on a whole new aspect in the past thirty years, and become a fixture in many countries. Their growing influence on the choices made by students and the behaviour of institutions would also be difficult to explain. Students, parents, and even governments tend to welcome them. A university fares poorly in the rankings when its professor-to-student ratio is high, it has lagged in adding to its library, its class size is high, its faculty is deemed relatively lacklustre, and services to students are lacking, etc. We may reasonably doubt that marginal differences in these aspects translate into a marked difference in the quality of education, but when the differences are large there can be no doubt. Of course, these quality differentials can often be attributed to differences in access to public and private resources. Nonetheless, the fact remains that the differentials exist and can be measured by various means.

INTERNATIONAL RANKINGS

The internationalization of universities that has been ongoing for at least two decades is quite remarkable for its form, scope, and pace. However, to truly understand what sets the current situation apart, it is useful to look at what was happening in the period from the 1950s until the 1970s.

The main poles of attraction for international students in that era were the United Kingdom for students from the Commonwealth, France for students from its former colonies and the Francophonie, Germany for students from Northern Europe, and the United States for students from everywhere. In the communist bloc, Moscow also had its own sphere of attraction.

In each of these countries, a small number of universities received the lion's share of foreign students, a significant proportion of whom were enrolled in graduate programs. In Britain, these were Oxford, Cambridge, the Imperial College of London, and the London School of Economics; in France, the Sorbonne and some of the *Grandes Écoles* and *instituts* played this role; in Germany the main universities were in Berlin, Munich, and Frankfurt; and in the United States, many universities, including Harvard, Yale, MIT, Stanford, Princeton, and Chicago, attracted foreign students. These universities did not actively recruit international students. On the contrary, most of them had extremely strict admission criteria and restrictive quotas. Foreign students educated in these establishments generally went on to become the backbone of the university systems in their home countries.

For reasons already mentioned, in the post-war period there was a surge of student enrolments throughout the industrialized world, especially between the mid-1950s and the mid-1980s. As a consequence, in many countries a tide of students swept into mass higher education systems, first at the undergraduate and then at the master's and doctoral levels. This is the global backdrop against which the new emerging economies of the twenty-first century must be understood. These economies, the uncontested leaders of which are China, India, and Brazil, have experienced spectacular growth during the past fifteen years. This growth is not only quantitative, but also qualitative, in the sense that these economies produce an ever-expanding array of goods with high value added and require a more skilled labour force. Since these emerging economies did not have an academic infrastructure capable of satisfying the demand for higher education, a large potential market appeared for universities in the developed world.

Clearly, many universities that sought additional revenues and an improved reputation saw an opportunity and seized it. International students, who generally pay higher tuition than domestic students, became a source of income that allowed these institutions to improve the services offered to the entire student body. Furthermore, upon returning to their home countries, these students frequently became ambassadors for their alma mater, further enhancing its name and prestige. Some countries even went so far as to articulate a national policy to promote international expansion of what they now treat as a higher education industry. Australia is a case in point for this, but other countries have striven to imitate it with varying degrees of success.

This is a completely new ball game. No longer is an elite of top international students seeking admission, mostly in graduate programs, to a small number of the most prestigious universities in the world. Rather, a very large number of universities of varying quality are chasing international students for all levels of education. We should point out that, while the prestige schools in the United States, the United Kingdom, Germany, and France that were attracting foreign students in the 1950s and 1960s have made few, if any, changes to their quotas and the rigour of their admission criteria, they continue to attract the cream of the crop among international students. It is the other universities that have launched themselves wholesale into international recruitment to, among other things, reap the windfall and enhance their reputations so as to alleviate shortfalls in their funding and competitive positions.

The significant increase in the international mobility of university students, the generally high cost of studying abroad, and the international scope of the market for academic reputation have all created the same need for information on the quality of universities that the United States experienced in the early 1980s. This set the stage for the first large-scale international rankings of universities, many of which, like the initial rankings of US universities, first appeared in academia. Of all these international rankings, two came out annually and became the most publicized, the most widely disseminated, and the most used by both students and the universities seeking to attract them.[3] One of them, the Academic Ranking of World Universities (ARWU), from Shanghai's Jiao Tong University, originated in academia and was first published in 2003. The other, associated with a general circulation newspaper (*The Times*), is the *Times Higher Education Supplement* (THES), which first appeared in 2004.

We see that this is a very recent phenomenon, but one that has nonetheless shaken up the universe of leading universities around the world. This new trend is reminiscent of some aspects in the development of evaluation and classification exercises that US universities went through. It is, for example, fostered by both academia and mass media. And while they strive to rank the same universities, their approach and criteria are very different. One uses reputational measures, including assessments from peers in various scientific disciplines, whereas the other eschews them. Surprisingly, it is the ranking that comes from the university setting that rejects these measures of reputation.

Academic Ranking of World Universities (ARWU)

This ranking was created by a group of researchers from the Jiao Tong University Institute of Higher Education in Shanghai to situate Chinese universities among the world's leading universities. In light of the many challenges involved in collecting data from the establishments themselves, this group decided to only use data that were already available at the international level and to avoid surveys of peers, leaving it with only six indicators.

The **Quality of education** is measured by the number of graduates from the institution who have been awarded a Nobel Prize or a Fields Medal.

Quality of faculty is assessed using two indicators. The first is the number of Nobel Prize or Fields Medal recipients, and the second is the number of faculty members featured in the list of the most cited researchers in twenty-one scientific fields, as compiled by Thomson Scientific, over a twenty-year period.

Research output is measured with two indicators. The first is the number of articles the faculty has published in the journals *Nature* and *Science* over the past five years. The second is simply the total number of articles published, according to data from Thomson Scientific, with a special weighting on articles in the social sciences.

The **Per-Capita performance** of an institution is measured by dividing the sum of the five indicators just described by the number of professors.

The institution that has earned the highest total is given a score of 100 for each indicator, and the totals of all the other establishments are pro-rated to assign a score from 0 to 100. Subsequently, the same normalization and prorated assignment of scores, both for the leading institution and for all other establishments, is used for the aggregate of all the indicators.

The authors of this ranking began by analyzing some 2,000 universities, of which only 500 were retained for their final ranking. They then listed the top 100 establishments in order, grouping the remainder by 50s up to the 200th, and then by 100s.

First released one year before the *Times* list, this ranking was highly publicized, but also subject to severe criticisms from all corners.[4] The first criticism was that all the indicators in this ranking were limited to the research aspect, and even there it performed very poorly. Moreover, many critics believe that measuring the quality of teaching by the number of graduates who have received the Nobel Prize or the Fields Medal is unconvincing for two reasons. First, there are nearly 20,000 universities in the world. The probability of a graduate from any one of them receiving a Nobel Prize is extremely low, notwithstanding the fact that many of the universities may, in fact, provide excellent training. Moreover, Nobel Prizes are usually awarded late in life. How can we be confident that the quality of teaching of the Nobel laureate's alma mater has been sustained over such a long period?

The first Quality of Faculty indicator used by ARWU, the number of faculty members in an establishment who have received a Nobel Prize or a Fields Medal, is faulted for the same reasons. Indeed, considering the number of Nobel Prize recipients who are still active in academia, the probability of finding even one within any of the 20,000 universities is vanishingly small. Furthermore, in light of the average age of these Nobel laureates, it is far from certain that they are still among the most active and innovative professors and experts in their field of specialization. Conversely, it might be thought that these Nobel laureates will always be strong advocates of an environment that fosters excellence and will thus push their respective institutions in that direction. This should have a positive, if indirect, effect on the quality of faculty in a university.

The second Quality of Faculty indicator, the number of professors who are on the list of the most cited researchers, also suffers from underlying biases. The first bias is its strong weighting toward the natural sciences, thus putting universities specializing in the social sciences at a disadvantage. The second bias is that any publication in a language other than English has a dramatically reduced chance of being cited. This might give universities in the English-speaking world, in particular those based in the United States and the United Kingdom, a certain edge. However, it must be pointed out that English has become the language in which the latest research in the sciences is published, regardless of where it originates.

Research Output is evaluated by two indicators, the first being the number of articles published by an institution's faculty members in the journals *Nature* and *Science*. The second is the total number of publications by the faculty as indexed by Thomson Scientific. We observe that the first indicator is more qualitative, while the second is quantitative. It has frequently been suggested that some measure of the impact of these publications should have been added to incorporate an element of quality into the second indicator.

Finally, with regard to the Per-Capita Performance indicator, we have little information on the source or the accuracy of faculty-related data for institutions. The definition of which positions are considered to belong to university faculties varies enough from one country to the next that the denominator used for this performance indicator raises a number of issues.

We have striven here to account for what we believe to be the most substantive criticisms of this ranking system. An already voluminous literature on the subject continues to grow daily, but with no apparent decline in interest in this annual ranking exercise.

Times Higher Education Supplement World University Rankings (THES)

One year after the *Academic Ranking of World Universities* was released, *The Times* published its own international ranking of universities in the *Times Higher Education Supplement*, in 2004, and the two international rankings that would become an annual fixture were in place. The THES ranking was conducted by the firm Quacquarelli Symonds (QS) with support from Evidence Ltd. The quality of the institutions was initially evaluated on the basis of the following indicators: a peer assessment, the number of citations of articles published by faculty members, the professor–student ratio, and the number of international professors and students. In 2005, an evaluation of recent graduates by their employers was added.

While this ranking was very influential in a large number of countries, the indicators it used were widely criticized.[5] We begin by summarizing the substance of the criticisms, and then look at changes made as of the 2010 edition.

While the choice of a consulting firm with no particular expertise in evaluating research universities was widely denounced, the use of **peer assessment** elicited the most vehement and justified criticism. First, we note that this criterion accounted for 50 per cent of the total score. Though reduced to 40 per cent in 2005, it was still very large. In addition, this initial indicator formed the basis on which 300 universities were chosen, of which 200 were then ranked. This indicator, which we have already noted played a role in the very first evaluations and rankings of US universities, was thus central to the published ranking and its reliability needed to match its weight.[6]

This was not the case. In fact, for the 2004 edition, QS selected 1,300 individuals from the university systems of 88 countries, who were assumed to be able to render an informed judgment. The response rate of those who were asked has not been released, but it appears that new evaluators had to be added to generate the published results. This is not very reassuring from the perspective of methodological rigour. In 2005, it appears that 2,375 "research-active academics" were added for this indicator, doing nothing to alleviate concerns raised about the first sample.

As an indicator of an establishment's quality, **employers' assessments** had no more credence in the eyes of critics. These employers were characterized by THES as "employers of internationally mobile graduates." This sample of employers, created by QS, omitted many categories of employers with the competence to pass informed judgment on the education quality received by new employees who had recently graduated from one of the universities under examination. There was also a suspicion that most of these companies were, in fact, clients of QS, which would be inconsistent with a rigorous selection of firm samples that were representative of the employers' population of high-quality graduates.

A number of analysts also questioned the relevance of **number of international professors and students** as an indicator of an establishment's quality. In his empirical study, Steiner even found that there is no correlation between indicators of the international character of faculty and students and those reflecting academic performance, except in the case of major private US universities.[7] Nonetheless, it seems that universities that accommodate a large number of international professors and students must surely be attractive in terms of both quality and their spirit of openness to the world. These are two characteristics of a great academic institution.

The **student–teacher ratio** is certainly a good indicator of the quality of teaching and training. The problem here is more related to the data quality. In fact, the definition of who is a university professor varies considerably from one country to the next, and it is far from obvious that the THES performed the necessary normalizations. Similarly, the number of students attending a university must not only be obtained, but it must also be normalized to account for the actual status of these students in any given year. Here again, there are questions regarding what was actually done. Now, if both the numerator and the denominator are suspect, we can have very little confidence in the resulting ratio.

The **number of citations per professor** is an indicator that has generally been well received. Even here, however, we find two problems that have no simple solution. First, there is an obvious bias in favour of English-language publications. Of course, since English is the international language of science, an article will be much more likely to be read and quoted if it is published in this language. Second, this indicator also favours the natural and biomedical sciences over the social sciences.

Before turning our attention to the modified indicators in the 2010 edition,[8] let us underline a criticism that applies to all rankings, including the two analyzed here, that create a single synthetic result for each university based on a weighted sum of sub-indicators. The assigned weights are always somewhat arbitrary, but they are definitive for the final result. A small alteration to these weights could completely redraw the landscape of university rankings. Furthermore, many of these indicators are highly correlated, to the point that some are redundant.[9]

We undertook an examination of the stability of the THES and ARWU rankings. Several factors can influence the quality of teaching and research and of university life. We will return to this subject, but for now, note that these are the basic factors that the rankings indirectly seek to quantify, each using its own set of indicators. Of all these factors, the following list should be noted: the number and quality of the professors; the extent and quality of physical and computer infrastructure; the scope and quality of auxiliary services; the quality of the students; the financial resources devoted to teaching and research; and organizational structures that can be more or less conducive to performance. These factors change over time, but they change slowly and the impact on an institution's quality is not immediate.

Rankings assess the quality of a university relative to others. Consequently, for a university's position in the ranking to change, there must not only be movement in the factors related to it, but this movement must differ from that of other universities that were previously higher or lower on the scale. As a result, we should not expect to see significant year-over-year changes in these rankings, provided the indicators of quality that are used accurately reflect real changes in the underlying factors. In this context, we would also point out that annual rankings seem excessive to us.

We looked at the stability of the results of these two rankings. First, for both rankings we examined the frequency with which each university that appeared at least once in the 2003–04 and 2010 rankings was present throughout.[10] The maximum frequency will clearly be eight (or seven, depending on the ranking). We would expect some dropping out and new additions, but this should mostly occur at the lower levels, so that most of the 200 should be present throughout the period and report the maximum frequency.

Let us first examine how many different universities went into the annual group of 200 over the sample period. In the case of the ARWU ranking, 238 different universities appeared in the top 200 over the eight-year period. As for the THES, even though the sample period was only seven years, 308 universities, or 29 per cent more than in the case of the ARWU, were required to fill the ranks of the top 200.

To gain a better understanding of the difference in stability between the two rankings, we created a table of the frequency with which universities appeared over the sample period. Table 2.1 below presents the results of these calculations.

We observe a considerable difference in stability between the two university populations. In the case of the ARWU ranking, 171 universities make the top 200 in each of the eight years, and only 18 are limited to a single appearance. In the THES ranking, for which the sample period is shorter by one year, only 117 universities are present in the top 200 in each of the seven years, whereas there are 60 that only appear once. In addition, we also wanted to know more about the stability of the rankings of those universities that remained in the group of 200 throughout the entire period.

To this end, for each university we computed the number of position changes and the sum of the rank distance moved over the entire period for both rankings. When summing up the rank changes we used the absolute rank value, because instability is the same whether the movement is upwards or downwards. These calculations allow us to not only evaluate the stability of each ranking, but also to see whether this stability varies with the position. A few aggregate numbers will suffice to reveal the enormous difference between the two rankings.

Table 2.1
Frequency of universities in ARWU and THES, 2003–2010

Frequency	Number of universities THES	Number of universities AWRU
8	–	171
7	117	11
6	33	7
5	22	7
4	23	4
3	22	8
2	30	9
1	60	18

The sum of differentials for all universities was 6,349 for ARWU and 14,011 for THES. This difference is all the more striking because in the case of THES there are only 117 universities over seven years, as opposed to 171 institutions over eight years for ARWU.

We repeated the calculations for the top twenty and bottom twenty universities in each ranking. For the top twenty universities in each of the rankings, the sum of rank differentials is ninety-one and their mean is 4.5 in the case of ARWU, whereas the corresponding values for THES are 575 and twenty-nine, respectively. Since we also have the number of movements, we are able to compute the mean value of all rank changes in a group. Thus, for the group of twenty top universities, the mean change in rank is 1.6 for ARWU and 5.2 for THES. In the case of the bottom twenty universities, the corresponding values are 9.5 for ARWU versus 24 for THES. So we see that, even in the case of universities at the very top, instability is decidedly greater in the THES ranking. The same calculations applied to the bottom twenty universities of both ranking systems confirm the difference in stability.

Another indication of the instability of the THES ranking is the inexplicable swings in rank that some universities experience. We counted the number of universities that, after appearing in the top forty, were subsequently ranked in the bottom 100, a drop of at least sixty places. In the case of ARWU, only a single university experienced such a precipitous fall, whereas in THES twelve did. The situation is no less revealing for the universities in the bottom forty. We also asked how many universities climbed by 100 places, for example from 180th to 80th position. We were unable to find a single

Table 2.2
Differentials in university rankings for each year in ARWU and THES

	ARWU	THES
Number of universities	171	117
Period (years)	8	7
Sum of differentials, all universities	6,349	14,011
Mean differentials, all universities	37	120
Sum of differentials, top 20 universities	91	575
Mean differentials, top 20 universities	4.5	29
Sum of differentials, bottom 20 universities	1,177	3,271
Mean differentials, bottom 20 universities	59	164

instance of such improbable movement in ARWU, while there were twenty in THES. It appears that the pre-2010 THES ranking was characterized by a large number of biases that affected not only its stability, but even its reliability.

THES strove to make adjustments to account for the widespread criticism of many of these elements, and the 2010 edition was completely redesigned to be, as *The Times* characterized it, "robust, transparent and sophisticated." *The Times* invested ten months in consulting with leaders in academia from all over the world to improve the methodology of its rankings. At the end of this extensive consultation, it not only modified and increased the number of indicators from six to thirteen, but also revised their weighting in the total score to incorporate the feedback and account for each indicator's reliability. *The Times* also improved how the indicators were aggregated to reduce the bias. In addition, to be retained in the ranking, universities must now officially agree to participate in the exercise, to provide data that are specifically relevant to them, and to review the use made of their own data when the indicators are constructed. Though *The Times* prides itself on this new ranking system, it also emphasizes that it will not hesitate to make any further changes deemed necessary and appropriate to ensure quality.

Before proceeding with a summary description of the thirteen indicators, consider the following observations about reputational surveys. We realize how roundly this indicator has been criticized in the past. For the 2010 ranking, *The Times* claims to have 13,388 participants in these reputational measures, and that this survey is now "statistically representative of global higher education's

geographical and subject mix." We note that the number of participants exceeded 16,000 in 2012. Since the survey results account
for 34.5 per cent of the total score (15 per cent for teaching and
19.5 per cent for research), their reliability is central to the credibility of the ranking. All in all, it appears clear that the measures
implemented have improved the quality of this indicator. Furthermore, its weight in the total score has been cut further, from
40 per cent to 34.5 per cent.

The thirteen indicators of the 2010 ranking are grouped into five
categories.

1   The quality of **teaching**, or alternately, of the **learning environ-
    ment**, is assessed using five indicators, the sum of which account
    for 30 per cent of the total score. The indicator with the greatest
    weight in this category (50 per cent of the category and 15 per
    cent of the total) is from a survey of individuals selected for their
    supposed ability to pass an informed judgment on the quality of
    the teaching in institutions with which they are familiar. While
    retaining this indicator, and even assigning a fairly heavy weight
    to it, *The Times* acknowledges that it is difficult to evaluate
    teaching quality, and that the same survey is probably more reli-
    able when it addresses research quality.

    The second indicator is the **faculty-to-student ratio** at the
    undergraduate level, which might also cover the quality of the
    supervision given in an institution. This indicator makes up
    15 per cent of the category, and thus 4.5 per cent of the total.
    This is far from the 20 per cent of the total this same indicator
    amounted to in previous rankings by *The Times*.

    A third indicator considers the **doctorate-to-bachelor's ratio** of
    degrees awarded. This indicator is designed to reflect the research
    environment to which undergraduates are exposed. The under-
    lying assumption is that a denser research environment will
    make the university experience more enriching. This indicator
    makes up 7.5 per cent of this category, and thus 2.25 per cent of
    the total.

    The fourth indicator in this category is the number of PhDs
    awarded per professor. It is clearly designed to reflect the **quality
    of accessible supervision** and the intensity of the research con-
    ducted in an institution. These two dimensions have a positive
    impact on students at both the graduate and the undergraduate

level. This indicator represents 20 per cent of the category, and thus 6 per cent of the total.

The last indicator used to measure the quality of teaching is **funding per professor**. The purpose of this measure is to indirectly evaluate the quality of infrastructure and the various services offered by the university. This indicator is assigned little weight in the category (7.5 per cent) and thus in the total (2.25 per cent).

2   In terms of volume, revenues, and reputation, **research** is evaluated from four indicators that make up 30 per cent of the total score. As in the case of teaching, the indicator with the most weight in this category is a survey of peers assessing the reputation of an institution in the area of research. This indicator makes up 65 per cent of this category, and thus 19.5 per cent of the total.

Added to this first indicator is **research funding per professor**. This is an essentially quantitative measure, useful for its ability to corroborate other, more qualitative, indicators. It makes up 17.5 per cent of this category, and thus 5.25 per cent of the total.

The third indicator in this category is simply the **number of articles per professor** published in the academic journals monitored by Thomson Reuters. The intention here is to measure the success of an establishment's faculty members in having their articles published in peer-reviewed academic journals. This indicator makes up 15 per cent of this category, and thus 4.5 per cent of the total.

The last indicator is the **the proportion of the establishment's total research budget that comes from the government**. Since the structures and details of how research is funded vary considerably from one country to the next, the usefulness of this indicator is not obvious. For this reason, *The Times* assigns very little weight to it, 2.5 per cent of the category, and thus only 0.75 per cent of the total.

3   Closely related to research, but constituting a separate dimension, the third category of indicators deals with **citations or influence of the research performed**. At 32.5 per cent of the total, this indicator carries a lot of weight in the ranking, so it is worthwhile to look at how it is constructed. The raw data are from 12,000 academic journals monitored by Thomson Reuters' Web

of Science Database, and were collected for each university over a five-year period, from 2004 to 2008. In addition, the data on citations were normalized by the mean number of citations in each of the 251 fields of research retained. This considerably lessens the impact that an institution's degree of specialization in a given field of research may have on its performance, thus addressing a criticism that was frequently levelled against earlier rankings.

4   The fourth category of indicators in this ranking is the **international composition of faculty and students**. The international-to-domestic ratio of faculty members accounts for 60 per cent of this category and 3 per cent of the total. For any given university, the reasoning underlying this indicator is that its ability to attract professorial staff from all over the world indirectly reflects how it is perceived internationally, while also testifying to its degree of openness compared with that of other major world-class universities.

The same principle applies to international students. This second indicator makes up 40 per cent of this category, and thus 2 per cent of the total.

5   The final indicator is the sole component of the fifth category: the **contribution of industry to the university's funding**. Even though *The Times* appears to believe that this indicator provides useful information about a university's capacity to innovate, the dismal quality of the raw data has led them to assign very little weight to it (2.5 per cent).

Overall, the 2010 edition of *The Times* ranking draws on a broader set of indicators and is a clear improvement in terms of reliability. Moreover, the fact that the ranked universities not only agreed to participate in the exercise, but also cooperated in the construction of some databases and verification of the results for certain indicators, provides some reassurance as to the professionalism of the overall operation and minimizes the potential for nonsense results. That being said, the considerable weight (34.5 per cent) that this ranking continues to assign to the results of a reputational survey provides fodder for ongoing scepticism, even though the number and quality of respondents has been greatly improved. This scepticism is particularly pronounced with regard to the teaching indicator.

Finally, we observe that in assigning 65 per cent of the weight to indicators related to research, this ranking predominantly, if not exclusively, favours the leading research universities. That raises the legitimate question of whether a university that is not one of the main universities in both research and training in graduate studies can plausibly aspire to be considered a world-class university. As we have already said, we believe the answer must be "no."

The new approach to ranking adopted by THES in 2010 had a marked impact on the level of comparability of the results from the two rankings. Indeed, while the rank correlation coefficient for these two rankings was only 0.58 in 2009, it rose to 0.77 in 2011, and even 0.85 for universities in the top 20 per cent.

In conclusion, we believe that this final configuration of *The Times's* rankings is a game changer. It appears to be destined to become the benchmark for international rankings.

REACTIONS TO UNIVERSITY RANKINGS

We have already indicated that there are clear signs of the influence these university rankings have had in some countries. In this section we will examine how these rankings, especially at the international level, might have affected the decisions and behaviour of actors who are directly and indirectly associated with academia. Of course, this includes the universities themselves, students, and their parents, but also governments, donors, and professors.

In our capacity as members of a major research university's upper management, we ourselves have reacted to these rankings, and have witnessed the reaction of other universities with which we were in contact, or even competition. The initial response of a university that feels it has been slighted by a ranking will be to question its quality and relevance. This can only go so far, however, since universities that have done well in the ranking very quickly learn how to capitalize on the results. These results can, for example, greatly facilitate an institution's efforts to recruit the best students, convince donors to invest in its excellence, sway governments in its favour in decisions on the inter-institutional allocation of public funds, attract the most promising professors, and raise its profile in the highly competitive market for academic prestige and reputation, on both the domestic and the international fronts.

This is, in fact, how international rankings of research universities are used. As a consequence, universities have begun to search for ways to improve their own rankings by paying more attention to the quality and availability of institutional data, reallocating funds to improve their position in some indicators, pressuring governments to increase funding to universities, actively soliciting support from their alumni, etc.

These somewhat anecdotal observations are borne out by an interesting poll conducted by Ellen Hazelkorn only a few years after the emergence of the two main international rankings.[11] The response rate to this international survey of 639 individuals and institutions was over 30 per cent, with 202 respondents in 41 countries. Over 70 per cent of the respondents confirmed that their institution had been featured in a national or international ranking.

A priori, we should not be surprised that fully 58 per cent of respondents were dissatisfied with their institution's position(s) in the ranking(s). In addition, 92.8 per cent expressed their intention to improve the domestic ranking, and 82 per cent the international ranking, of their institution. What is more striking, because it is mathematically impossible, is that 70 per cent of the respondents would like to see their institution in the top 10 per cent of universities in their home country and in the top 25 per cent of research universities internationally. While the statistical representativeness of this poll is open to debate, it does demonstrate that underneath the purely anecdotal there appears to be a real phenomenon of research universities showing sensitivity to the results of international rankings.

This poll also clearly revealed that universities are not only sensitive to how they place in these rankings, but that they also make use of their results – provided they are favourable. We see, for example, that 50 per cent of institutions say that they have used these results in their advertising.

Of course, they also take steps to attempt to improve their showing. Thus, we learn from this same poll that 56 per cent of respondents have an in-house process for reviewing the rank obtained by their institution – in more than half of cases, this involves the vice-chancellor, president, or rector. Most respondents state that they have launched strategic initiatives or reached academic decisions designed to help improve their placement. Moreover, 76 per cent of respondents admitted that they closely monitor the rankings of other universities in their country, and 50 per cent those of other universities around the world. Several establishments state that they consulted the rankings before establishing a strategic partnership with another university. It is also likely that top-tier researchers do the same before considering a position or a collaboration with another university.

Furthermore, we cannot preclude the possibility that governments follow these rankings closely. Recent decisions made in France in the context of *Plan Campus* were quite clearly designed to improve the rank of French institutions in research universities' international rankings. The former president of France explicitly said as much. Furthermore, even if this is not openly acknowledged, it is highly likely that the decisions of various governments will increasingly be influenced by international university rankings. Rauhvargers provides us with some very convincing examples. Here are two: since 2008, to be eligible for the status of "highly skilled migrant" in the Netherlands, the candidate must have a master's or PhD degree from a recognized Dutch university or from a university ranked among the top 200 by THES, ARWU, or QS. Since 2012 the University Grants Commission of India has required that bilateral program agreements can only be signed with universities in the Top 500 of THES or ARWU.[12]

There can be no denying the impact that national and international rankings have on the behaviour of universities, students, governments, and donors.

Nor should we underestimate the extent to which the universities themselves increasingly use the results of these rankings to establish their strategic orientations and inform their day-to-day decisions. If the impact of these major international rankings was already borne out by a poll just a few years after they began, we can only imagine where we stand five years later.

Thus, it is clear that academia, while continuing to cast a critical eye on these rankings and suggest improvements, will increasingly learn to live with them, even if they remain seriously annoying in some regards.

CONCLUSION

The processes by which programs and institutions are evaluated after taking root over the past decade have, in essence, satisfied an expanding demand for information. The scrutinized institutions pervade the lives of growing societies and the individuals that live in them. Covering ever more countries, these ranking operations have gradually improved as they reacted to a constant barrage of criticism and increasingly relied on the collaboration of the ranked universities. This same process, in place for a decade on the international level, has yielded fruit, especially in the case of THES. However, it seems to us that the annual repetition of these exercises is absurd, serving the interest of the evaluators' publicity more than of their clientèle's needs. As we have said, the factors that determine the quality of an academic institution only change slowly, and annual changes of rank are essentially attributable to the statistical white noise that a five-year cycle would eliminate.

The various analyses of the two international rankings that we performed yield one major conclusion: The pre-2010 THES ranking is worthless. The exceeding instability of this ranking's year-over-year results are compounded by the extreme and inexplicable movements of a large number of universities. The overall impact of these observations is to demolish the reliability and, by extension, the credibility of this ranking.

And to what can we attribute this great instability? Its source is as unique as it is clear. The first reputational survey conducted for the THES ranking, which determines what universities are retained and their position, is at the root of these wild fluctuations. As we have already mentioned, as of 2004 the components and samples of this survey were regularly changed, which only increased the instability of the results. In addition, the number of "experts" called on to assess the quality of the teaching and research faced an overwhelming task in light of the very large number of universities they had to consider at the international level. Reputational surveys may yield credible results within a national university system in which the various members generally know each other very well, but this knowledge of the milieu is considerably lessened at the international level, especially when an expert is called on to evaluate the teaching and research performances of institutions that are not among the thirty universities with strong international reputations.

The THES ranking methodology was significantly improved, as we emphasized above, so much so that our analyses clearly reveal that its results largely converged with those of the ARWU, which only uses quantitative indicators. Indeed, the number of quantitative indicators used by the 2010 THES ranking was increased, the reputational survey of graduates' employers eliminated, and the reputational survey of research and teaching vastly improved at the same time as its weight in the overall evaluation was reduced.

As for ARWU, though the criticisms we have already articulated remain valid, our analyses show that this ranking was more stable and reliable. Unlike in the THES, we did not observe inexplicable and unreasonable movements among the research universities assessed by this ranking year after year. For all these reasons, we limit ourselves in what follows to post-2010 rankings from both the THES and the ARWU.

For our purposes, we will treat the combined results of THES and ARWU as yielding a credible, if imperfect, portrait of the pool of world-class universities. It is on the basis of this pool that we will attempt, in the remainder of this book, to uncover the characteristics of word-class universities and, in particular, explain their international distribution.

3

THE INTERNATIONAL DISTRIBUTION

In this chapter we turn our attention to an entirely different dimension of the international rankings of the best research universities: their distribution by country. We immediately note that the United States has dominated these classifications from the beginning. This raises a number of questions. Is the United States truly as dominant as the data suggest? Are these results primarily attributable to the US's large population and relative wealth? How should we understand the positions of the other countries? To answer these questions, we must begin by building an explanatory model and then empirically testing its predictions.

EXAMINING THE INTERNATIONAL DISTRIBUTION

According to the results in the 2012 edition of the ARWU and THES, seven countries account for 90 per cent of research universities in the global top fifty, 80 per cent of the top 100, 73 per cent of the top 200, and 59 per cent of the top 400. As a result, we decided to use this dominant group as a sample for testing the predictions of our model based on macroeconomic variables. Table 3.1 presents the distribution of the universities representing these seven countries by category of rank.

What does this table tell us? US universities clearly stand out in both ranking systems and in all categories. Those from the United Kingdom generally post a solid second place. Considering the small size of their populations, Canada and Australia are each represented by a respectable contingent of universities in the top 100 and even the top 50.[1]

Table 3.1
Distribution of world-class universities by country, 2012

	Top 50		Top 100		Top 200		Top 400	
COUNTRY	THES	AWRU	THES	AWRU	THES	AWRU	THES	AWRU
United States	30	35	48	52	77	84	106	113
Germany	1	0	4	4	9	13	23	29
France	0	2	4	3	7	8	11	16
United Kingdom	7	5	10	9	31	19	48	32
Japan	1	2	2	3	5	8	12	15
Canada	3	2	5	5	8	8	18	16
Australia	2	0	6	4	8	7	18	15
TOTAL	44	46	79	80	146	147	236	236

Sources: Data from the websites of the two organizations.

In these two rankings the number of institutions in each category is almost identical for all the countries in our sample. Thus, the relative weights of institutions from these countries that stand out among samples of leading research universities are roughly equivalent, if not equal, in these ranking exercises. Of course, there are a handful of differences between the rankings, but not enough to affect the big picture.

THE EXPLANATORY MODEL

In industrial and post-industrial societies, the acquisition of new skills and knowledge drives innovation by firms and entrepreneurs. A firm's growth, or even survival, depends on its ability to integrate new knowledge, compelling it to equip itself with a more or less formally structured capacity for research and development (R&D). This evolution is given impetus by the parallel development of the service economy, which also requires expertise and knowledge.

Faced with the challenges of governing increasingly complex societies while offering their citizens adequate public services, governments must also capitalize on the benefits yielded by research. Post-industrial societies are built on complex planning and management, not only of the various aspects of innovation (including the social), but also of scientific, technological, and environmental risks.

To continue developing, modern societies must thus build on two essential platforms: an increasingly skilled labour force and a constant injection of new knowledge from a multitude of scientific and technological disciplines. We will see how the research university, as reinvented in the United States from its German roots, has become a vital instrument for satisfying these two needs.

Thanks to remarkable advances in scientific knowledge, research universities have flourished to meet an exponential growth in demand throughout the twentieth century. The post-industrial societies that give rise to this demand partially fund these institutions in concert with their increasing reliance on knowledge.

Let us return to the central question of this chapter: What is the significance of the inter-country distribution of the best research universities? We postulate that a principal determinant of this distribution is the global distribution of demand for the main outputs of these universities. In other words, we should find the greatest concentrations of high-calibre research universities in those countries that are most deeply invested in knowledge and where the demand for researchers, specialized workers, and new knowledge is strongest. Comparable levels of demand will be a function, for example, not only of the value of an economy's output, but also of the specific composition of that output. It seems evident that, for an equivalent value of production, a natural-resources-based economy will require a less highly skilled workforce than one that is specialized in knowledge-based goods and services.

It is also clear that societies in the early stages of industrialization will have few, if any, research universities. Moreover, individuals from these countries, having acquired their training in a foreign research university, will very often remain abroad rather than return to their country of origin, where there will be little demand for their skills and expertise.

We conclude from the preceding that at least six factors play a central role in the dynamics of the development and international distribution of research universities.

1   The **total population** of a country constitutes the principal source of potential demand for higher education and graduate studies, including, of course, that part of this demand that is specifically met by research universities. *Ceteris paribus*, among post-industrial economies and societies, a country with twice the population of another should have twice the level of demand for university education at the various levels.

2   The **size of the domestic economy**, as measured by **gross domestic product** (GDP), will have a positive effect on the demand for skilled labour and scientific and technological knowledge. For approximately equal populations, if one country's economy is twice as large as another's, it should have twice the demand.

3   A country's **relative wealth** can be measured by **per-capita** GDP. *Ceteris paribus*, in relatively wealthy countries the demand for highly skilled labour and scientific and technological knowledge should be greater and, by extension, foster the emergence and dissemination of numerous research universities. Indeed, in the case of the wealthiest countries, consumer demand for new goods and services with a high value added should make up a relatively large part of the demand that shapes production decisions.

    Beyond its character as a profitable investment, higher education is desirable in its own right for the intrinsic benefits it can confer. Education enables individuals to acquire greater self-knowledge, be better equipped to understand the world around them, and contribute to local and international cultural exchanges. Empowered to be better citizens, on both the national and the international level, they will have the means to play a not negligible role in the transmission of traditional and new knowledge to future generations in both the private and professional spheres. In wealthier societies, the inherent value of higher education naturally fosters a greater demand for this type of training.

4   Governmental science, technology, and innovation policies vary from one country to another. Public policies aimed at university research funding, development of governmental research, direct financial support to private-sector R&D, fiscal incentives sustaining industrial research activities, appeals to enterprises making intense use of new knowledge, etc., all strengthen social demands for a highly skilled workforce and for new knowledge. These policies support research universities' strategic external benefits and ultimately their relative intensity. In our model, **domestic R&D spending as a percentage of** GDP outlines this factor's impact.

5   It is also worth noting that government policy increasingly targets measures to create a highly skilled workforce. We have attempted to identify the impact of these later policies in terms

of the proportion of a country's labour force with a university (tertiary A) degree.

6　We round out our model of these five macroeconomic variables by adding a sixth. This is an interaction variable, which we call **economic density**, obtained by multiplying GDP by per-capita GDP for each country. Its appeal is that it captures in a single measure many of the factors that have an impact on the demand for university education, especially with regard to research universities. By combining relative wealth (measured by per-capita GDP) with the size of an economy (measured by GDP) we are, in a sense, weighting the size of an economy by a dual factor. This allows us to jointly consider the impact of high incomes on the demand for higher education and on the composition of consumption affecting the industrial structure that will be more centred on the knowledge economy.

The justification for this analytical model thus reduces to the following: The size of a national system of research universities will be positively correlated with the population level and the size, total wealth, and research intensity of the economy – all of which drive the demand for a highly skilled work force and new knowledge. We further assume that, *ceteris paribus*, in any system there is a positive correlation between the total number of research universities and the number of world-class institutions.

Using this analytical model, we can now attempt to explain the international distribution of world-class universities found in the ARWU and THES rankings. If our model does not fully explain this distribution, it must be that there are relevant factors that we have omitted. Even while significantly increasing our understanding of the international distribution of world-class research universities, these factors may fall short of providing a full explanation.

EMPIRICAL RESULTS

To test the assumptions of our model we have chosen six industrialized countries whose performance, in terms of how many world-class institutions they harbour, we compare with that of the United States. They are: the United Kingdom, France, Germany, Japan,

Canada, and Australia. These are countries whose overall development is comparable and which have a long academic history.

The measures used to quantify the impact of the aforementioned factors for each selected country are: population; GDP in US dollars evaluated at purchasing power parity (PPP); per-capita GDP in US dollars evaluated at purchasing power parity; domestic R&D spending as a percentage of GDP; and the percentage of the age 25–64 population group with a university (tertiary A) degree. We use two of these variables, GDP and per-capita GDP, to create an interaction variable that we call economic density.

For each of these variables and for each country in our group, table 3.2 shows the characteristics of the population and of the economy as well as its ranking, as a function of these same variables, relative to the United States.

We first observe that the populations of these countries vary widely, from 21 million in Australia to 315 million in the United States. The potential demand for university education could thus be as much as fifteen times greater in the United States than in Australia; similar ratios position the five other countries relative to the United States. On the basis of this indicator alone, we should not be surprised to find a greater number of research universities and, by extension, a greater number of world-class research universities in the United States than elsewhere.

As we have already said, if the potential demand for university education is to materialize, there needs to be a demand for highly skilled workers to absorb the graduates and also a demand for new knowledge to create a variety of opportunities for scientists within a society. The size of the economy is a first indicator of the extent of these demands.

In every country, the variables for GDP and population move in the same direction, accurately reflecting the relatively similar development levels of countries in this group: the larger the population, the larger the GDP. Thus, in these countries there is an excellent chance that latent demand will translate into real demand for a university-trained, highly skilled labour force.

However, the relative wealth of these populations varies somewhat, as is indicated by per-capita GDP which is, for example, nearly 30 per cent lower in France than in the United States. In this context, our interaction variable between the size of an economy and the

Table 3.2
Macroeconomic indicators

	United States	Germany		France		United Kingdom		Australia		Japan		Canada	
	Number	Number	% relative to US (100)	Number	% relative to US (100)	Number	% relative to US (100)	Number	% relative to US (100)	Number	% relative to US (100)	Number	% relative to US (100)
Population (millions)	315	82	26.0	62.0	19.7	62	19.7	21	6.6	127	40.3	33.6	10.7
GDP (billions)	14,100	3,330	23.6	2,649	18.8	2,175	15.5	925	6.6	5,070	40.0	1,336	9.5
GDP per-capita	46,000	36,300	79.0	33,600	73.0	35,155	76.4	39,500	25.9	32,400	70.4	37,808	82.2
GDP × per-capita GDP (billions)	648,600,000	120,879,000	19.0	89,006,400	13.7	76,462,000	11.8	31,537,500	4.9	164,268,000	25.3	50,500,800	7.8
Gross domestic expenditure on R&D as a % of GDP	2.77	2.64	95.3	2.02	72.9	1.77	63.9	1.97	71.1	3.42	123.5	1.84	66.4
University (ter. A) degree as %	31	17	54.8	18	58.0	28	90.0	26	83.8	25	80.6	26	83.8

Source: OECD: Population: 2009; GDP 2009; GDP/POP 2009; Gross domestic expenditure on R&D as % of GDP: Domestic Expenditures on R&D (as a percentage of GDP) 2008.
University degree: Percentage of the 25–64 age group with a university tertiary A degree, 2010.

relative wealth of its population proves valuable for explaining the distribution of research universities, as recorded by international rankings, among these seven countries.

For the proportion of 25 to 64-year-olds with a university tertiary A degree (bachelor's, master's, and PhD), Germany and France lag behind the United States more than the other countries in our group, all of which have similar results. For this variable as well, the situation of the United States is fully compatible with the strong positions its research universities occupy in the global rankings.

Japan's **economic density** is only 25 per cent that of the United States, whereas its population and economy amount to 40 per cent. The same general pattern is seen among the other countries in our group, though the magnitude of the observed gaps varies considerably from one country to the next.

The variable **domestic expenditures on R&D** as a share of GDP reveal two clusters of countries on the basis of R&D intensity. On one side, we find Japan, the United States, and Germany, characterized by a very high research intensity. On the other, France, Australia, Canada, and the United Kingdom post research intensity results that, while not weak, are not as strong as those in the first group.

The data in table 3.3 show the number of universities from a given country in a specific category relative to total US universities in the same category. For a given country, this will allow us to compare the difference between these proportions with the difference between its economic density and that of the United States, while accounting for the other macroeconomic variables that have been used.

Let us first examine the case of Japan. Since its indicator of economic density is 25 per cent of the corresponding value for the United States, we would expect this country to have a total number of universities in these rankings corresponding to at least 25 per cent of the US total. Moreover, the fact that research intensity in Japan is significantly greater than in the United States, as measured by gross domestic expenditure on R&D as a percentage of GDP, could even lead us to expect a better showing of Japanese research universities in these rankings.

However, as we see in table 3.3, Japan only has, at best (ARWU ranking), 15 universities in the top 400 world-class research universities, corresponding to 13.3 per cent of the US total. Furthermore, looking at the different categories, this percentage falls to 9.5 (ARWU) or 6.5 (THES) for the top 200, 5.8 (ARWU) or 4.2 (THES)

Table 3.3
Country performance relative to the United States

	Top 50		Top 100		Top 200		Top 400	
COUNTRY	THES	AWRU	THES	AWRU	THES	AWRU	THES	AWRU
United States	100	100	100	100	100	100	100	100
Germany	3.3	0	8.3	7.7	11.7	15.5	21.7	25.7
France	0	5.7	7.7	5.8	9.1	5.8	10.4	14.1
United Kingdom	23.3	14.3	20.8	17.3	40.2	17.3	45.3	28.3
Japan	3.3	5.7	4.2	5.8	6.5	9.5	11.3	13.3
Canada	10.0	5.7	10.4	9.2	10.4	9.2	17.0	14.1
Australia	6.7	0	12.5	7.7	10.4	7.7	17.0	13,3

Source: Computed from the data in table 3.1.

for the top 100, and a paltry 5.7 (ARWU) or 3.3 (THES) for the top 50. Thus, when comparing Japanese with US universities, we observe a net underperformance in the number of world-class institutions. We find that there are fewer world-class universities than Japan's relative economic density and research intensity would lead us to expect.

The case of Germany is no less interesting. Its economic density leads us to believe that it should have at least 19 per cent of the US total. Germany's R&D intensity, which is for all practical purposes equivalent to that of the United States, should boost its standing. So what do we find regarding its distribution of world-class universities relative to the other countries in our study?

Germany has, at best, 29 universities in the top 400, 26 per cent of the corresponding US value. Thus, with regard to the number of universities ranked among the top 400 by ARWU, Germany clearly surpasses expectations (7 percentage points above the expected 19 per cent). At 22 per cent, this over-performance is also seen in the THES rankings, though to a lesser extent. However, in both rankings this edge vanishes when we look at the top 200 before becoming a net underperformer in the top 100, and even more so in the top 50. Indeed, Germany is practically absent from this last category. Only in the THES ranking does a single German university make the cut.

Overall, in comparison with the results for US research universities, despite their overrepresentation in the pool of 400 world-class institutions, and contrary to our expectations, German universities do not succeed in placing in the top categories. Just as in the case of

Japan, German universities are absent from the highest categories of international rankings, even though their economic density and research intensity, as well as the number of their universities in the top 400, would all augur well for their performance.

The situation of the United Kingdom is remarkable for a completely different reason. According to our interaction variable, economic density, the number of UK universities in the top 400 should not exceed a total of approximately 12 per cent of the US total, amounting to at most fourteen world-class institutions. Nonetheless, this country manages to place thirty-two (ARWU ranking), or even forty-eight (THES ranking) research universities in the top 400. In doing so, even its weakest performance (in the ARWU ranking) corresponds to 28.3 per cent of US universities in the same category, which is well above the percentage (12 per cent) of its economic density relative to the United States.

To a lesser extent, this over-performance persists in the top 200, top 100, and even top 50 categories of research universities of both the ARWU and THES rankings. It is abundantly clear that the United Kingdom posts the strongest performance of the seven countries being studied (including the United States, whose research universities provide the point of reference) in its relative ability to field a large number of world-class universities, which, moreover, stand out for their presence in the very highest categories of the rankings.

The situation of France is somewhat more difficult, except for the category of top 400 research universities. It barely attains the proportion we would expect on the basis of, for example, its economic density relative to the United States. While not among the very highest, we have already commented on France's solid research intensity, which may have helped its showing. Nonetheless, in comparison with the results obtained by US universities, French institutions post a significant underperformance that extends throughout the category of the top 200, top 100, and top 50, regardless of the ranking considered. For the higher categories, French universities report results that are, *ceteris paribus*, below what we would expect on the basis of its economic density relative to the United States. In this regard, France's situation is comparable to that of Germany.

The total population of the two remaining countries in our sample is significantly lower than the average of these five. This is, in particular, the case with Australia and its 21 million inhabitants. While its economic density relative to that of the United States suggests it should have something on the order of six or seven universities in the top 400, Australia is, in fact, represented by fifteen or eighteen, depending on the ranking used. Compared with the results for US universities, we see this over-performance of Australian institutions carrying over into the top 200 and top 100 before weakening in the top 50.

With a population of 33 million, Canada is a small country by the standards of our group. On the basis of its economic density relative to that of the United States we would expect a maximum of eight or ten Canadian institutions in the top 400. Moreover, Canada is characterized by one of the lowest research intensities in the group. Only the United Kingdom is lower in this factor.

In fact, Canada has no fewer than sixteen (ARWU) or eighteen (THES) universities in the top 400. This over-performance can be seen to persist, though to a lesser extent, through the top 200 and top 100. In these two categories, Canada posts a higher proportion of research universities than we would expect relative to US universities in the same category. Canada also has its fair share of research universities in the top 50. Like Australia, we find that Canada performs very well.

We can now draw a few conclusions on how successfully this model of macroeconomic variables explains the inter-country distribution of the best world-class research universities as classified by the ARWU and THES rankings. Overall, the empirical results corroborate our expectations that the countries with the highest economic density tend to have a greater number of universities in our two international rankings. Nonetheless, we remain confronted by two issues: Some countries surpass the expectations formed on the basis of our macroeconomic variables, while others fall short. Second, the predictions of our model are even less satisfactory in the higher categories of the two chosen ranking systems. This initial approach, though useful in some respects, must clearly be complemented by a more detailed analysis of actual higher education systems.

WHAT'S NEXT?

It seems clear to us that the next step is to take a closer look at the various organizational and institutional features of national higher education systems to pursue our investigation more deeply.

We are not the first to have taken this path. Several researchers have already looked at the specific characteristics of national higher education systems to better understand the factors that determine their performance. While their initial standpoints may not have focused on exactly the same issues as we have, their work and conclusions might still prove useful. In the following chapters we will strive to understand the various organizational and institutional features of national higher education systems as they foster or hamper the performance of research universities likely to distinguish themselves on the international level.

To pursue this train of thought, we have chosen to examine some specific national university systems. The selected systems – for reasons that will become clear in the following chapters, they are the university systems of the US, the United Kingdom, France, and Canada – will provide more informative results on the specific factors that determine their positioning on the international scale of world-class universities. A selected country's specific type of positioning may, however, be shared by university systems in any number of other industrialized countries.

4

THE UNIVERSITY SYSTEM
IN THE UNITED STATES

In the previous chapter we compared the performance of six industrialized countries with that of the United States, which we had chosen as a benchmark. But how does the United States compare with this subset of the main industrialized countries?

The population of the United States represents 45 per cent of the total population of the seven selected countries, its GDP amounts to 48 per cent of theirs, and its economic density is 55 per cent. It appears perfectly reasonable that fully 50 per cent of the world-class universities in the countries of our sample should be located there, but what do we find in the two international rankings presented in the previous chapter? On average, for the AWRU and THES rankings, the United States accounts for 47 per cent of the 236 universities that these seven countries place in the top 400, 55 per cent of the universities from the same countries in the top 200, 63 per cent of their universities in the top 100, and 70 per cent of their universities in the elite group of the top fifty world-class research universities.

It is this progression from a strong lead posted by US universities in the broadest category of world-class universities to an ever-increasing dominance at higher ranks in the hierarchy that we will now seek to explain. To do this we examine the particular characteristics of the US university system that might affect its performance. We begin this chapter with a brief overview of recent developments in US universities focusing on the environment within which research universities function and trends in the relationship between research and teaching.

Next, we will delve more deeply into certain organizational elements of this system and its research universities: the organization and financing of basic research, structures, and current sources of funding of academic operations and, finally, the ways and means by which the main actors (professors, students, and key administrators) arrive and evolve in these institutions. The critical aspects of each of these components will be highlighted.

In this chapter we will lay the groundwork for a comparative analysis of four selected university systems. In fact, in the following chapters we will closely follow the approach developed here in our examination of the US system.

A BIT OF HISTORY[1]

US research universities are at the very heart of the modern university. From the turn of the nineteenth century through the first half of the twentieth, they diligently clung to a vision of integrating teaching and research in higher education. During the second half of the nineteenth century, American academics and scientists returned from stays in Europe full of enthusiasm about the German model, motivated to start new universities at home that would dedicate a large share of their resources to basic research while coordinating this research with teaching, in particular programs of advanced training in research at the graduate, and especially doctoral, level.

It is generally recognized that one of the first US universities to achieve this vision was Johns Hopkins University in Baltimore. A private university founded in 1876, this institution was resolutely focused on the missions of a modern research university: expanding knowledge through research activities and developing advanced graduate training programs through research, the cornerstone of which would be the doctorate – or PhD, as it's called in the United States. Johns Hopkins University served as the benchmark for the design and delivery of modern and innovative PhD programs throughout the United States.

Although Johns Hopkins University and other US research universities drew inspiration from the German experience when designing curricula and advanced research training programs, the academic mould that shaped the organization within which these elements were to take shape did not have much in common with the corresponding German structures. Thus, we see that basic research was solidly anchored in the US university system from the beginning. This strong bond persists – the United States has never relied on a system of basic-research institutes operating alongside universities and financed from the same government funds to the same extent as some European countries.

Not all universities were mandated with conducting research, but those that were dedicated themselves to the task with great energy and persistence. It should be noted that, in the early days, research universities that systematically integrated research with teaching were on the fringe of US institutions of higher education.

From the end of the nineteenth century and into the first decades of the twentieth, the efforts of US research universities to pursue basic research and develop scientific knowledge received very generous funding from wealthy private foundations. Seasoned observers and specialists were acutely aware of how the United States was lagging behind Europe in fundamental science in many disciplines, so a number of private foundations provided scientists with the infrastructure and resources they needed to make up this lag. Many disciplines in the arts and sciences in various research universities received substantial funding to develop their basic research programs. These major funding bodies were less interested in specific practical applications than in providing support to universities that were actively advancing knowledge in a variety of fields and contributing to training in and through research.

Organizational Innovations

Unlike in Germany, training programs in North American universities were the domain of teachers and researchers grouped into departments. For a given scientific discipline, these groups of professionals collectively assumed responsibility for teaching programs at both the undergraduate and graduate levels. In the specific case of research universities, their responsibilities extended to programming and delivering activities devoted to scientific discovery, exploration, and experimentation while also supporting the discipline's research training environment.

Groups of professors and researchers brought together by their disciplinary affiliation exercised decision-making power within their departments. Based on the autonomy and collective responsibility of the specialists in an academic discipline, university departments gradually asserted themselves as key academic units for the future of US universities. The university department is a core structure in the

US system, and was a major American organizational innovation around the middle of the nineteenth century.

Another organizational innovation marked the development of US research universities. Very early in their history, they created a separation between the tasks associated with undergraduate and graduate studies. The interaction between research and teaching was primarily emphasized for graduate studies. Such a concrete and significant integration was not meant to be imposed on all elements of an institution, or even on all institutions within the US system.

A further component of this academic labour division soon followed: the creation of "graduate schools." In the case of undergraduate studies, departments' core relationships are with the faculty to which they belong (e.g., Faculty of Arts, Faculty of Sciences). However, for graduate studies, especially at the PhD level, these same departments are also closely linked to another university faculty, called the graduate school. This latter, a horizontal faculty, in a sense, has functions that extend across all departments, schools, and faculties of a university, fulfilling objectives related to institutional priorities in the area of graduate studies and links between research and advanced training in research. The functions it performs include coordinating, promoting high standards, exercising quality control, and providing general support to units and actors at the graduate levels.

This vertical division of academic labour in US research universities has played a key role in the remarkable development of these institutions.[2] We must bear in mind that the growing dominance of US research universities is principally due to a series of major organizational innovations that date back to the fledgling research university movement.

Graduates from US higher education programs were looking for advanced training in research in a discipline belonging to the arts and sciences. They wanted careers as research professionals in academia or in a position in which active participation in research was an asset, or even a requirement. From the earliest days of these research universities, and for a long time thereafter, the main job market for new PhDs was in universities.

Two segments of this market were the most active. On the one hand, there were the research universities themselves, in which departments consisting of groups of teachers and researchers worked to develop scientific specializations worthy of a high-quality department. Academic organization, as it shaped the structure of departments, encouraged the proliferation of research professionals, professionals with PhDs who were tasked with providing both teaching and supervision to students. Professors thus collectively assumed the various administrative tasks associated with the effective functioning of the departments. In this fashion, the departmental structure replaced the system that was widespread in many European universities, that of a prominent professor holding a chair in a specific discipline.

On the other hand, the value placed on the spirit of discovery would eventually lead to a sweeping reform of general undergraduate education. An expectation was created that teaching would be up to date and incorporate new knowledge, particularly in light of the fact that students were able to choose some optional courses in devising the program that would lead to their bachelor's degrees. Professors with PhDs offered the new curriculum for this general undergraduate education. The way university education was construed in the United States thus made it easier than in Europe to link research and education together, especially Germany with its gymnasium system. Groups of professors expedited the introduction of research results and experimental frameworks, both theoretical and analytical, starting with bachelor's programs. Students seeking advanced training in research were first required to master the challenges presented by a general undergraduate education, that usually embraced several related scientific disciplines.

A Rapid Expansion

Throughout the twentieth century, and particularly during the postwar period, higher education in the United States expanded rapidly, affecting all segments of the academic job market. With university attendance rates reaching 50 per cent of the relevant age groups, mass higher education had to leave its mark. In fact, we see that growth in the market for higher education at this time was a powerful engine of the development of the university system, particularly the new US research universities.

The market for researchers in academia was complemented by a non-academic demand. Research professionals were notably needed in certain industrial sectors, which were already generating and applying scientific and technological knowledge. These market forces combined to create an environment that fostered the development of research universities, which very quickly surpassed their European counterparts, even those in Germany.

The Second World War presented US research universities with a whole new major reality, and they in turn, beyond helpful scientific equipment and infrastructures, provided the government of the United States with unexcelled clusters of experts and scientists – who were essential to its massive and ambitious military research projects. Key discoveries with far-reaching ramifications for science and technology resulted. The biggest change was that the federal government became a very important funder of research conducted in academia, especially in research universities, entrenching the central role public funding would play in the basic research performed by these institutions. From thereon in, whether private or public, the main source of funds for all institutions was the federal government.

At the end of the Second World War a type of social contract was concluded between research universities, specialized scientific milieus, the firms and organizations of civil society, and the federal government. Vannevar Bush, the president's science adviser at the time, played a key role in elaborating this social contract, which had, and still has, a decisive impact on the development of research universities.

Research universities were mandated to conduct basic research, mostly financed by the federal government through its major research funding agencies, including the National Science Foundation, founded in 1950, and the National Institutes of Health, which have been very active since the mid-1950s. The scientific and academic communities maintained full control over the directions, priorities, and the evaluation of basic research. There was a ready consensus that, with the return to peace, the federal government no longer needed to exercise such hands-on guidance of basic research conducted in academia. Purely applied research could be left in the hands of business, civil society organizations, and government, in accordance with their needs. Furthermore, in specific sectors associated with particular needs in American society, such as agriculture, health, and security, the federal government promoted the development of major laboratories specializing in basic research. This course of action, like the development of private non-profit research organizations supported by philanthropic agencies, was by no means intended to subvert the central role played by research universities in the production of basic research,

A period of strong growth in research and development followed. Prior to 1950, the percentage of US GDP that was devoted to research and development amounted to less than 1 per cent. By the mid-1950s it had surpassed 1.5 per cent, then continued growing to 2.73 per cent in 1960 and 2.98 per cent in 1965. In the early 1970s, this percentage stabilized at approximately 2.5 per cent of US GDP. Also, in 1950 expenditures on higher education did not exceed 1 per cent of GDP. In 1960 they surged to 1.31 per cent of GDP, and then continued rising to 2.22 per cent in 1965 and 2.56 per cent in 1970.

Naturally, basic research performed by US research universities also expanded greatly during this period. In only a few years, between 1960 and 1965, expenditures on basic research rose an amazing 25 per cent.[3] This trend was accompanied by a significant growth in advanced training in research. The number of individuals who obtained PhDs from US universities also grew precipitously, especially after the end of the Second World War. During the 1930s, a little more than 25,000 PhDs were awarded by these institutions. In the 1940s, this number edged up to a little over 30,000, followed by an explosion in the 1950s when the total reached nearly 83,000. In the following decade, this almost doubled to over 160,000, doubling again in the 1970s to 320,000 PhDs awarded.[4]

The next major impetus to increased academic research and advanced training in research came from the American political desire to catch up to the Soviet Union after the successful launch of Sputnik in 1957. The scientific and technological policies adopted required the support of research universities. This is how these core sources of new knowledge increasingly transformed into locations in which graduate students and post-doctoral fellows became researcher-employees under groups of professors. On top of their mandate as science incubators, US research universities had to manage the tensions inherent in their primary mission of integrating research into teaching. To keep up with the growing demand for new technological and scientific knowledge, they were increasingly drawn to research practices that, while firmly anchored in the university, could diverge from their teaching mission to some extent.

In short, the time of the Second World War and the following "thirty glorious years," from 1945 to 1975, were critical and probably unique in the growth of US higher education. This period was principally marked by the spillover effect of the post-war boom on the development of universities, which were expected to absorb a large contingent of veterans. This is also when the contribution of US research universities became essential to both the conduct of research and the training of researchers. The PhD, a degree that is largely associated with these institutions, is inextricably associated with their success and with the remarkable development of the United States.[5]

Today[6]

The severe economic downturn of the 1980s changed everything. Its fallout had a lasting impact on our research issues, setting the stage for how US research universities function and perform today. The major recession of the first decade of the twenty-first century further exacerbated these institutions' challenges.

Since the 1980s the share of GDP dedicated to R&D has remained fairly constant at between 2.5 per cent and 2.8 per cent, ultimately reaching 2.79 per cent in 2008.[7] However, this masks some important shifts, including a remarkable growth in the share of R&D funded by industry. Since 1980 this increase has been on the order of 200 per cent, whereas the contribution of the federal government grew by a mere 20 per cent. Overall, federal money accounted for 70 per cent of investments in R&D and industry's contribution was less than 30 per cent in the mid-1960s, but soon these numbers were reversed. By 2000, industry was providing 68 per cent of R&D funding, whereas the federal government's share was 27 per cent.[8]

Another change was that research performed in academia accounted for an ever-expanding percentage of GDP, rising from 0.23 per cent of GDP in 1980 to 0.303 per cent in 2000 and 0.36 per cent in 2008. To compensate for the weak growth in government funding during these years, US research universities tended to focus more on their own resources. During the 1980s, for example, funds allocated to research by the universities themselves increased by one-third. From 2004 to 2009, while total domestic R&D spending increased by 27 per cent, the portion assumed directly by the universities surged by 44 per cent even as subsidies from the federal government faltered at a mere 17.9 per cent.[9]

Private non-profit foundations have always provided valuable support to research and its associated training in universities. This was no less true during the 1980s. However, more recently the fall-out of the recession had a marked impact on gifts to universities. They have been declining just like university endowments, as observed by the National Research Council's Committee on Research Universities. Though smaller, the contribution of industry to research in academia doubled during this period, rising from 4 per cent of total university research funding in 1980 to 8 per cent in 2000. At the same time industry's own, self-financed level of basic research stagnated, or even declined.[10]

These global shifts in the financing of R&D and university-based research reflect other major changes to the mission of research universities in the United States. Over the course of the past decades they have played an increasingly central role in economic development. While retaining their role in teaching, they have been able to cement their direct role in contributing new knowledge to the economy and to various organizations and firms in the industrial sector. This research aspect was an important way in which academia made a contribution to society and its knowledge-based economy.

We can distinguish two paths along which university research formed links with industry and its R&D sector and fostered the expansion of the new economy. On the one hand, and mostly in the field of natural sciences, university-based research consolidated corporate research efforts. The development and production of goods and products, or even services, arising from this transfer of scientific and technological expertise, remained the exclusive purview of the business sector.

However, on the other hand, and most particularly in the fields of biotechnology and biomedical sciences, university research and industry became more intertwined. In particular, scientific discovery in its own right, and not the products to which it gives rise, became the object of patents. Under these conditions, the basic research underlying a patent may result from collaboration between universities and industrial laboratories. As a result, universities' investments in this research could not be fully disengaged from their interests. Against this background, the commercialization of university research became a matter of course, even though the financial yield to research universities has not been as high as expected.

Such trends have altered the landscape of university research in a handful of disciplines. The contribution of universities to the development of the knowledge economy and its industrial and organizational sector through the production of new knowledge in these disciplines enhanced their legitimacy and credibility. However, it was not without changes that affected the university research scene.

Indeed, the very structures that framed the production of university research were transformed. Among other things, Organized Research Units (ORUs), most commonly outside of the traditional academic structures of departments and faculties, were significantly expanded. In the 1980s and 1990s institutes, centres, and groups of teams and laboratories within academia, while not new, proliferated and became more productive and visible, sometimes in partnership with external agencies. These were dedicated to research efforts that were less directly embedded with teaching. Universities also strove to adopt structures to promote technology transfers, patent applications, and the launch of companies to capitalize on faculty members' scientific and technological discoveries.

Also, as basic research became an engine of the knowledge economy, we note that it did not migrate to government-funded research centres and laboratories that operated alongside universities. On the contrary, it became more deeply rooted in universities, which received a lot of assistance from the federal government and its research funding agencies to sustain their more direct economic role. The 1980 Bayh–Dole Act, which conferred on universities the property rights of patents resulting from research funded by federal governmental agencies, contributed significantly to this trend.

The same principle applied to specific grants provided by the National Science Foundation in the fields of natural sciences, physics, and engineering, and the National Institutes of Health in biomedical and health sciences. It should be noted that progress in the biomedical and health sciences was particularly strong during this period. This was largely thanks to the specific grant programs that encouraged universities to undertake research contributing to economic development and to form partnerships as needed.

We observe, in passing, a key aspect of the type of research taking place in the Organized Research Units described above. Because it is rooted in academia and partially supported by federal funding agencies, this research is subject to peer review. Consequently, the university-based research that is at the heart of the knowledge economy industrial and organizational sector is of very high quality. The pedigree of much of the new science and technology that forms the knowledge economy bedrock is unimpeachable. This large-scale development of new synergies between research activities in academia and the outside world was another typically American innovation that remained virtually unique to the US for many years. One characteristic that stands out with respect to recent developments in research in the United States is the basic research dynamism. The knowledge-based economy in the United States, where it is particularly vigorous, also draws heavily on basic research, which primarily originates in research universities and absorbs approximately 70 per cent of US research funds. US research universities, nurturing a tradition of research within their faculties that hosts professional training, devote 14 per cent of their research funding to the most theoretical and general aspects of applied research. R&D proper only accounts for 2 per cent of their research budgets.[11]

Over the course of their development, and especially since the Second World War, US research universities have seen a significant diversification and remarkable expansion of their missions. Clark Kerr, a key actor and seasoned observer of the US research university scene as well as the former president of the University of California public system, described universities who assume these roles as "multi-versities."[12]

Much more recently, Neil Smelser used the term "structural accretion" to describe the unique evolution of an institution, especially a research university. Over time, missions and functions multiply even as core founding principles and traditional functions are retained. According to Smelser, this type of complex mutation of an entity that nonetheless remains constant and relatively homogeneous is specific to universities. In other areas, institutions confronted with these types of developments cannot adapt to them without sloughing off some of their earlier activities or functions, or even abandoning part of their founding mission. This notion of structural accretion is apt for capturing this particularity of research universities: transformation alongside retention of their founding missions.[13]

In short, despite the permutations in their missions, US research universities continue to aim for and achieve (in most cases at least) an integration of research and teaching. This is attested to by their sustained dynamism in the annual production of training in and through research and the advancement of knowledge. At the same time, they are home to research activities that are produced within organized research units removed from faculties and departments. However, these research units, which are typically non-traditional (for instance, multidisciplinary research centres), frequently contribute research that must fully respect the university-mandated requirements. While focusing on spurring knowledge in a specific field, the research units have done much to stimulate research within and (especially) across disciplines. In many cases their contributions to doctoral and post-doctoral education are renowned.[14]

To recapitulate, despite the many tensions they face in light of the complexity and diversity of their missions (about which we will say more in chapters 8 and 9), US research universities, or at least an impressive number of them, appear to be rising to the challenge. This is amply demonstrated by their standings in international rankings of world-class universities.

PRESENT CHARACTERISTICS OF THE SYSTEM

We have collected data to shed some light on current issues facing US research universities and identify the attributes of a system that has placed such a large number of institutions very high in international rankings. Which institutions should we focus on? We will not cover all universities, or even all research universities, in the United States – that would cast our net too wide. We decided instead to focus on a sample that is large enough to be representative of our target population. What we are looking for are data on the factors that shape the functioning of these universities and thus help explain their international ascendancy. We will not attempt to conduct a thorough analysis of each institution for purposes of comparison with all the others in the sample.

We began by selecting all US universities, whether public or private, covered by data collected by The Center.[15] This organization gathers annual data on research universities in the United States and presents assorted information on the best performers as a function of predetermined parameters. These data cover a variety of information on the activities of research universities. We were most interested in information in the Center's database about funding allocated by the federal government to the top 200 research universities in 2008.[16]

This initial sample, which we selected because it satisfies a key characteristic of research universities – funding allocated on the basis of peer review – consists of 200 universities, 143 of which are public. In addition to the data from The Center, we also acquired information about our sample from the National Science Foundation and the National Center for Science and Engineering Statistics. Since we were unable to find similar and comparable data for all of the 200 institutions retained by The Center, we had to pare our sample down to 176 universities.

From this group we next created a subsample of the thirty-seven research universities that, collectively, awarded 50 per cent of the PhDs granted by US universities between 2002 and 2006. Since the PhD is the signature degree awarded by research universities, this subsample allows us to focus on a particularly strategic aspect. Consider the statement by L. Thurgood et al. From an emerging power on the international scene in 1900, by the beginning of the twentieth century the US had become the world's leading power. The remarkable growth of doctoral education within US research universities figures among the numerous factors nurturing this strength.[17]

The thirty-seven universities in this subsample, both public and private, were identified by a recent evaluation of US research PhD programs conducted by the National Research Council.[18] We were able to gather all the data required by our analysis for thirty-six of these universities.

Note that 113 of the 176 universities we selected are in the top 400 of the ARWU and THES 2012 rankings. The top 200 and top 50 world-class universities from both of these two rankings, include, respectively, 93 and 38 research universities from our sample. Our samples are thus representative of US research universities identified in the ARWU and THES rankings. We point out that a great number of universities in our samples, just like those in the fifty best world-class universities according to both the ARWU and the THES ranking system, are members of the prestigious Association of American Universities (AAU), which has very high standards for research and advanced training in research.

Also, the institutions in our two samples only represent a small fraction of US institutions of higher education. At the beginning of the twenty-first century the US higher education system consists of some 4,000 establishments, of which over 2,300 universities award at least a bachelor's degree, according to The Center. Research universities are only a small fraction of that total. Recall that the Carnegie Foundation identified no more than 300 of them at the beginning of the century. Nonetheless, we believe that the 176 universities in our sample are representative of the pool of research universities from which world-class ones are selected.

Research Activity

Examining the external research funds obtained by both private and public universities in 2008 makes one thing abundantly clear. If we abstract from research funds that the universities generate independently, which are not accounted for in these tables, we observe in table 4.1 and table 4.2 that public universities receive a very large proportion of their funding from government: 70 per cent from the federal government and nearly 10 per cent from state governments. Private universities also receive their share: 80 per cent of their research funding is from the federal government, but much less, of course, from local administrations. As we see from the following tables, both classes of university receive comparable levels of funding from other sources, such as non-profit foundations.

These tables clearly indicate that professors in US research universities, as well as the institutions in which they work, receive a major part of their research funding from agencies financed by the federal government but we see that this research funding distribution by institution is by no means guaranteed. Rather, it depends on the success the faculty members have with these research funding agencies on the basis of a peer review process. The pool of public research funds is not unlimited, and there is stiff competition between professors who regularly submit funding applications. We observe in passing that, contrary to popular perception, funding from private business amounts to no more than approximately 8 per cent of the total, which is consistent with Geiger's reported findings.

The success of US research universities thus springs from a body of high-quality professors who distinguish themselves in national competitions for research resources from funding agencies. This should not be surprising. It is also worth noting that this state of affairs creates pressure on institutions to make the effort to attract, recruit, integrate, and then retain the best specialists, as well as good students, into graduate studies (in particular doctoral and postdoctoral), to the extent that the latter could be instrumental in swaying a professor to opt in.

This snapshot of total research funding from external sources becomes more telling when a denominator is introduced. In that vein, table 4.3 illustrates the relative amounts of research funding from external sources per professor in each of our two samples. Thus we see that professors in private US universities obtain research funding at twice the average of that available to their colleagues in

Table 4.1
Funding of university-based research by source and category of university, Group of 37,
United States, 2008–2009, in thousands of US$

Group	Federal	State/Local	Industry	Other Sources	Total
IN ABSOLUTE TERMS					
24 public of the 37	8,094,287	1,192,253	1,009,317	1,072,732	11,368,589
12 private of the 37	5,813,721	178,614	420,367	732,345	7,145,047
Total	13,908,008	1,370,867	1,429,684	1,805,077	18,513,636
AS A PERCENTAGE BY SOURCE OF FUNDING					
24 public of the 37	71.2	10.5	8.9	9.4	100
12 private of the 37	81.4	2.5	5.9	10.2	100
Total	75.1	7.4	7.7	9.7	100
AS A PERCENTAGE BY CATEGORY OF UNIVERSITY					
24 public of the 37	58.2	87.0	70.6	59.4	61.4
12 private of the 37	41.8	13.0	29.4	40.6	38.6
Total	100	100	100	100	100

Note: The 24 universities covered are public universities from the Group of 37 with the highest
number of PhD graduates. The missing university is City University of New York Graduate Center,
for which we do not have all the relevant data.

the public system. These data also reveal that this trend carries through to funds from industry and other sources, such as private non-profit foundations. Only state-level funding is disbursed preferentially, on a per-capita basis, to professors in public research universities.

As we see in both tables 4.4 and 4.5, these trends remain unchanged to all intents and purposes if we replace the number of professors in the denominator with the number of graduate students or PhD graduates. In fact, private universities are able to provide their graduate students with considerably more generous support from research revenues than public universities. This differential is widely recognized in the area of advanced training in research; PhD graduates in private universities operated in a much richer financial milieu, enhancing the potential of these institutions.

These funding differentials cannot be attributed solely to the relative performance of professors in private universities – the difference in disciplinary resource bases and the intensity of some disciplines in these universities may also be a factor. Nonetheless, the careers of professors in the major private universities receive more support

Table 4.2
Funding of university-based research by source and category of university, Group of 200, United States, 2008–2009, in thousands of US$

Group	Federal	State/Local	Industry	Other Sources	Total
	IN ABSOLUTE TERMS				
120 public of the 200	17,502 748	2,833,908	1,929, 951	2,438,002	24,704,609
56 private of the 200	11,859,072	377,128	938,287	1,453,240	14,627,727
Total	29,361,820	3,211,036	2,868,238	3,891,242	39,332,336
	AS A PERCENTAGE BY SOURCE OF FUNDING				
120 public of the 200	70.8	11.5	7.8	9.9	100
56 private of the 200	81.1	2.6	6.4	9.9	100
Total	74.7	8.2	7.3	9.9	100
	AS A PERCENTAGE BY CATEGORY OF UNIVERSITY				
120 public of the 200	59.6	88.3	67.3	62.7	62.8
56 private of the 200	40.4	11.7	32.7	37.3	37.2
Total	100	100	100	100	100

Note: In light of the diverse sources of data we drew on, we were only able to use 176 of the 200 universities studied by The Center. Of these, 120 are public and 56 are private.

from the funds that the university institutions themselves invest in research. In fact, the private universities' capitalized endowment funds, which greatly exceed those of public universities, enable them to better support the activities of their professors and graduate students and support their successful applications to funding agencies.

There can be no doubt that the high quality of the major private research universities is a primary characteristic of the US university system. Their very existence stimulates the performance of public universities. However, the major private research universities would not be able to single-handedly absorb all the brightest American and foreign students into their graduate programs or hire all the excellent professorial candidates that emerge from US and foreign universities. Thus, there is a niche for public research universities – which they have occupied.

This explains why our subsample of the thirty-seven US research universities that made the greatest contribution to training PhDs between 2002 and 2006 contains twice as many public (twenty-five) as private (twelve) universities. All signs indicate that it is mostly the

Table 4.3
External research funds per professor and graduate student, United
States, 2008–2009

Group	Per professor	Per graduate student
24 public of the 37[1]	$288,111	$60,740
12 private of the 37	$576,353	$70,289
120 public of the 200[2]	$233,757	$53,927
54 private of the 200	$457,228	$59,403

1 The 36 universities covered are those from the group of 37 with the highest
number of PhD graduates. The missing university is City University of New York
Graduate Center, for which we were unable to obtain all the relevant data.
2 In light of the diversity of our data sources, we were only able to use 176
of the 200 universities selected by The Center. Notes: Professorial staff include:
"non-tenured faculty," "on tenure track," and "tenured faculty"; graduate
students (full time). Source: National Science Foundation/National Center
for Science and Engineering, Statistics Survey of "Academic Research and
Development Expenditures: Fiscal Year 2009." National Center for Education
(NCES), IPEDS Employees Survey, Fall 2009. National Center for Education
Statistics (NCES), IPEDS Survey "Award/Degree levels offered Year 2009."

biomedical sciences that allowed private US research universities to
benefit from the expansion of research activities in academia between
the 1980s and today. These sectors account for nearly 40 per cent of
private universities' total research funds.[19] Finally, of the thirty-six
US universities in the ARWU top fifty in 2012, there were exactly
eighteen private and eighteen public institutions; whereas the corresponding numbers for THES 2012 were fourteen public and fifteen
private.

In sum, the role played by private research universities in the US
system has invigorated the performance and funding of their public
counterparts. The US National Research Council Committee on
Research Universities confirms that public universities are now a
centrepiece of the national system in that they award most PhDs and
conduct most basic research. Consequently, it has focused on a series
of measures designed to consolidate their immediate future by
addressing the issues they face in the short term.[20]

Sources of Operating Funds

It is easy to see that a university's operating funds are a key determinant of its output. To fulfill its many missions with dynamism and

Table 4.4
External research funds per PhD graduate, United States,
2008–2009

Group	Per PhD graduate
24 public of the 37[1]	$770,334
12 private of the 37	$1,137,746
120 public of the 200[2]	$815,845
54 private of the 200	$1,123,515

1 See table 4.3
2 See table 4.3

innovation, rather than merely adequately, a research university requires a deep well of resources. It has been estimated that the operating costs of a research university that seeks to integrate research into teaching and training in and through research are six times as high as those of an institution specializing in undergraduate education.[21]

But more than the quantity of resources is at stake. Analysts of university systems have already observed that a diversity of income sources constitutes a strategic input into their development and that excessive dependence on one or two main sources of operating funds, aside from research and capital asset funds, curbs their autonomy and undermines their ability to innovate. This is particularly true in that some sources of income, notably operating subsidies from government at the national and local level, are tied to very specific agendas, making them difficult to predict in the medium and long term.

We have already pointed this out in the case of research funding, but it is also true for operating funds, particularly in the case of public US research universities. The economic crisis and the resulting budgetary restraints imposed on various levels of government in the United States immediately following the "thirty glorious years," and then again in the 1990s, were reflected in cuts to university public funding. The fallout of the 2008 financial shock was also felt in all sectors, including government funding of universities.

Under these conditions, a diversity of operating fund sources is unquestionably desirable. What do our data have to say about this?

Table 4.5 presents the operating fund sources of US public research universities in the year 2009.[22] Since our interest is in the global

Table 4.5

Funding of operating expenditures by source and category of public university, United States, 2008–2009, in thousands of US$

Group	Govt. grants	Tuition fees	Philanthropy	Other income	Total
IN ABSOLUTE TERMS					
24 public of the 37[1]	13,924 171,558	9,877,085,359	2,093,246,319	4,893,271,258	30,787,774,494
129 public of the 200 The Center[2]	39,435,361,259	23,658,042,684	4,363,514,243	10,841,352,638	78,298,270,824
AS A PERCENTAGE BY SOURCE OF FUNDING					
24 public of the 37	45.2%	32.1%	6.8%	15.9%	100.0%
129 public of the 200 The Center	50.4%	30.2%	5.6%	13.8%	100.0%

1 The 24 universities covered are public universities from the group of 37 with the highest number of PhD graduates. The missing university is City University of New York Graduate Center, for which we do not have all the relevant data.
2 In light of the diversity of our data sources, we were only able to use 129 of the 143 public universities (among the total of 200 universities) retained by The Center.

structure of this funding, and since it can only evolve very slowly over time, there is no significant methodological penalty in considering only one year. Governments, more specifically the governments of the various states, provide a considerable share of these operating funds, though this never amounts to more than half of their revenues. Next in line is tuition, which generally accounts for one third of public universities' operating funds. Other incomes are from ancillary businesses, other educational activities, publications, use of the university logo, etc. Revenues from philanthropic foundations are relatively marginal for public universities, whereas those from supplementary sources, taken together, are quite important.

Table 4.6 allows us to compare private and public universities in terms of their sources of funding for academic operations. The challenges involved in gathering the relevant information – data for the operating budgets of private universities are mostly gleaned only from documents they make public – have forced us to restrict our comparison to a limited number of institutions: to wit, the fraction of private universities in our sample that post the best performances in advanced doctoral research training. A broader dataset would have been unnecessary for our purposes.

Table 4.6
Funding of operating expenditures by source and category of university, Group of 37,
United States, 2008–2009, in thousands of US$

Group	Govt grants	Tuition fees	Philanthropy	Other Sources	Total
	IN ABSOLUTE TERMS				
24 public of the 37[1]	13,924,171,558	9,877,085,359	2,093,246,319	4,893,271,258	30,787,774,494
12 private of the 37	6,289,378,000	5,295,342,000	11,953,522,000	4,410 832,000	27,949,074,000
Total	20,213,549,558	15,172,427,359	14,046,768,319	9,304,103,258	58,736,848 494
	AS A PERCENTAGE BY SOURCE OF FUNDING				
24 public of the 37	45.2	32.1	6.8	15.9	100
12 private of the 37	22.5	18.9	42.8	15.8	100
Total	34.4	25.8	23.9	15.8	100
	AS A PERCENTAGE BY CATEGORY OF UNIVERSITY				
24 public of the 37	68.9	65.1	14.9	52.6	52.4
12 private of the 37	31.1	34.9	85.1	47.4	47.6
Total	100	100	100	100	100

1 The 36 universities covered are those from the Group of 37 with the highest number of PhD graduates. The missing university is City University of New York Graduate Center, for which we do not have all the relevant data.

What does this table tell us? First, it confirms the impressive volume of resources available to private universities. The total revenues of a dozen of them nearly equal the amounts received by their competitors in the public system, which have twice their number of establishments. Their operating fund sources are also very diversified. It is not surprising that financing received from the government only covers a little less than a quarter of operating expenditures. In fact, their main income sources are their vast endowment funds and grants from a variety of philanthropic foundations. The share of their operating expenditures covered by other sources, such as those enumerated above, is comparable to that of their public sector competitors.

Paradoxically, tuition represents a smaller share of private universities' operating revenues than of public universities. That finding must, however, be qualified with the observation that private universities' declared revenues from tuition are net of discounts granted and specific scholarships that the university provides to the students either on admission or over the course of their studies.[23] Even though a smaller proportion of their operating expenditures is financed by tuition, each private university in our sample nonetheless obtains more money from tuition than a comparable public institution.

More comprehensive data on tuition, presented in table 4.7, shed further light on this source of revenue for US universities. Nationwide, in 2009, private universities stood out in terms of the mean, maximum, and minimum tuition collected by universities in the various states. Unsurprisingly, they came out on top – even the lowest tuition found among private universities far exceeded its level at their public counterparts. As to the mean, it is three times as high at the undergraduate level. This gap shrinks somewhat at the graduate level, though even there tuition charged by private universities is nearly twice that of public universities.

The data presented so far describe the current state of events, but it is worthwhile to examine them from a completely different perspective. How has the financing of US research universities evolved over time and how has the diversity of their funding sources allowed them to weather the negative impacts of troughs in the business cycle?

Public research universities, especially the most prestigious ones, continue to receive large operating subsidies from state governments. According to our data, which admittedly only pertain to some of them, nearly half of their total revenues are from that source. However, this situation does not fully reflect the substantial decline in government funding that started at least as far back as the early 1980s and has accelerated since the 2000s. We find that average cutbacks in state government funding to public universities amount to 25 per cent. By the early 2000s, this decline had reached the point that the best-financed half of public universities spent the same amount on operating costs as the worst-financed half of private research universities.[24]

The recession of the past few years has only exacerbated this trend. In 2012 alone, for example, government grants fell by at least 7.6 per cent from their 2011 levels. But the severe recession isn't the only problem. Regional and local government contributions to higher education fell by 6.9 per cent from the end of the 1980s to

Table 4.7
Tuition fees paid in the various states of the US, 2009

	Undergraduate		Graduate	
	PUBLIC	PRIVATE	PUBLIC	PRIVATE
Mean tuition	$5,129	$19,369	$7,190	$13,702
Mean maximum tuition	$9,382	$29,169	$40,917	$21,218
Mean minimum tuition	$1,744	$9,968	$2,961	$7,769

Source: National Center for Education, IPEDS, Survey of Tuition Fees, 2009.

1998, and then a further 6.6 per cent by 2008.[25] We understand the National Research Council Committee's concern for the immediate future of public research universities, whose resources are supposed to enable them to fulfill both regional and national missions. To accomplish this, their state government funding would at least have to return to its 1987–2002 levels, adjusted for inflation.[26]

To alleviate the worst impacts of these cuts, significant changes were made to tuition levels, among other things. Although these amounted to 22 per cent of operating costs in the early 1980s, their value had climbed to 37 per cent by the beginning of the 2000s. Any growth in revenues available to universities is thus primarily attributable to an increase in tuition.[27]

Most public research universities took advantage of the leeway they had been granted, which varied from one state to the next, to increase tuition and ancillary fees on students from their own state. More often than not, they asked more of students nearing the end of their undergraduate studies, those in professional programs, and especially graduate students. Out-of-state, and in particular international students were charged even higher tuition levels.[28] In the case of the latter, the most prestigious public research universities began competing head-to-head with their counterparts in the private sector. The historically low tuition fees charged out-of-state students by prestigious public US universities gave them a competitive edge that they quickly learned to turn to their advantage.

We should note that the federal government is not involved in funding universities' operating costs – that is strictly under the jurisdiction of the states. Nonetheless, it does play an important, if indirect, role in supporting university attendance among certain specific age and demographic groups. This was already the case when the GI

Bill of the post-Second World War period facilitated veterans' access to university. Then, in the early 1970s, generous programs of financial aid to students – known as the Federal Pell Grants – targeted the neediest students, especially with grants. But with the government belt-tightening of the 1980s, these grants were soon transformed into student loans that involved other economic agents, such as the banks. Without this vital support, the level and diversity of income available to the institutions, whether public or private, would have been reduced considerably.[29]

We observe that US research universities rely on a diversity of sources to fund their operating costs. This diversity provides them with a certain degree of autonomy with regard to government funding but, although this is true of both public and private universities, it is less so for the former. Tuition levels play a central role throughout the American academic system and they have risen sharply across the board since at least the beginning of the 1980s. According to some experts, including R.L. Geiger, this is part of a broader trend of privatization of higher education in the United States. In this area private universities experienced extremes. They also harnessed the massive resources in their endowment and private philanthropic funds in support of their missions and their faculty and student bodies.

Finally, we must bear in mind that for research universities to perform well they need operating funds that are not only substantial, but also represent a diversity and flexibility in their sources. Notwithstanding the sporadic shortfalls in operating funds that US public research universities have confronted in recent decades, they continue to have access to a generous revenue stream and flexibility in terms of its sources and disposition. These are the features that allow the institutions we are examining to position themselves in the highest categories of world-class universities' international rankings.

Human Resources

For US research universities, as multi-versities or institutions of an imposing girth that offer a broad array of undergraduate programs and invest heavily in their institutional priority of graduate education integrated with research activities, students and faculty are absolutely essential. If there aren't enough of them, despite the considerable difference in that regard between public and private schools, no university can truly fulfill its mission.

The issues affecting students and professors are numerous and complicated, but for our purposes it is sufficient to concentrate on a few specific elements. First we will focus on how universities acquire these resources through the recruitment and selection process. Institutions need to attract individuals with a passion for learning and a strong aptitude for assimilating, transmitting, and generating knowledge if they are to fulfill their missions. But they must also retain these individuals while capitalizing on opportunities to support their career paths, encourage their activities, and motivate them to constantly surpass themselves.

If a university is to fully benefit from the strategic resources represented by students and professors, managers must step up to the plate. They are key actors in the organizational arrangements and decision-making mechanisms by which institutions plan and manage, in a more or less holistic fashion, how they will obtain the human resources that are their raison d'être.

We will, once again, restrict our examination to specific issues that are relevant to the university administrator. We want to find out whether the way in which universities delegate authority to administrators sheds any light on the positions these institutions attain internationally. We will attempt to document their roles in light of the broad orientations set by their institutions' missions. These orientations will create the conditions for success in obtaining and retaining human resources and providing the necessary measures and incentives to support them.

STUDENTS

Now we turn our attention to the student bodies of US research universities. We begin by noting the enormous size differentials among the institutions. On average, as table 4.8 shows, public research universities have a larger student body than their private sector counterparts. In both our subsample of the thirty-seven universities with the highest output of PhDs and in the rest of the sample, public universities have nearly twice as many students as private universities when all levels are considered.

We also observe the large contingent of students in the graduate levels at private universities. There they represent between 40 per cent and 50 per cent of the student body, as the table makes clear.

Table 4.8
Full-time university students by level of studies and category of university, Group of 37
and Group of 200, United States, 2009

Group of 37	First level	Higher levels	Total
	IN ABSOLUTE NUMBERS		
24 public of the 37[1]	655,521	187,167	842,688
12 private of the 37	94,725	101,653	196,378
Total	750,246	288,820	1,039,066
	AS A PERCENTAGE BY LEVEL OF STUDIES		
24 public of the 37	77.8	22.2	100
12 private of the 37	48.2	51.8	100
Total	72.2	27.8	100
	AS A PERCENTAGE BY CATEGORY OF PUBLIC AND PRIVATE UNIVERSITY		
24 public of the 37	87.4	64.8	81.1
12 private of the 37	12.6	35.2	18.9
Total	100	100	100
Group of 200	First level	Higher levels	Total
	IN ABSOLUTE NUMBERS		
133 public of the 200[2]	2,027,496	502,140	2,529,636
55 private of the 200	324,757	239,156	563,913
Total	2,352,253	741,296	3,093,549
	AS A PERCENTAGE BY LEVEL OF STUDIES		
133 public of the 200	80.1	19.9	100
55 private of the 200	57.6	42.4	100
Total	76.0	24.0	100
	AS A PERCENTAGE BY CATEGORY OF PUBLIC AND PRIVATE UNIVERSITY		
133 public of the 200	86.2	67.7	81.8
55 private of the 200	13.8	32.3	18.2
Total	100	100	100

1 The 36 universities covered are those from the Group of 37 with the highest number of PhD graduates. The missing university is City University of New York Graduate Center, for which we do not have all the relevant data.
2 In light of the diversity of our data sources we were only able to retain 188 of the 200 universities selected by The Center.
Source: National Center for Education Statistics (NCES), IPEDS Survey "Estimated enrollment Fall 2009."

Conversely, between 70 per cent and 80 per cent of the student population of public universities is at the undergraduate level. However, in each type of institution the average number of graduate students is quite similar across these two categories.

These distributions of students between the private and public sector are reflected in the degrees conferred. Two-thirds of the degrees awarded by public research universities are bachelor's degrees, whereas between 35 per cent and 40 per cent are awarded by their private sector counterparts, depending on the sample. Among all degrees awarded by an institution, more PhDs are awarded in the private than in the public sphere. However, since there are more of them, public universities still award more PhDs than private universities.

A recent study by the National Research Council's Committee on Research Universities is revealing about this issue of size – not of the universities as such, but of their doctoral programs. This recent study, like similar ones conducted between 1982 and 1995, reveals a positive correlation between the size of the student body and faculty in doctoral programs and their position in this ranking. Seventy percent of PhD programs are in institutions that offer teaching characterized by large student bodies. The same proportion, i.e., 70 per cent of all programs, are in public research universities. The 2010 study found that for most disciplines, larger doctoral programs tend to attract students with the best SAT scores, who are most likely to receive merit-based financial assistance in the form of fellowships.[30]

Let us note the reality that underlies this observation. A doctoral program size does not merely refer to the number of students, but also to the size of the teaching and research staff. Thus, it reflects the organization of disciplinary fields into departments with large bodies of students and professors who contribute to creating a rich and diversified academic environment of advanced training in research. We have already observed that the department-based structure is a key element of the US system, which originated during the nineteenth century.

Not just anyone can enter a doctoral program in a US research university, whether public or private. Any student desiring higher education, especially advanced training in research, must pass a battery of tests known as Graduate Record Examinations (GRE), which include a demanding quantitative reasoning element. It is, in fact, an incontrovertible rule of academia in the United States that all graduate school applicants must take these tests, which form the basis on which their candidacy to a research university will be accepted or rejected. This standard applies to both American and foreign candidates. The best research universities select the candidates who have scored best on these tests. Competition among universities to recruit the best students is fierce, and over time many practices and institutions have arisen that reflect this reality.

From the perspective of a student who has done well on the entrance examinations, a university's attractiveness will be a function of its programs' reputation for quality, but also of its tuition, as well as of the various forms of financial assistance offered to the best students. This assistance will consist of fellowships, both internal and external, preferential tuition rates, and the availability of teaching assistant (TA) and research assistant (RA) positions. It is not uncommon for the most proactive and wealthiest, and especially the most reputable, universities to extend an invitation to the best candidates (even before they have applied) to visit the institution and meet the professors and researchers who would be responsible for their education. This practice is particularly widespread for the best candidates seeking advanced training in research and who stand out for their academic track record and GRE scores.

The weight that each university gives to these various entrance examinations in selecting its graduate school students will, of course, vary with its priorities and strategic vision. One thing is certain, however. The quality of the student body contributes considerably to the reputation of an institution. We have noted above how the US higher education system is particularly fond of assessments and rankings in all their manifestations. In the market for reputation, an institution whose students have obtained particularly high admission test scores will benefit from this confirmation of its excellence.

Therefore, recruiting and selecting the best students for its graduate programs, and especially for its advanced training in research, is not a trivial matter for a US research university, whether private or public. In the case of the latter, the state government might intervene to rein in the pursuit of the best students by reminding the institution that its primary mission is to educate state residents. But the constraints imposed on public universities by state governments are obviously less restrictive in the case of graduate students, especially at the doctoral level.

A US research university has to attract and recruit very good students into its graduate school. However, it must also be able to retain them and see them through to graduation. We have already established that, in comparison with their public counterparts (which have posted respectable results in their own right), private US research universities in our two samples have the means to offer their graduate students, particularly those in advanced training in research, a richer learning environment thanks to their greater per-capita resources in terms of the sums invested in research.

Turning our attention now to operating funds per student, in 2008–09 private US research universities attained very high levels ($186,460), giving them a comfortable lead over their public competitors. However, at the international level, the average income of $36,535 per student received by public universities is enough to place them in a select group of institutions that are very well-situated to offer their students an excellent learning environment.[31]

In 2006 these additional resources made it possible for private universities to offer students a ratio to full-time professor of 13.2, which was lower than that of their public competitors (19.32). But, once again, on the international scale we see that the latter perform quite well by this measure.[32]

Within these institutions, guiding and retaining students at the graduate level is also a matter of academic structure. As we know, professors responsible for basic research as well as teaching at all levels are grouped into departments by discipline. They are also called on to work within a vertical division of academic labour which, in the US, has taken the form of close and sustained links between departments and the graduate school. Such a division of academic labour has contributed greatly to the increased visibility and size of student bodies at the graduate level, along with the attention that must be paid to retaining them.

Most US research universities, whether private or public, rely on the services of a graduate school to monitor output and performance in graduate studies and advanced training in research. In addition to making the university the main locus of basic research, it was by creating this vertical division of labour between undergraduate and graduate levels that the United States gave birth to the research university. That it succeeded is confirmed by its dominant position on the international scene in the training of PhD graduates.

And, as if they were really needed, ongoing evaluations, especially those that examine all US PhD programs, like the one recently conducted by the National Research Council, remind all public and private research universities in the United States that considerable challenges remain to be addressed in terms of their core missions of conducting research and providing advanced training in research. Attracting the best students and awarding enough PhDs in a reasonable time frame is a moving, but always relevant, target.

FACULTY MEMBERS

In the previous section we emphasized that the research resources available to US research universities, whether public or private, depend in large measure on the research grants obtained by their faculty members. We also observed that per-professor annual research funding from external sources is quite generous for professors in the public universities in our samples, and even more so for professors in the private universities.

We conclude that these institutions need to recruit and retain very good specialists in many scientific disciplines. These specialists, in turn, select an institution on the basis of the quality of its human and physical research infrastructures. They gravitate toward establishments that are able to recruit good students at the graduate level, especially doctoral and post-doctoral, and that can offer solid scientific and technological infrastructure, including high-quality spaces of specialization and a wide variety of equipment, such as high-powered computers and new information technology infrastructures. Underlying the research output of a good university there is, thus, a pool of talent motivated by competition and by the evaluations that give access to resources disbursed by funding agencies and their committees of peers.

We see that in academia, selecting and hiring professorial staff that represent various scientific disciplines and have an aptitude for conducting innovative research, in some cases across disciplinary boundaries, is not a simple matter. In the North American context, selection and hiring fall within the purview of individual institutions as a function of their priorities, institutional choices, and resource endowments. Most typically, a shared decision-making process on hiring a professor will first be made by faculty members in the department. They create a short list that is submitted to the faculty administration and then to the institution's central administration for final approval. In general, there are no intermediaries to interfere in this system of decision-making autonomy by which a university acquires its professorial resources.

The explosive development of research universities since the middle of the last century has been accompanied by a profound transformation in professors' career paths in US academia. This transformation can be traced back to the emergence of research professionals in universities, specifically in research universities, during the first part of the twentieth century. University staff positions have been increasingly occupied by research professionals who devote considerable effort to both conducting research and training graduates mostly for the academic market.

An upshot of this has been greater emphasis on the research component of a professor's job description. Without abandoning the role of teaching, the new success standard in a professorial career is the ability to make a mark in one's field of specialization. The focus has increasingly shifted to being recognized as an authority by peers on the basis of published work, research, and discoveries. Peer recognition generally makes it easier for faculty members to maintain their status and reputation as top-notch scientists while also ensuring access to research funds. These faculty members then train their own students in the same spirit, as colleagues who will some day make their own contribution.

In a landmark publication, David Riesman and Christopher Jencks call this momentous shift in the professorial career in American universities and society the "academic revolution."[33] This turning point became even more inescapable when, at the height of the Second World War, the intensity of investments and expenditures in research and the phenomenal growth in basic research reached previously unattained levels. The remarkable post-war expansion of scientific activity and higher education, especially at the doctoral level, set the stage for the emergence of this academic revolution. Clearly, the ideal site for a professorial career that embraces the imperatives of research and the critical contribution of developments in science as a success measure is the research university.[34]

The extent to which international rankings of first-rate universities, which we looked at in previous chapters, rely on the ability of professors to advance scientific knowledge in their disciplines will have become apparent. This is why elements such as research funding allocated by committees of peers, publications in high-impact journals, and the recognition represented by prestigious awards are frequently among the variables used by international rankings of research universities. In their own way, these rankings entrench the changes to professors' tasks and career paths initiated by the academic revolution, which emphasizes a very specific measure of professional success in academia.

We have already looked at some features of US doctoral programs that are considered large as measured by numbers of students and faculty members. Professors in the largest quartile of programs generally demonstrate higher research productivity. In fact, for all families of scientific disciplines, professors in programs belonging to this quartile report greater per-capita output in terms of scientific publications, the mean number of citations per publication, the mean number of awards and distinctions, and the percentage of professors receiving research grants. Finally, the proportion of tenured professors tends to be greater in the largest programs of this top quartile than in other programs.[35]

Over time, this measure of professional achievement in academia has become a quasi-universal gauge of professors' performance. It should be noted that this standard originated with research universities. Applying this standard across the board to all academic institutions can cause us to forget the characteristics that distinguish research universities from all other higher education establishments.

In conclusion, our analysis suggests that US research universities would not perform as well internationally if they were unable to recruit and retain some of the best tenured faculty members – while also supporting their production. The financial squeeze these institutions (especially public universities) have been subject to in recent decades has created real challenges on the domestic front, but internationally the conditions under which they recruit, select, and retain faculty members remain very competitive. This is a key feature, of course, because they constitute the pool of institutions that nurture the very highest ranks of world-class universities.

Academic Governance

Sound management practices are required to attract excellent students and accompany them through to graduation in a reasonable time frame while recruiting and retaining top-notch faculty members. Following in the footsteps of Johns Hopkins University in

Baltimore, most of the US research universities in both of our samples can be proud of their excellent records in both teaching and research and of promoting a structural model that is characteristic of a first-rate research university. They are also guided by a shared vision that is nourished by structural relationships between various actors and management levels which helps them attain the best possible performance.

For our purposes we need not delve too deeply into the details of the overall management of US research universities. However, we cannot deny the fact that some key aspects of their governance contribute to the positions these universities attain in international rankings.

It should be borne in mind that the governance and administration of US research universities, whether public or private, is in the hands of governing bodies comprising members from both inside and outside of the institution. Moreover, these institutions' administrative coordination and governance are not ultimately provided by a branch of government, such as a department of education, or of higher education.

Even the overall administration of public universities, which have closer links to state government, is completely independent. They also have their own governing bodies, helping them retain an arms-length relationship with the relevant departments. Although the United States government has a department of education, this federal agency does not exercise any direct control over the activities of US academic institutions, specifically research universities. The centre of gravity of decision-making powers in universities is in the institution itself.

In some senses this centre of power is diversified. US universities, and especially research universities, normally have a three-tier academic and administrative structure. The top tier consists of the board of directors and the central administration, in conjunction with various technical and academic services; the faculties into which the various scientific and professional disciplines are grouped constitute the middle tier; and the last tier is made up of departments, schools, and various research units. The efficiency of their relations and their willingness to work together to achieve the university's mission, as well as the historic roots of the various institutions, are instrumental to the future of research universities, whether public or private, as well as their ability to place among the top ranks of world-class research universities.

Key distinctions must, of course, be made between public and private research universities. Both types of institutions share, more or less, the governance structures described above, but the links public universities maintain with the relevant agencies of state governments may prove more constraining. For example, in a number of states we have seen the administrators of public research universities have to adapt to budgetary belt-tightening. This has clearly had an impact on their global operating funds, and most particularly on their expenditures on teaching. These public universities have had to show dynamism and leadership in their relations with their respective state governments during the financial difficulties of recent decades. In the short term they have proposed solutions to ensure access to more revenue, in particular by charging more for tuition and for the services dispensed by their medical clinics.

Thus, research universities' governance and management abilities play a central role, as a key characteristic that enables these universities to stand out in international rankings. This explains why there is currently a drive to grant even more autonomy to research universities, especially in the public sector, to help them deal with new challenges by increasing their flexibility in such matters as establishing tuition levels, managing financial and fixed assets, setting rules governing intellectual property, and monitoring resources provided as research grants. While some fear that individuals from outside academia might have too much influence on boards of governors, many believe that the representation of various elements from local, regional, and national public life should be expanded.[36]

Another feature of the academic governance of research universities merits attention: the culture of leadership and governance that the principals of an institution foster. This is one of the variables that we can evaluate using results from a study of US research universities with international renown conducted by Amanda H. Goodall.[37] After having served in the academic administration of one of the great universities, the London School of Economics, Goodall became interested in the high officers that govern contemporary research universities. She sought to determine whether differences in the leadership style of these universities would explain the differences in their output and performance. To answer that question, she used the ARWU international ranking of world-class research universities, 2004 edition, focusing on institutions in the top 100. Of these, fifty-one were US research universities. On the basis of this sample,

Goodall's study further illuminates the governance of institutions with strong representation in our two samples.

What are her findings? Most presidents of the universities in her study were career academics. Looking at the citations received by these leaders for their output in scientific writings over their entire careers, Goodall observes that the presidents of the top twenty best performing and most prestigious institutions were the most cited. In fact, she finds a very high and significant correlation coefficient between the rank of each of these 100 institutions, on the one hand, and the number of scientific citations received by the published work of their respective presidents, on the other.[38] We will see in the chapter on UK research universities that Goodall was able to establish, on the basis of that subsample, an even more direct and causal relationship between the scientific credentials of the presidents and the success of the institutions they direct in rigorous and systematic evaluations of the research performance of the main British universities.

For the moment, let us bear in mind that the most prestigious world-class research universities are directed by academics who are also experts in their field, and whose authority is equal to their responsibilities. This leadership calibre carries over to all faculty members and to various levels of the administration, reflecting a credible leadership, a thorough understanding of what makes a great university, the ability to set high standards that have been internalized by their author, and clearly signalling to the entire institution what is required if it is to fulfill its mission.[39]

CONCLUSION

Let us now draw a few conclusions from our examination of the US university system. We begin by recalling the extent to which a large number of organizational innovations set the course for the remarkable evolution of the US university system and its research universities. This clearly puts paid to the simplistic vision that the dominance of US research universities can be solely attributed to the volume of resources available to them.

We turn next to an essential dimension of US research universities: their unique role as the hub of basic research, which is partially funded from government revenues. With regard to the distribution of roles between universities, business, and government-run laboratories, it was the strategy of the president's chief scientific adviser during the post-war period, Vannevar Bush, to favour expanding the capacity of US research universities to enable them to be the principal producers of basic research. Within these institutions we found and continue to find the actors and the characteristics of basic research that make leading contributions to the advancement of knowledge and, in the context of a society founded on the application of knowledge, play a vital role in economic development.

The importance of research universities to American society rests on their ability to select the best students, in particular for graduate studies, and on their advanced training in research at the doctoral level. This level – and its strong association with advanced research capacity – was once the defining area in which the United States built its reputation, but increasingly it has been under international assault from constantly expanding university research capacities in a number of countries. Also observe that US research universities are very active in selecting the best professors, whose credibility in their respective disciplines enables them to harness the resources required for providing a graduate education that is aligned with research activities. They benefit from wide decision-making latitude not only in the selection of their human resources, whether students or faculty, but also in the use of incentives to support their careers, whether in training or in generating new knowledge.

Public US research universities are, overall, less well-endowed than their private competitors. But a strong case can be made that, on the international scale, the top representatives of this class in the United States still benefit from operating conditions that are generally far superior to those of the best world-class universities in many other countries. This is a matter to which we will return. As we will see, this state of affairs is attributable more to how resources are concentrated in a handful of research universities in the US system than to the size of their resource pool relative to that available in the other systems we will examine. We should also be aware that the diversity of revenue sources for US research universities gives them greater latitude in the strategies and choices they can implement to support their respective missions. We have seen how this diversity enabled some of these institutions to expand their income base and reallocate their resources through more cross-subsidization across various budget items to maintain their academic output in terms of research and advanced training in research, despite the economic downturn.

All of these organizational characteristics working together create the conditions for many US research universities to climb to the highest and most prestigious levels on national and international rankings of institutions. There are challenging issues on the horizon for this higher education system and its research university component that we will return to in another chapter. The following chapters will discuss the conditions, usually different though not without some similarities, under which research universities elsewhere function and generate their output. The characteristics of higher education systems in the United Kingdom, Canada, and France will shed new and contrasting light on the paths followed by other research universities that are, theoretically, also among the best at the international level.

APPENDIX

Table A-4.1
Operating cost per full-time student, in US$, United States, 2009,
public universities

Group	Cost per full-time student
24 public of the 37[1]	36,535
120 public of the 200 The Center[2]	31,836

1 We were only able to use 24 of the 25 public universities in the group
of 37 universities with the largest number of PhD graduates. The missing
university is City University of New York Graduate Center, for which we were
unable to obtain all the relevant data.
2 In light of the diversity of our data sources we were only able to use 120
of the 143 public universities (among the total of 200 universities selected by
The Center).

Table A-4.2
Operating cost per student in US$, United States, 2008–2009,
private universities

12 private universities of the 37	Cost per full-time student
Johns Hopkins University	310,041
Stanford University	389,948
Massachusetts Institute of Technology	258,628
University of Pennsylvania	255,071
Columbia University in the City of New York	157,345
Harvard University	196,285
Yale University	230,249
University of Southern California	43,212
University of Chicago	229,650
Northwestern University	95,940
Cornell University	129,218
Princeton University	166,175
Average of the 12 private universities	186,460

Source: Data on public universities: National Center for Education (NCES), IPEDS
Finance Survey, Fiscal Year 2009. Data on private universities: Financial Report,
Fiscal Year 2009. Data on students: National Center for Education Statistics (NCES),
IPEDS Survey "Estimated enrolment Fall 2009."

5

THE UNIVERSITY SYSTEM
IN THE UNITED KINGDOM

Research universities in the United Kingdom[1] are unique. According to our model of the distribution of research universities by country as a function of macroeconomic variables, only the United Kingdom is overrepresented in the highest categories of the ARWU and THES rankings. This result is all the more surprising because this performance even bests that of US research universities in the top echelons of these rankings.

Therefore, we will look more closely at the conditions under which institutions of higher education, and particularly universities, operate in the United Kingdom. This should allow us to identify the specific characteristics of this system that create the conditions for its institutions to stand out as world-class research universities.

We begin our examination of the unique features of the UK university system by reviewing its historical development to understand the soil in which the institutions specifically mandated with being research universities took root. Next we will look at the current organization of universities and their various missions to shed some light on the fundamental structural characteristics of this system. We will see that the recent history of these institutions, in particular research universities, is characterized by some developments that are quite distinctive.

Following the course we set when examining the US university system, we will examine the conditions under which UK universities currently operate by paying special attention to how research activities are structured and funded, sources of operating revenues, and the entrance on the academic scene of students, professors, and the principal administrators. We begin with some detailed and up-to-date

data on UK universities and the subgroup identified as research universities – a limited pool that is the source of UK world-class universities.

A BIT OF HISTORY

The universities of the United Kingdom have had a stellar reputation
for hundreds of years. The prestigious colleges of federated institutions such as Cambridge and Oxford Universities are renowned for
their pursuit of academic excellence. For centuries, these two institutions completely dominated the UK university scene, which did not
have any other universities of any consequence prior to the second
decade of the nineteenth century, aside from the universities established in Scotland during the fifteenth and sixteenth centuries. This
began to change with the founding of the University of London
(1826) and the University of Durham (1834).

Cambridge and Oxford have always stood out for the small size
of their colleges and their pedagogical approach, which is centred on
undergraduate programs. Their high degree of selectivity primarily
focuses on training a well-educated mind, promoting and striving
for academic excellence. While similar in some ways to a liberal education in the US undergraduate system, the teaching at Cambridge
and Oxford colleges is distinctive in its reliance on tutors, resulting
in a very low student-teacher ratio. This approach to undergraduate
studies is also much more specialized and circumscribed than the
equivalent level of liberal education in the North American system.
This close relationship between professor-tutors and students formed
the locus of an autonomous academic organization revolving around
the college – a structure that proved impervious to the formation of
departments grouping professors and students, as we find in the
United States.[2]

Primarily devoted to educating clerics and members of traditional
liberal professions, Cambridge and Oxford also have a history of
supplying England with its government clerks and socio-political
elites. Of course, as the number of universities in the United Kingdom
increased, this influence was bound to wane, but even today the
imprint of these two institutions on social and political elites is very
pronounced.[3]

These university structures, benefiting from a long history of organizational independence, never had to compete with other higher

education institutions that might have marginalized their contributions, as was the case (more on this to come) in France.

The late nineteenth and early twentieth centuries saw a growing demand for new knowledge and a highly skilled labour force to work in modern industries that were receptive to new technologies. We know, of course, that the United Kingdom was, to a very large extent, at the very heart of modern societies' industrial revolution. However, the response of the higher education system did not entirely escape the influence of the institutional model transmitted by Oxford and Cambridge. The so-called red-brick universities movement – their characteristic architecture setting them apart from Oxford and Cambridge's prestigious colleges – sprang up at the beginning of the twentieth century in key industrial cities and regions, embodying a philosophy of teaching that departed from the emphasis on intensive tutoring. For the most part, they followed in the footsteps of the Scottish model, in which tutoring as the basic pedagogical unit was secondary to the departmental structure.

Nonetheless, these institutions, which contributed to the first significant expansion of higher education in the United Kingdom, mostly remained true to the values and traditions represented by the Oxford and Cambridge model. Small new universities with a low student-to-professor ratio, they also emphasized undergraduate education, strict admission criteria, and academic excellence. Despite the fact that they appeared in a world in which research, as an activity of discovery and experimentation, was receiving a great deal of attention in Germany, these institutions concentrated their efforts on undergraduate education with an openness toward the more applied and technical aspects of training a highly skilled labour force.

Another factor that proved telling was that, for a very long time, universities in the United Kingdom drew the resources they needed to function from their immediate social milieu and their student bodies. These were independent private institutions that were largely self-financing by means of resources received from organizations of civil society, endowment funds, and the tuition paid by their students. Thus, by the end of the First World War, half the revenues of UK universities were from private sources and the other half from public – one third of those from the national government and the remainder from local authorities.[4] By this time the university system in the United Kingdom had embarked on a very different path from that of the other systems in Europe, which were already highly dependent on their national governments.

Slower Expansion of University Attendance

These developments can only be understood with reference to the social contract, on which there was a virtual consensus among the principal administrators and actors on the university scene and social elites – including the responsible political entities – regarding the fundamental pillars of the UK higher education system and its university component. This consensus has allowed these universities to integrate into the modern world without abandoning their organizational features. This shared vision was structured around small institutions with low student-to-professor ratios that were highly invested in the quest for academic excellence, initially at the undergraduate level but then expanding to encompass the graduate level, locally called postgraduate studies.

This ideal type of university also explains why the United Kingdom was slower than other countries to attain high levels of university attendance among the relevant age groups. The impact of this selectivity and the small universities made itself felt for many years. By the end of the 1930s, for example, an average of 2,000 students attended each of the twenty-four universities in the United Kingdom. The mode of the student size at that time, i.e., the most representative student body size within institutions, was 1,000 students. Even at the beginning of the 1960s, this mode still ranged between 1,000 and 2,000, and in the early 1980s it ranged between 3,000 and 5,000 students. This is a far cry from the mean, or even the mode, of contemporary French and US universities.

In the post-war period, and especially the 1960s, university student bodies grew dramatically in many countries. First observed in the United States, this trend became known as mass higher education. Even in Europe, by the beginning of the 1980s, countries were admitting 20 per cent to 30 per cent, and sometimes more, of the relevant age groups into university. During that same time period this value fluctuated between 12 per cent and 14 per cent in the United Kingdom.[5]

Clearly, the political agenda needed to address the issue of expanding access to higher education. Reports on the subject persistently drove home this point, and the Robbins Report in 1963 contributed to the founding of new universities in Essex, East Anglia, Sussex, York, etc. More recently, the committee chaired by Lord Browne once again shone a spotlight on this issue in 2010.[6]

This very issue of access, incidentally, formed the backdrop against which a network of polytechnics and teachers' training colleges was created in the mid-1960s with support from the government. Officially part of the higher education system and evolving at the same time as the autonomous university sector, these institutions (often closely linked to local authorities) underwent a series of transformations. Subsequently, in the 1990s some of them capitalized on decisions made by the government – under the Further and Higher Education Act of 1992 – to reinvent themselves as the newest crop of universities. In this way, the UK higher education system became both more unified and more regulated.[7] By the end of the twentieth century it had been substantially revamped. Indeed, because of new funding rules progressively introduced starting in the mid-1960s, this latest crop of universities – frequently referred to as the post-92 universities – are part of a renewed UK university system.

Increasing access played a crucial role in the significant changes to government funding of higher education and to the relationship of universities with public authorities that developed during the twentieth century. New conditions for university funding also played a major role. A single statistic captures these developments. As we noted above, at the end of the First World War direct government subsidies accounted for one-third of universities' total revenues. By 1946, 80 per cent of their income was from that source.[8]

It should be noted, though, that for some fifty years the relationship between this funder and the institutions was mediated by the powerful University Grants Committee (UGC). From 1920 to the mid-1960s, this committee acted as a buffer between the universities and government agencies – serving as the game master of government funding for universities. This system sustained the foundational pillars on which higher education was built in the United Kingdom. In fact, the actions of this committee had the net effect of prolonging the social contract we mentioned earlier. Relations between universities and the government converged toward a pattern that still prevails in government funding of university-based research in many countries: The universities retain a certain degree of decision-making, academic, and administrative autonomy with regard to their development strategies and the allocation of their resources while depending on government agencies for these resources.

The autonomy of universities is thus inextricably linked to the fact that decision-making bodies mostly comprise academic representatives. The UGC, whose membership was drawn from the academic community, functioned in the same way until the mid-1960s. The universities dealt with this committee, whose direct access to ministerial authorities responsible for government finances was unencumbered by political interference. Indeed, during the period in which this committee exercised its powers, the Department of Education and Science did not play a central role in university funding or operations, polar opposite to the highly interventionist approach taken by the corresponding ministry in France.

During the first half of the twentieth century, the UK university system underwent a real process of nationalization in step with the proportional increase in government funding. Then, during the mid-1960s, the government decided that the UGC would begin reporting directly to the Department of Education and Science. The result was an erosion of the Committee's privileged relationship with the Treasury. From then on the UGC's decisions and interventions reflected a new approach, resulting in the abandonment of the social contract between universities and the government. What is more, the department responsible for the Committee began increasing the burden of directives governing the funding, and then the operation, of universities, which were largely dependent on government monies. Under the Department direction, the Committee multiplied national guidelines and standards for various organizational aspects of universities, which were then used to determine the level of government funding and, by extension, to impose binding controls on the operations of those institutions.

The process had run its course by the late 1980s when the UGC was finally disbanded. It was succeeded by the Universities Funding Council (UFC), a body that was even more unambiguously a formal extension of the Department of Education and Science. Over some twenty-five years, from the mid-1960s to the late-1980s, higher education in the United Kingdom thus experienced a sweeping makeover characterized by efforts and policies designed to rationalize the system. The budgetary crises the government of the United Kingdom weathered in the 1970s and 1980s reinforced this trend. Clearly, even before it was disbanded, the UGC had been stripped of much of its earlier function as a buffer.

The Universities Funding Council exercised a more interventionist management of the universities that were eligible for government funding. Moreover, also during the late 1980s, the government issued new rules governing the financing of universities. Grants to universities were frozen and they were required to increase the tuition charged to international students to levels that actually covered the cost of the education provided.[9]

Evolution of Research Organization

Another important characteristic of this system is how basic research is organized within universities and UK society and the role played by research universities. We have seen how this is important to the creation of a pool of universities that can give rise to world-class research universities. We note, as have others before us, that the university in the United Kingdom was somewhat belated in treating research as an activity of discovery, experimentation, and the generation of knowledge. However, when it did, it pursued these endeavours with the same drive for excellence that marked its tradition of teaching.[10]

In the name of industrial and commercial development the government of the United Kingdom had begun to fund laboratories and national research institutes by the beginning of the twentieth century. Thus, after World War One, some fifteen laboratories were dedicated to meeting the needs of the day for applied research. For a brief period, it even appeared that research activity had escaped the confines of academia to flourish in external institutes, as was notably the case in France and Germany.

But this was not to be. Against the backdrop of a growing perception that scientific research was becoming too beholden to government departments, the principle that the government should fund research indirectly through granting councils, as advocated by Haldane, was adopted in 1920. These research councils cover a variety of scientific disciplines: the first (medicine) was created in 1920, followed by agriculture, nature, and the environment (1949), science (1964), and the social sciences (1965). Following in the footsteps of the US university system, funds are disbursed by these councils on the basis of merit and the recognized expertise of the recipients, which is established by a competitive process and peer assessments.

Concurrently, the drive for excellence and new knowledge, in particular within the excellent inner circle of the colleges of Cambridge and Oxford, contributed to opening UK universities to research at the highest levels. We observe, in fact, that these institutions created academic laboratories for conducting basic research during the first third of the twentieth century. Subsequently, universities that were established during the nineteenth century, drawing heavily on the Scottish model, also showed a growing interest in academic research.

Research conducted in academia thus became a central and strategic element of research activity in the United Kingdom, in particular in the area of basic research. Since at least the middle of the twentieth century, there can be no doubt that university-based research has played a vital role in higher education and in all research conducted. There are, of course, research institutes in the UK, some of which perform basic research and are funded by the research councils or by private foundations from the health and welfare milieus, called "charities." Some of these are found outside of the university sector or operate in partnership with academic research bodies. Nonetheless, unlike in other European countries, in the United Kingdom these institutes are not a cornerstone of government-funded research.

Today

It is undeniable that the UK research universities included in the international ranking exercises ARWU and THES are evolving in a modern higher education system with organizational features that are, of course, rooted in history but are also shaped by the present. Changes that have occurred since the end of the 1980s are central to these developments.

These changes affect most of the key organizational elements of universities in the United Kingdom. They include the processes by which university education is funded, the government resources they receive for research, and the administration of the differentiated tuition rates they charge their various clientèles. All of this occurs against the backdrop of constitutional changes affecting the various components of the United Kingdom.

One result of devolution, which has coloured the recent history of the United Kingdom, has been that constitutional responsibilities for education, including higher education, were delegated by the 1992 Act to the constituent countries. The supplementary constitutional agreements of 1998 further entrenched devolution of powers within the United Kingdom. However, the central government still controls the budgetary resources provided to each of these countries, as they do not currently have the power to levy taxes on their territories.

As a result, the countries of the United Kingdom fund their higher education sector with the global transfer payment they receive from London. The unified Universities Funding Council, which was responsible for the entire higher education system in the United Kingdom, was soon replaced by four bodies, one for each constituent country (HEFCE: Higher Education Funding Council for England; SFC: Scottish Funding Council; HEFCW: Higher Education Funding Council for Wales; DELNI: Department for Employment and Learning of Northern Ireland).

During the late 1980s and early 1990s there was a major shakeup of the UK university system. First, the government decided to incorporate what has been called the idea of "the market" into the university funding process.[11] Next, following the lead of HEFCE in England, higher education funding bodies introduced a principle of increased competition between institutions, especially with regard to research funding. Finally, higher education in the United Kingdom, especially in the university sector, became increasingly preoccupied by global measures of quality assurance covering more than a single institution, giving rise to periodic evaluations of academic units and their offerings.

The economic downturn of the late 1980s severely stressed government budgets, which fund higher education, among other things, and this spending was slashed. Annual government funding of universities, principally for teaching but also for research – not counting the merit-based allocations to professors in the form of grants and contracts, primarily obtained from research councils – fell to the point where, by the early 1990s, it represented less than 50 per cent of universities' total income.

These institutions were thus compelled to turn to the private sector for more of their funding. The government's intention, especially in England, was to restore private contributions as a significant source of university funding, as it had been prior to the Second World War. Philanthropic donations and endowment funds play a role, of course, but they are not the only source targeted by the government under the "market" idea.[12] Tuition fees are a more reliable source of private income – especially when they are from international students or students enrolled in graduate (so-called postgraduate) studies, who are not covered by government-established cap. We will have more to say on this matter below. Tuition paid by undergraduate students must also be counted as an additional private source to be developed.

At the turn of the last century tuition came under direct government control, as exercised by HEFCE. In 1998, for the first time, the council capped the amount of tuition that universities could charge undergraduate students who are residents of the United Kingdom or a country of the European Union at one thousand pounds sterling (£1,000) per year, indexed to the inflation rate for subsequent years. This measure did not apply to postgraduate or international students, but it did curb universities' autonomy in setting tuition levels.

Then, under pressure from the government, in 2006–07 HEFCE raised the maximum for undergraduates to £3,000, again indexed to inflation. The system provides for deferred repayment, allowing students to pay their tuition after graduation according to a formula that pegs instalments to income. In addition, the government has set up a system of loans and fellowships specifically covering tuition that complements the equivalent system already in place to compensate student living expenses. Thus, when students join the labour market, they can repay the student loans incurred for their tuition and the general cost of education at an annual interest rate not exceeding the inflation rate.

HEFCE uses a formula to assign quotas of students to each institution, especially in the case of undergraduate studies, on the basis of which it allocates funds according to a schedule of disciplines. Neither international students nor postgraduate students are factored into this quota, which determines how much money each institution will receive to fulfill its teaching mission. The sum of all these quotas dictates how much government funding is allocated to recurring institutional subsidies and to the loans and fellowships provided to UK students.

While HEFCE was working out its position in the matter of tuition and quotas, other quality assurance issues arose. Near the turn of the century, in 1997, the Quality Assurance Agency (QAA) was created as a quasi-autonomous non-governmental organization, though it maintained links to the government. Notwithstanding the devolution of powers in the higher education area, its activities cover all universities in the United Kingdom. Funded by contributions from higher education institutions, it is described as a "light touch" regulatory agency with no statutorily binding powers. Nonetheless, it conducts periodic evaluations of universities by means of on-site inspections and by releasing reports and recommendations that are made public. It also ascertains that the institutions themselves regularly proceed with systematic evaluations, including bringing in external auditors, to ensure adherence to the standards and codes of practice that it promotes for university education.

More recently, HEFCE announced two or three new measures that will have an impact. On the one hand, following the publication of a White Book by the Department of Business, Innovation and Skills, the ministry to which HEFCE now answers, as of 2012–13 it only subsidizes students enrolled in programs providing training that is either clinical or involves laboratory-based experimental science.[13] This excludes students in the social sciences and humanities from its recurrent funding scheme.

On the other hand, it has also raised the tuition cap to £9,000 per annum.[14] Universities desiring to set their rates in the top range of £6,000 to £9,000 are obliged to submit an institutional plan for increasing access for students from underprivileged socio-economic backgrounds and underrepresented ethnic groups. This plan must be approved by the recently created Office for Fair Access (OFFA).

Aside from tuition levels, universities have another measure they can use to attract students. For many years the educational system in the UK has had a system of national rankings (based on academic records) for students graduating from secondary school and seeking admission into higher education. This component of the admissions system is centralized and administered by the University and Colleges Admissions Service (UCAS), to which candidates submit applications that contain their academic records and a document describing their educational goals. Universities can admit students they have duly selected into their full-time regular programs, provided these students meet the admission criteria set by UCAS. However, institutions may still require higher academic achievement from their candidates than the standards set by UCAS.

Hence, HEFCE has announced that, as of 2012–13, graduates from secondary school who rank at the very top of their cohort according to the documents submitted to UCAS will not be counted for purposes of the quota. They will, in a sense, be off the books when the institutional quota is calculated, but they will nonetheless be counted for subsidies to the teaching function if they are in an eligible discipline.

Other major aspects of recurring funding for higher education have been affected by similar developments – driven not only by assessments, but also by competition for resources between institutions. Rules of attribution for the grants made by HEFCE to universities, as well as by funding councils in the other constituent countries of the United Kingdom to their institutions, make provision for funding a research component that is conditional on an assessment. This is a core subsidy called Quality Research. This funding, designed to pay for the research portion (set at one-third) of the work performed by professors, is accordingly pro-rated to their incomes. It also provides financial support to postgraduate students in the form of fellowships or contributions that reduce the burden of tuition. Yet another part of the budget managed by HEFCE is called "postgraduate research student funding – PGR funding stream," under which universities are able to obtain funding for the supervision of students in research training or post-doctoral studies.

The beginning of the 1990s saw the first of HEFCE's systematic evaluations of the research activities of departments in UK universities. These were performed by panels of peers and commonly referred to by the acronym RAE, for Research Assessment Exercise.[15] These operations were repeated on a regular basis and became the foundation on which research funding decisions were made. For a given unit, an analysis of the research output of all the professors, the quality of the environment, and the work of the postgraduate research students yields a quality score falling into one of four groups, with a fifth group to indicate whether the quality is inadequate for any kind of ranking. This score determines whether a research university qualifies for a QR (quality research) subsidy and, potentially, additional funds for the supervision of students in advanced training in research. Depending on the outcome of this evaluation, a university and its units may only receive one of these subsidies, or none at all. Also, this same score dictates how much financial assistance, if any, will be forthcoming for research until the next research assessment exercise.

Over the past couple of decades, HEFCE has conducted four such operations: in 1992, 1996, 2001, and 2008. We note that, even after the devolution of powers in the area of higher education, the other constituent countries of the UK have continued to subject their universities to these exercises. In the framework of higher education planning operations conducted by the Department of Business, Innovation and Skills, HEFCE was encouraged to become increasingly discriminating in the matter of financial decisions based on research assessments.

Consequently, HEFCE announced that, for the year 2012–13, it would only consider academic units that had received a rank of three (internationally excellent) or four (world-leading) when assessing research for the purposes of allocating recurring funds.[16] Funding agencies in the other constituent countries retain the option of following their own course in acting on these assessment exercises. Overall, they are more inclined to support institutions whose research quality falls below the threshold for recurring subsidies set by the HEFCE.

PRESENT CHARACTERISTICS OF THE SYSTEM

We now return to our central research question: Why do research universities in the United Kingdom perform so well in the ARWU and THES rankings – in some cases placing in the very highest categories? Clearly, the tradition of excellence that is the legacy of Oxford and Cambridge plays a role. To begin our exploration let us specify which UK institutions we will be considering.

We start with data on the operating conditions of the 165 higher education institutions in the United Kingdom. However, we will also work with a specific subsample of these universities. Like many other higher education systems, UK universities participate in a number of associations. The most prestigious of these, which includes the leading research universities, is called the Russell Group. In 2012–13 it represented a total of twenty-four universities in the United Kingdom. Although most are in England, there is at least one member institution from each constituent country. In 2009–10 research universities belonging to the Russell Group received nearly two-thirds of the external research funds disbursed by government granting agencies and foreign organizations, three-quarters of the funds from charities, and 60 per cent of those from business, and conferred the bulk of doctoral degrees.

Thus, these institutions are home to the lion's share of basic research and advanced training in research. This trend confirms a phenomenon that we have already observed and commented on: True research universities are relatively uncommon within any given higher education system that is characterized by institutional diversity. Also, these research universities concentrate within their walls a large share of the system's capacity for research and advanced training in research. We will see how recent public decisions by the constituent countries of the United Kingdom have very frequently been designed to strengthen either one or the other of these trends.

Institutions in the Russell Group are very well represented in the 2012 edition of both the ARWU and THES rankings of world-class research universities. Both of these lists feature nine of them among the 100 best universities internationally, and a further nine in the next category of ranks, 101 to 200. The THES ranking adds a few more UK research institutions to these two categories – which might be explained by the greater weight it assigns to subjective data on institutional reputation.

Our data are mostly drawn from information collected and maintained by HESA – the Higher Education Statistics Agency. Founded in 1993 by an agreement between government departments, university funding agencies, and universities and colleges, HESA is an arm's-length official data collection agency. However, under contractual arrangements it maintains constant contact with the relevant government departments – meeting their specialized information needs. It also receives subscription fees from universities and colleges in the United Kingdom, which have access to its data. We found that its databases on student bodies and university funding, for example, were particularly useful to us for working with both our subsample (the Russell Group)[17] and the entire UK university system.

Research Activity

From the mid-1980s until today, R&D spending as a percentage of GDP in the United Kingdom, as in other OECD-member countries, has tended downward, from a little over 2 per cent in 1985 to 1.8 per cent in 2008. Per-capita expenditure on R&D is lower in the United Kingdom than in the United States, France, and Canada.

Moreover, 26.5 per cent of R&D in the United Kingdom in 2008 was performed in academia. Rising to 28 per cent in 2009, this percentage still lagged behind the corresponding value for Canada but exceeded its value in the United States and France. Direct participation in R&D by the government is particularly weak in the United Kingdom in comparison with France, the United States, and Canada. Finally, we note that investments in research performed in UK universities amounted to 0.47 per cent of GDP in 2008 – rising to 0.52 per cent in 2009. This contribution made by university research in the United Kingdom, as measured by the funds invested in it, proves greater than the corresponding value in the United States. Also, across all sources, intramural research spending in the UK university sector exceeds that of Canada and France, but lags behind that of the United States.[18]

Unlike countries in which governments invest substantially in institutes or centres that parallel the university system, the United Kingdom expects its research universities to make a significant contribution to the generation of new knowledge. This feature, which is solidly anchored in the nation's higher education history, strengthens the position of the research universities in the system. Just as in the case of US research universities, the key role UK research universities play in the national research effort provides them with access to a high level of resources that act as a push factor, setting them apart on the international level.

In the United Kingdom, the funding of university-based research is governed by a dual model. On the one hand, universities have access to potentially recurring annual income from university funding councils. We have already noted how the Higher Education Funding Council for England and analogous agencies in the other countries of the United Kingdom attribute resources to the universities for purposes of research. Recall that these mechanisms rely on rigorous periodical Research Assessment Exercises (RAES), with the assigned scores dictating the amounts allocated.

This first component of the dual model is complemented by other funds made available to universities in the form of grants and contracts that are generally awarded on the basis of merit following an evaluation of research projects and researchers. The lion's share of such complementary contributions from external sources takes the form of grants from the seven research councils. These are directly disbursed to professors after their applications have been evaluated by peers who, in turn, submit their recommendations to the research granting councils. In fact, as we see in table 5.1, the merit-based grants and contracts aspect of the dual model constitutes a significant source of the external research funds that flow into UK universities.

In the case of research universities, this amounts to a considerable sum of money: nearly US$7 billion, with institutions in the Russell Group accounting for US$4.5 billion. The sheer magnitude of these numbers is the first thing that stands out, being comparable to levels observed in public research universities in the United States. In the United Kingdom, this governmental source distributes grants and contracts – especially from research councils (which account for over half of external research funding) – primarily to research universities, but also to all universities in the system. Nonetheless, the research universities in our subsample collect the lion's share of the merit-based grants provided by research councils – 66.4 per cent going to universities in the Russell Group.

Resources from philanthropic organizations, including substantial contributions from "charities" in the case of UK universities (notably the Rowntree Trust, the Leverhulme Trust, and several in the biomedical field, including the British Heart Foundation, Wellcome Trust, etc.), are the second largest source of funds for university research. Once again, we find that universities in the Russell Group appropriate the bulk (three-quarters) of these funds. These top-tier universities also benefit greatly from foreign research funds, the third-largest income source for research universities – a considerable proportion of which are from EU research support programs. All things considered, business contributes relatively little to research conducted in university settings. However, even in this case there is a clear bias in favour of research universities in the Russell Group.

The extent to which the competitiveness of professors in the leading UK research universities constitutes a fundamental input into their research output cannot be overstated. By attracting faculty members who have acquired a reputation in their disciplines on the basis of their publications, merit-based grants, and contracts received, especially from research councils, these universities position themselves to make a mark both domestically and internationally.

However, the impact of an academic faculty's excellence in the area of research extends beyond the aforementioned resources gathered from grants provided by research councils. It also smooths the

Table 5.1
Funding of university-based research by source and category of university, United Kingdom, 2009–2010, in thousands of US$

Group	Government	Business	Philanthropy	Foreign	Other	Total
			IN ABSOLUTE TERMS			
Russell Group	2,401,367	255,725	1,061,105	737,256	191,929	4,647,382
Other	1,213,895	171,863	340,931	396,179	113,109	2,235,977
All universities	3,615,262	427,588	1,402,037	1,133,434	305,038	6,883,358
		AS A PERCENTAGE BY SOURCE OF FUNDING				
Russell Group	51.7	5.5	22.8	15.9	4.1	100
Other	54.3	7.7	15.2	17.7	5.1	100
All universities	52.5	6.2	20.4	16.5	4.4	100
		AS A PERCENTAGE BY CATEGORY OF UNIVERSITY				
Russell Group	66.4	59.8	75.7	65	62.9	67.5
Other	33.6	40.2	24.3	35	37.1	32.5
All universities	100	100	100	100	100	100

Notes: External research funds include all external subsidies and research contracts. These values converted into US$ using purchasing power parity (PPP) based on 2009 OECD GDP numbers.
Source: HESA, Finances of Higher Education Institutions 2009–2010, Tables 4 and 5.

way for recurring research funding and support to students in advanced training in research received from university funding councils, especially HEFCE, and earmarked for English research universities. These contributions are a function of scores obtained by the universities' various academic departments during the RAEs. In 2009–10, research components that were eligible for recurring funding amounted to 22 per cent (£1,906,321K) of total annual subsidies of £8.5 billion (£8,655,053K) doled out by university funding councils, including HEFCE. This was not far short of the global budget of over two-and-a-half billion pounds sterling (£2.682 billion) made available to UK research granting councils in support of activities of discovery – a budget that mostly went to universities.[19]

Needless to say, the amounts disbursed by the funding councils to institutional support for research in 2009–10 were based on the results of the 2008 Research Assessment Exercise conducted by the

HEFCE in collaboration with the other UK funding councils. These subsidies were alloted to some 130 different institutions, but three-quarters of the institutional support for research provided by the funding councils went to twenty-six research universities. It should come as no surprise that the research universities of the Russell Group ranked at the top of these twenty-six universities.

In addition, the Russell Group's achievements in these measures of university-based research institutional success are spearheaded by an inner group, called by some the "golden triangle" of South-East England universities. These consist of Oxford, Cambridge, the Imperial College of London, University College of London, and the London School of Economics and Political Science. These universities alone generally receive nearly one-third of both the research funding from research granting councils and the recurrent support for the research element provided by HEFCE.[20]

There can be no doubt that the rules governing the dual UK research funding model favour the performance and output of research universities endowed with faculty members who are very competitive in obtaining resources allocated by peer assessment. This model, which is not unlike what we observed in the case of the United States, relies on assessments and competition that differentiate between individual faculty members first and then between the institutions themselves. Its overall impact is felt throughout the UK higher education system.

This funding model for research represents a strategic choice to create concentrations of the best and brightest of the UK's researchers – as authorities in the constituent countries stated quite openly. As a result, UK institutions were propelled into diversification and a concentration of their respective missions: One group became more focused on teaching while another, smaller, group (as our data confirm) went in the direction of becoming research universities in the sense we have been using the term.

Sources of Operating Funds

The previous chapter devoted to the US higher education system revealed the extent to which the level and diversity of universities' sources of operating revenues are key contributors to their output. According to OECD data, on the international level the United Kingdom is not among the countries making the greatest investment in higher education at the tertiary, or university, level. In 2007 it devoted the equivalent of 1.3 per cent of its gross domestic product to this network – half of this effort (0.7 per cent) being from the public sector – while the mean of OECD countries was 1.5 per cent.[21] A similar finding has prompted authorities in the United Kingdom to promote investment in this sector, seeking to encourage, as we noted, private sector input to compensate for the limited availability of government funds.

Augmenting these resources is on the political agenda even more now that the government, which controls the number of undergraduates admitted each year through a system of quotas imposed on the institutions, has come to the realization that it is not opening enough new places relative to the number of eligible candidates. The percentage of qualified candidates who are unable to gain admission to a full-time undergraduate program is increasing, and currently stands at 36 per cent. It is believed that there is a large contingent of qualified candidates who are simply unable to find a place in a higher education institution.[22]

What is the situation of research universities in light of these findings? Ignoring fixed asset funds and research grant funding provided to professors, we observe in table 5.2 that research universities receive one-third of the amounts made available to all universities in the United Kingdom.

We see that in 2009–10 recurring subsidies received from university funding councils accounted for less than half the operating revenues of universities (45 per cent). In the case of research universities, this percentage was even smaller. Moreover, tuition makes up approximately one-third of research universities' operating revenues in our sample; in the case of other universities this percentage is nearly 44 per cent. Conversely, UK research universities receive a greater proportion of their operating revenues (nearly 25 per cent, versus 10 per cent for other institutions) from other sources, such as philanthropic donations, endowment funds, local authorities and various government departments, and the European Union (excluding research grants funds, of course). A few of the most prestigious research universities, in particular Oxford and Cambridge, also earn supplementary income from their university presses, trademarks, and bookstores.

All things considered, the distribution of these operating revenue sources is like that of the most prestigious public research universities in the United States. Here, as there, government subsidies account for a little less than half of universities' total income. Broadly

Table 5.2
Sources of operating funds, United Kingdom, 2009–2010, in thousands of US$

Group	Govt. subs.	Tuition	Other income	Total
1 Russell Group	4,634,984	3,491,130	2,471,732	10,597,845
2 Other	9,206,069	8,842,765	2,117,045	20,165,880
All universities	13,841,053	12,333,895	4,588,777	30,763,725
Group	Govt. subs.	Tuition	Other income	Total
1 Russell Group	43.74%	32.94%	23.32%	100.00%
2 Other	45.65%	43.85%	10.50%	100.00%
All universities	44.99%	40.09%	14.92%	100.00%
Group	Govt. subs.	Tuition	Other income	Total
1 Russell Group	33.49%	28.31%	53.86%	34.45%
2 Other	66.51%	71.69%	46.14%	65.55%
All universities	100.00%	100.00%	100.00%	100.00%

Note: Funding of operating expenditures does not include external funding of research grants, but it does include profits from ancillary business ventures. GDP values from the OECD (2009) converted into US$ at PPP.
Source: HESA, Finances of Higher Education Institutions 2009–2010, tables 4 and 5.

speaking, tuition contributes approximately one-third of the required income, while revenues from other sources amount to one-quarter.

Research universities in the United Kingdom, like their public US counterparts, draw on a variety of income sources to cover their operating costs. This gives them greater flexibility in cross-subsidizing their basic teaching and, partially, research activities to reflect their priorities, strategic plans, and institutional choices – in the case of research, this includes the research element of recurrent institutional subsidies from funding councils. As we know, postgraduate studies, and especially advanced training in research, are expensive.

Thus, for this UK university system, which is in many respects characterized by government interventionism, a diversity of income sources remains a key variable for any institution hoping to stand out at the international level. However, this diversity's impact is circumscribed – despite receiving a large share of the total revenues in the system, research universities face limits on their decision-making autonomy. Nonetheless, the option of cross-subsidization allows them to concentrate the required resources on their priorities, provided they have previously demonstrated an ability to sustain excellence and have established a strong institutional reputation.

We must also note that this type of diversity in funding sources encourages research universities in the United Kingdom to perform well in the ARWU and THES international rankings. As in the case of public US research universities, this reality strengthens the capacity of their UK counterparts to post strong performances in a highly competitive world.

Human Resources

The previous chapter raises some questions: does a given institution, in particular a research university, select the students and professors that populate its ranks as a function of its priorities and strategic development choices? How can it provide sound supervision and incentives to assist them in their career trajectories?

STUDENTS

As we have already seen, the traditions and legacy of UK universities make them unique: Very selective access to higher education gives rise to a very particular conception of the academic milieu. For many years the emphasis was on keeping establishments small, creating a low student-to-professor ratio, and emphasizing education centred on a well-formed and independent mind, especially at the bachelor's level.

In the mid-1990s, B.R. Clark drew a rather sombre picture of the unity of research and training offered by UK universities at the postgraduate, especially the doctoral, level. Strongly influenced by a bias toward undergraduate studies, and also constrained by low university attendance, Clark maintained that the organizational design of academic departments and universities failed to provide the structuring environment required for proper development of training at the postgraduate level.[23]

However, since then considerable progress has been made in the matter of university attendance, and most specifically in university programs at the tertiary level – i.e., programs of at least three years and giving access to the most demanding professions in terms of qualifications and advanced training in research. Not only is the postgraduate student body growing, but it is growing faster than the undergraduate student body. The main beneficiaries of this trend have been the so-called "taught master's" programs, but "research master's" and doctoral programs are also experiencing healthy expansion.[24]

What do our data tell us about attendance in research universities? We see in table 5.3 that we are still dealing with institutions that had slightly fewer students in 2009 than their US counterparts. On average, they have some 22,000 students, approximately one-third of whom are at the postgraduate level. These are comprehensive research universities, supported by numerous faculty members and offering a broad array of training programs, though some of them stand out for providing an education that is much more specialized, either in the natural and biomedical sciences, or in various disciplines in the social sciences.

Overall, as we see in table 5.3, a large proportion of the students admitted into UK universities are at the bachelor's level (80 per cent), but in research universities this share is smaller (70 per cent). The remaining 30 per cent in the case of institutions in the Russell Group is divided into, on the one hand, slightly fewer than 20 per cent of the students in master's postgraduate studies, mostly consisting of "taught postgraduate" programs. On the other hand, the high proportion of the Russell Group's student bodies (approximately 10 per cent) at the "higher degree research" level – to wit, research master's and doctoral programs – is what differentiates these research universities above all others.

This distribution of students across all levels gives UK research universities an edge over their US public rivals, where total enrolment in comparable graduate studies is generally equivalent to 20 per cent of the total student body.[25]

Students enrolled in research master's or doctoral programs benefit from the government's policy of concentrating the best and brightest of the UK's researchers into certain universities, where they make up approximately 10 per cent of the student body – approximately four times the relative weight of higher degree research postgraduate students in the United Kingdom's other universities. This has given a greater critical mass to students in advanced training in research who are attending research universities.

At the undergraduate level there is a national system for processing applications in which the student can specify a list of universities he or she would like to attend. However, the final decision regarding admission is left to the universities. Furthermore, for postgraduate studies, which are not regulated by a national admissions system, universities have more leeway in the area of student recruitment and admissions.

Table 5.3
Distribution of students, full-time equivalent, by level of studies and category
of university, United Kingdom, 2009–2010

Group	First level	Second level	Third level	Total
IN ABSOLUTE NUMBERS				
Russell Group	309,702	78,966	41,810	430,496
Other	1,190,144	221,378	36,235	1,447,734
All universities	1,499,846	300,344	78,045	1,878,229
AS A PERCENTAGE BY LEVEL OF STUDIES				
Russell Group	20.6%	26.3%	53.6%	22.9%
Other	79.4%	73.7%	46.4%	77.1%
All universities	100.0%	100.0%	100.0%	100.0%
AS A PERCENTAGE BY CATEGORY OF UNIVERSITY				
Russell Group	71.9%	18.3%	9.7%	100.0%
Other	82.2%	15.3%	2.5%	100.0%
All universities	79.9%	16.0%	4.2%	100.0%

Notes: 1 full-time student = 3.5 part-time students, numbers rounded. First level includes the
categories "First degree" and "Other undergraduates." Second level includes the categories "Higher
degree (taught)" and "Other postgraduate." Third level includes the categories "Higher degree
(research)," doctoral, and "research master's." "Further education students" are not included. These
are mostly students in continuing or post-secondary non-university education.
Source: HESA, Students in Higher Education Institutions 2009–2010, table 11a.

Consequently, despite the fact that their relationship with government funding councils might stipulate certain conditions governing
the minimum number of students they must accept or placing a cap
on tuition fees, universities in the United Kingdom benefit from
sweeping autonomy in the most important decisions related to
admissions. They are required to manage a trade-off between quantity and quality, since a larger student body might generate more
operating resources, in particular from tuition charged to foreign
students. It is also worth noting that their allocation for operating
expenses requires that students be seen through to graduation within
a fixed amount of time.

Bearing in mind that UK research universities exercise a great deal
of autonomy in the area of recruitment, selection, and admission of
students, it is, of course, nonetheless true that university funding
councils impose some rules governing the number of students admitted and the tuition charged to undergraduates. But the quality of the

students admitted clearly bears the stamp of a culture of selectivity, in particular at the postgraduate level.

UK universities compete to attract candidates with very strong academic records and a demonstrated proclivity for advanced training in research – a phenomenon that is even more pronounced among the subgroup of top universities. The twenty-four institutions of the Russell Group alone account for over one-third (36 per cent) of this student population.

Research universities are also distinguished by the higher overall per-student operating costs they incur. For all practical purposes, they spend twice as much per student (nearly US$27K) as the other institutions (US$14K). In this case, as in the case of all research universities, these differentials are partially explained by the greater cost of postgraduate training in advanced research that is given in institutions that actively pursue new knowledge production activities. However, internationally, this level of expenditure per British student falls short of that of public US research universities.

In his analysis of advanced training in research and the necessity of linking it with milieus that are actively pursuing scientific discoveries, Clark observed that these issues rarely make it onto the political agenda in the United Kingdom. At the time, few reports or political platforms had been devoted to them and few institutional initiatives were devoted to improving the organization of these educational sectors.[26] In this regard as well, things have changed. As Green and Powell observe, the Harris Review of the mid-1990s finally proved to be the trigger for effecting changes in postgraduate studies and training in research within UK universities.[27] In the aftermath of the Harris report there have been others, from committees and specialized public institutes, that exclusively address postgraduate education in the United Kingdom and its most urgent institutional issues.[28]

Academic administrators and government decision-makers responsible for funding and planning higher education in the United Kingdom are less and less able to ignore the management of postgraduate education, from admission to the graduation of students. This trend is accentuated by the significant changes mentioned above that more specifically address policies for funding research and its various associated types of formation. University funding councils are paying greater attention to these issues, both in the conduct of rigorous periodic assessments and in decisions regarding the allocation of additional resources directly targeted at the missions of research universities.

Also, following in the footsteps of the North American experience, we observe the progressive introduction of a vertical division of academic labour into the UK university system – often in the form of graduate schools. In 2010, over 70 per cent of the 165 higher education institutions in the United Kingdom had at least one graduate school. More attention is thus being paid to the development and supervision of students in postgraduate programs and studies, including those in advanced training in research, and to better organization and academic consistency in the administration of programs.[29]

Furthermore, the Quality Assurance Agency issues codes of practice and orientation guides that set out quality standards that institutions must meet in the area of postgraduate education. These cover both "higher degree taught" and "higher degree research" programs. Since the middle of the last decade the QAA's on-site assessment visits have covered advanced training in research programs in an increasingly systematic fashion. University funding councils now consider these assessments when allocating recurring funding to research universities for their activities of scientific discovery and for the supervision of students enrolled in advanced training in research.

Another initiative, in this case by several research granting councils in the United Kingdom, underscores this trend toward a policy that is more attentive to research focused training. To foster doctoral education in particular, these councils have created Doctoral Training Centres (DTCs) whose goal is to promote – by means of special funding targeted at cohorts of students – the emergence of critical masses of very good students within environments that are characterized by research excellence. DTCs also emphasize acquiring knowledge and skills that create the ability to work in a variety of settings – not only universities – where knowledge is generated, as well as using interdisciplinary scientific strategies. In the short term, research granting councils offering Doctoral Training Centres plan to concentrate a greater share of their student fellowship resources in them.[30]

UK research universities that are present in international rankings have adopted a new academic culture for their programs of postgraduate education. Some twenty years after Clark's indictment of the state of postgraduate programs and studies in the United

Kingdom and the failure to better integrate research activities and training, we observe real progress and a political and institutional consciousness more committed to the importance of postgraduate education. The missions of the research universities focused on this type of training are supported by policies and practices that encourage recruiting the best students, including from abroad, and supervising and retaining them in research-intensive environments while ensuring that they are supported by professors committed to research.

Thus, we might venture to say that UK research universities have a long tradition of active and selective management of their student populations and holding on to them in their programs. This tradition is increasingly expanding into more structured and consistent efforts to organize postgraduate education and advanced research training. These research universities access the pool of students, an essential resource for any university, by competing with other institutions to attract the best candidates. From this perspective, these institutions exercise direct control over admission into the programs they offer as a function of their policies and institutional priorities.

FACULTY MEMBERS

The government-funded process of scientific discovery that occurs in the UK university environment is a matter of competition and assessment. Previous sections of this chapter have established and documented this finding. Key players in this publicly funded research system are professors who work in the Units of Assessment (UOA), i.e., the different university disciplinary departments that participate in periodic research assessment operations conducted by HEFCE. To obtain government research funding, these departments and their professors need to receive good reviews from their peers on various RAE panels that carefully evaluate their output, including through on-site visits.

In any national system, the quality of a research university's academic faculty is an inevitable determinant of its ability to adequately fulfill its missions. This variable is all the more important in an environment in which access to the resources required for attaining a critical mass of professor and student-researchers, as well as the best conditions for scientific discovery and training in research, involves a whole series of assessment operations. Ultimately, a research university that desires high-quality professors in a variety of disciplinary departments, and consequently in the UOAs that participate in periodic assessments, must learn to capitalize on opportunities to recruit and select its faculty members as they present themselves.

UK research universities, which are imposing institutions with large faculties, have proven themselves adept at that game. In comparison with other institutions in the UK higher education system, we have already noted that they receive – thanks to the quality of their faculty members – a share of both public and private research funding that far exceeds their relative weight in the system.

Consequently, their students learn in an environment that is rich in research resources per professor. Table 5.4 illustrates the wide gap that separates research universities from other UK universities. Considering only external research funds awarded on the basis of merit, we find that they receive over three times as much per professor as other institutions, and five times as much per full-time postgraduate student. Perhaps most important, in these universities the learning environment benefits from twice the external research funds per full-time doctoral student than in other institutions – setting the stage for the exceptional scientific discovery environments that are required for doctoral education.

We should also bear in mind that, in addition to the aforementioned resources, these research universities receive recurring funds for the maintenance of research infrastructures and the supervision of students that reflect the ranking of their units by RAEs. Members of the academic faculties in these institutions are a key component of their ability to acquire the best possible resources. We clearly see that the five institutions in the golden triangle, which we have already mentioned – Oxford, Cambridge, the Imperial College of London, University College of London, and the London School of Economics and Political Science – jointly make up the flagship of the universities in the Russell Group. They bring up the average of all these universities both in terms of merit-based external research funds obtained and the ensuing volume of publications.[31]

Universities in the United Kingdom also clearly have a handle on their professorial requirements. The recruitment, selection, and hiring of members of a university's academic faculty are first and foremost under the auspices of the basic academic units, disciplinary departments, and equivalent structures. It is up to the various levels of academic administration to make the funds required for these

Table 5.4
Research spending per professor and postgraduate student, United Kingdom,
2009–2010, full-time equivalent, in US$

Universities	Per professor	Per postgraduate student	Per PhD student
1 Russell Group	82,925	38,479	111,155
2 Other	25,415	8,680	61,708
All universities	47,793	18,191	88,197

Note: Professors are full-time equivalent and correspond to the category "Academic Professionals."
Postgraduate students includes both master's and doctoral students. GDP values from the OECD
(2009) converted into US$ at PPP.
Sources: HESA, Finances of Higher Education Institutions 2009–2010, tables 4 and 5; HESA, Staff in
Higher Education Institutions 2009–2010, table 5; HESA, Students in Higher Education Institutions
2009–2010, table 1.

staffing choices available, to exercise the ultimate decision-making
authority, and to ensure that the choices made by the academic units
meet the quality standards.

This is, thus, a sphere of action that an institution can occupy
equipped with its strategic development plan, its institutional priorities, and a clear definition of its short- and medium-term objectives.
It will not have to accommodate some outside decision-making body
imposing the taking on board of external scientific staff with which
it has no direct relationship.

However, we need to bear in mind that the recruitment of academic faculty by UK universities is limited by internal constraints.
Since the end of the Second World War there has been a national
system that sets the salaries of professors in higher education. In
fact, nation-wide collective agreements are negotiated by representatives of faculty members, the University and College Union (UCU),
and of employers in higher education, the University and College
Employers Association (UCEA). These agreements set the salary
scales for various tiers of university professors.

However, any given institution maintains a very real independence
when choosing into what tier to place a newly hired professor.
Between these tiers and pay scales, and their implementation by any
university, there is enough flexibility to allow the institutions a great
deal of leeway. For example, several research universities use bonuses
as performance incentives for their professors.

It appears, moreover, that the national framework that determines
compensation for professors under the agreements with the UCU are

more binding for the first years of a professorial career and for institutions that are either quite new or are not classified as research universities. Professors in the latter are most active in research and their salaries ultimately appear less constrained by the official national compensation grids. It should be noted, however, that academic faculty members of UK universities acquire tenure very rapidly, generally by the end of their first year. Moreover, the interests of research-oriented professors lie not only in their salaries, but also in the quality of infrastructures and of the professionals who will support their research programs. In this regard, the pool of resources available to UK research universities and their allocative flexibility in this matter gives them an edge in the recruitment of high-quality professors.

It is also clear that over time UK universities have had to revise their student-to-professor ratio. As we have seen, government cutbacks throughout the United Kingdom have left their mark on the resources invested in higher education. This ratio rose from 9.5 to 11.5 students per professor between 1980 and 1989. Of course, these global results conceal major variations across broad disciplinary sectors and institutions.[32] *Ceteris paribus*, research universities have fared better in this regard than institutions that are more oriented to teaching – notwithstanding the persistence, even acceleration, of this trend toward higher ratios since the beginning of the 1990s.

Despite the external constraints on the autonomy of UK universities in the area of faculty member resources, we note that this is one aspect of their operations that they have well in hand. Here they wield much more direct decision-making authority, and consequently power, especially in the case of research universities, than many other European universities. This factor thus gives a clear edge to any UK research university that reaches a high position in international rankings and succeeds in remaining there.

Academic Governance

For the purposes of our study, the governance of an institution raises a series of questions. Do the academic administrators manage to directly control access to the human resources of their university? Are they able to devise a game plan for the priorities that govern teaching and research so as to provide solid support to the key actors in their institutions and guide them to better yields, even a stronger international position? Can they count on the collective will of the principal driving forces of the milieu to promote high standards and a culture of excellence? Do they have the elbow room to redirect any potential diversity in their revenue sources into expenditure and investment choices that support improved performance?

Since universities in the United Kingdom are, strictly speaking, generally private – or shall we say quasi-private? – with their charters and administration delegated to the boards of governors, we might be tempted to jump to a hasty, but ultimately unfounded, conclusion to that effect. While it is true that these universities have the status of private legal persons, in some sense, no one in the United Kingdom actually believes that the higher education system is truly private. Quite aside from the large proportion of their income universities receive from government sources, the reach of government regulation further puts paid to that notion.

The various university funding councils and many other independent bodies – such as the Quality Assurance Agency (QAA), the Higher Education Statistics Agency (HESA), and the Universities and Colleges Admission Service (UCAS), to name but a few – amount, for all intents and purposes, to a government regulatory system, though their boundaries are often vague and porous. There are, moreover, persistent objections to the lack of an arms-length relationship with the government in the case of most of these agencies, despite their nominal independence. The prevailing mood is clear: Appealing to the private status of these universities, or of research universities, or even of the most prestigious institutions, Oxford and Cambridge, would elicit strong opposition.

Tony Bruce concludes his systematic and detailed study of higher education in the United Kingdom in the context of constitutional change and the devolution of powers with some interesting comments on the organizational dynamics underlying the system. Other than England, which harbours the lion's share (80 per cent) of UK higher education institutions, none of the other three constituent countries sought to introduce the idea of "the market" invoked by the English government and the HEFCE for the management of their own higher education system. Their respective policies increasingly diverged from those of England, notably in the case of tuition fees and finding a new balance between public and private in the funding of higher education.

In addition, while paying lip service to the notion of autonomy of universities, the authorities in these three countries (Scotland, Wales, and Northern Ireland), leaning on more power gained through devolution policies, have formulated action plans to harness their universities to their short- and medium-term socio-economic goals. In so doing, they have become much more interventionist in the area of higher education and the management of universities, seeking to revamp the composition of, and the powers exercised by, their boards of directors, among other things. In fact, universities in these three countries are increasingly treated as public services devoted to the pursuit of national agendas as defined by the government of the day. Bruce concludes that there is an imminent threat to the autonomy of these universities, and that the end result of this trend is toward a more traditional European model of higher education.[33]

There is no disputing that the government of England uses the agencies and councils to which it delegates government funding and some regulatory functions over higher education to elicit from universities, especially research universities, the support required to sustain a knowledge-based national economy. This has been made manifest many times in recent years.

However, we must bear in mind that, even while they have stitched together a regulatory framework that imposes real constraints, authorities in the United Kingdom have found a way to leave a considerable degree of decision-making latitude to the universities, just as they have promoted an atmosphere of competition and emulation between them, in particular with regard to activities in scientific discovery and advanced training in research. They also extended this autonomy to the new post-92 universities – previously identified as polytechnics and continuing education colleges – which they strove to disentangle from the legacy of the more traditional English university education system.

So much so, in fact, that in the case of UK research universities the situation is clearer: Their principal administrators manage institutions that exercise direct and full control over decisions governing access to a broad array of human and financial resources, the absence of which would leave them unable to produce such remarkable yields. The leadership and governance style that the principals of an institution cultivate is thus a key variable that we can examine, in the case of UK research universities, by drawing on the results of a recent study, to which we alluded earlier when examining the governance of US research universities.

Recall that Amanda H. Goodall summarized the results of the work she has conducted in recent years on research universities' governance in an article with the evocative title "Why Socrates Should be in the Board Room in Research Universities."[34]

In the case of UK research universities Goodall has been able to establish an even more direct relationship between the scientific credentials of the vice-chancellors and the success of the institutions they direct. She bases this on the results obtained for departments or assessment units of fifty-five research universities during three successive evaluations – the 1992, 1996, and 2001 HEFCE Research Assessment Exercises – of leading UK universities' research performances. Normalizing her data by holding factors such as total revenues, the institution's size, and the age and disciplinary affiliation of the vice-chancellor constant, she has generated results that speak for themselves.

During the period she examines, research universities in which the number of departments classified as excellent increased from one assessment to the next were headed by vice-chancellors with stellar scientific careers. In fact, the five and ten research universities with the greatest growth in the number of departments ranked as global leaders in their disciplines post high-correlation coefficients between these outcomes and the very large number of scientific citations their leaders earned over the courses of their careers. Also, the five and ten institutions that experienced the steepest decline in the rankings of their respective departments in these research assessment operations had leaders with less outstanding academic records.

In fact, the vice-chancellors in charge of the ten research universities that had made the most progress reported three times as many scientific citations as those whose institutions regressed the most. Taking the point even further, Goodall documents a systematic decline in the number of departments classified as excellent in these research universities that parallels a gradual decline in the scientific citations of their principal academic administrators.

University administrators who were recognized authorities in their fields exercised a pronounced driving effect on the principal academic actors and the various levels of a given institution's governance. Drawing on nearly twenty-five interviews conducted with men and women who had exercised the highest functions in research universities – fifteen of whom were in the United Kingdom – our colleague explored the mechanism of this coattail effect. As we have seen, Goodall maintains that it arises from credible leadership, a deep understanding of what makes a great research university, and the ability to set, for the various components of the institution, standards that are high but well internalized by the person who first formulated them and oversees their implementation. Sending a clear signal as to what really matters for completely fulfilling the mission of a great research university will have all the more effect to the extent that the individual who articulates it renders it credible.[35]

CONCLUSION

The case of UK research universities is of great interest for our study. There are marked similarities between them and corresponding institutions in the US system, especially those in the public sector. They undeniably exercise decision-making autonomy in many areas, allowing them to make choices and set the priorities they choose in keeping with a long and strong tradition of striving for excellence. Thus, they have the means to ensure, in their own right, their present and future in terms of the selection and recruitment, as well as the policies governing the supervision and retention of students and professors. These research universities also benefit from a diversity of income sources that is conducive to emulation and competition in their relationships.

However, at the same time, these UK research universities are evolving in an environment in which market effects and the drive to compete are for the most part mediated by government. Their access to resources and their competitive relationships bear the mark of a mixed system in which the relative autonomy of the institution coexists with a governmental regulatory framework. In many ways, the institutional mix and the delicate balance between autonomy and regulation underlying the functioning of UK research universities located in England are remarkable. On this matter, it might be said that research universities in the other UK constituent countries appear to be facing a growing imbalance between autonomy and regulation. They belong to university systems whose operating conditions are increasingly polarized by the rise in government intervention.

6

THE UNIVERSITY SYSTEM IN CANADA

In previous chapters we have seen that there are marked differences between countries in their ability to produce world-class universities, even when their situation is normalized to account for the broad macroeconomic factors that play an important role in the demand for a highly skilled workforce and new ideas. We then examined the institutional and organizational characteristics of the functioning of US universities to identify a subset of features that might contribute to their standing among the best world-class research universities. In the previous chapter we underscored the importance of the institutional and organizational arrangements that have helped UK research universities reach the top of international rankings.

Despite a shorter history and smaller size, the Canadian university system has performed very well in terms of the number of world-class research universities it has spawned. We will examine the unique features of this system that might explain its performance on the international scene. The Canadian system has been profoundly influenced by those of the United Kingdom and the United States, and very peripherally by that of France.

As we did in the case of the other systems studied, we begin with a brief historical overview and then turn our attention to the broad characteristics of the Canadian system with regard to the organization and funding of research. Next, we will look at the functioning of this system in terms of its size and diversity of funding sources, among other things. We conclude with some of the most important issues raised by the ways and means by which students and professors arrive and evolve while also taking note of factors associated with governance in this university system.

A BIT OF HISTORY

In contrast to the long university traditions of European countries, the history of universities in Canada is quite short and mirrors the development of this young country in a North American context at a time when the sciences were coming of age and taking shape and research was gaining entrance into academia. For over one hundred years, until 1759, Canada was a colony of France. Here Monseigneur de Laval had founded the Séminaire de Québec for training priests in 1663. With its links to France cut off following the British conquest of 1759, this institution was obliged to broaden its mission to include education in the liberal professions – on site and in French. Lacking the name and the status, the root of Canada's university system can nonetheless be traced to here, though it was not until the middle of the nineteenth century that it seriously began to develop.

The situation was radically transformed by the Conquest. The English-speaking population subsequently ballooned in the wake of the American War of Independence as a large number of American loyalists, who did not want to sever their ties to the Crown, emigrated to the Canadian colonies. These swelling ranks of anglophones gradually recognized the need for universities patterned after those in the British homeland to deter young Canadians from pursuing their studies in the United States. Two higher education institutions were thus founded with a royal charter, the first in Lower Canada in 1821 (McGill University) and the second in Toronto, in Upper Canada, in 1827 (King's College, which became the University of Toronto in 1850). Initially affiliated with religious orders, the University of Toronto soon asserted its independence and became secular and autonomous.

Inspired by the most advanced academic systems of the time in Germany, the United Kingdom, and the United States, McGill strove for an international standing from the beginning. After a somewhat tumultuous startup, as is typical of new and first institutions, it came under the leadership of a first-class scientific mind, John William Dawson, who held the position of principal for thirty-eight years, from 1855 to 1893. Placing McGill on the international academic map began in 1857 when, at Dawson's invitation, the American Association for the Advancement of Science held its first meeting outside the United States in Montreal.[1]

This institution also benefited from a geographical location and economic conditions that were particularly propitious. Montreal was the nucleus of Canada's industrial revolution during the mid-nineteenth century. By the end of that century, no less that 75 per cent of Canada's wealth was concentrated in Montreal, most of it in the hands of the city's anglophones. Dawson, like his successors, knew how to turn this fact to good use for the institution he headed. Business leaders and Canada's titans of industry sat on McGill's board of directors, and their substantial and frequent gifts ensured the development of this premier Canadian university. The Molsons and Smiths were just two of the wealthy Montreal families that supported McGill. At the beginning of the twentieth century, William Macdonald, the Canadian tobacco magnate, took over and gave more than CAN$14 million in donations to McGill, an enormous amount of money at the time. Since recurring and predictable government funding did not exist, McGill's development followed a path similar to that of private US universities, with which it had close ties. It should not come as a surprise that McGill served as a model for many other Canadian universities – founded to meet the demand of a growing population.

During the nineteenth century Toronto lacked the wealth, economic development, and population of Montreal.[2] Nonetheless, the university that had been created there in 1827 was Upper Canada's answer to McGill in Lower Canada, even if the anglophone elite aspired to make McGill the leading university for both colonies. The people of Upper Canada did not quite see it that way, and the University of Toronto, which was the new incarnation of King's College, became Canada's second centre of university studies. After developing an undergraduate system based on the UK model, and still desiring to shield young Canadians from colleges in the United States, reputed to be hostile toward the British monarchy, it was decided that the best approach to developing graduate studies was the US model which, as we have seen, drew heavily on its German forerunner. The founding in 1876 of Johns Hopkins University and the creation of its PhD program had a profound influence on the University of Toronto.[3] Many of its graduates went to Johns Hopkins for their doctoral studies, and quite a few of them remained in the United States. Moreover, there were professors at the University of Toronto who had already earned their PhD and urged their own university to set up such a program. Consequently, a research PhD program was established in 1897 along the lines of the one at Johns Hopkins. This was how Canadian universities fell under the sway of the US model for graduate studies – an influence that has only grown in light of the remarkable success of the US model, as we saw in chapter 4.

McGill and Toronto, which successfully blended university traditions from the United Kingdom, Germany, and the United States to create a Canadian version of the research university, were thus pioneers of this type of institution in Canada. During this same period two other anglophone universities were founded and enjoyed a certain prominence, without, however, rivalling the influence of McGill or University of Toronto: They were Dalhousie in Halifax and Queen's in Kingston.

In Lower Canada, where the French-speaking population was concentrated, Queen Victoria bestowed a royal charter on the Séminaire de Québec in 1852 granting it the right to award degrees and endowing it with all the "rights, privileges, powers and duties of a university." The upshot was a Catholic university run by clergy, Université Laval, which extended its hegemony over French-language postsecondary education in 1878 by opening a campus in Montreal – whose French-speaking population was greatly expanding during this period. In 1920 this campus became the fully autonomous Université de Montréal, but not without a share of hard-fought turf wars.

Compared with McGill and the University of Toronto, the two francophone institutions were weighed down by a series of handicaps from the beginning. First, they were Catholic institutions in a highly conservative social milieu, led by clergy who often had no academic expertise. Rome exercised a great deal of control over these universities, and they essentially identified with the European network of Catholic institutions that was worlds away from the great German, UK, and US traditions that were blazing the trail for modern universities. In addition, little if any of the vast wealth concentrated in Montreal, which was such an asset to McGill, was available to these two francophone universities, which had to depend on the Catholic Church for their survival. Finally, they could not gain much from the French university model, as it generally had little to offer. Thus, Canada saw a two-tier development of universities, and it was not until the early 1960s that francophone universities in Quebec begin to catch up to their leading anglophone counterparts.

Evolution of University Funding

A brief historical overview of university funding in Canada will shed some light on the current state of affairs that we will examine in this chapter. Clearly, when these Canadian universities were founded there was no government policy for funding this type of institution. In a tradition that was characteristically North American, philanthropy played a central role. Furthermore, the most affluent Canadian industrialists not only contributed out of their personal fortunes – their wealth was, in any case, not comparable with that of their US counterparts – but they also weighed in with their considerable political influence to encourage governments to support these new institutions. As a complement to tuition fees and philanthropic gifts and bequests, government funding in the form of grants was sporadic. For example, it might top off the budget for a building project or erase an operating deficit.

The British North America Act (BNA) of 1867 established the division of powers and responsibilities between levels of government in this new federation. Education fell to the provinces, while research was a shared responsibility. This division of responsibilities did not immediately affect the sporadic funding of universities by governments. For a long time, the government funding of universities was an annual, ad hoc decision, creating a need for continuous lobbying of politicians by university administrators. It was not until the 1960s that provincial governments, specifically in Ontario and Quebec, established a formula that was explicit and based on a series of objective criteria for university funding.

The federal government, which was shut out of education by the BNA Act of 1867, responded to increasing demands from universities that it contribute to their finances to help them deal with the costs occasioned by a sharp increase in students.[4] Thus, in 1951 direct federal funding was established on a per-capita basis. This lasted until 1966, by which time it amounted to CAN$100 million. By and large, this jurisdictional overstepping by the federal government was tolerated by the provinces. Only Quebec refused to allow its universities to accept direct funding from the federal government – with the effect of exacerbating the pronounced disadvantage of these universities relative to their counterparts elsewhere in Canada for many years.

In 1966, however, under pressure from Quebec and a few other provinces, the federal government opted to respect the constitution and transformed its direct subsidies to universities into transfer payments to the provinces earmarked for funding universities. Over time, the formula was modified so that this funding, rather than being on a per-capita basis, covered 50 per cent of the costs incurred by provincial governments for universities. This formula, which was very beneficial to the provinces, only lasted one decade – the federal government found it increasingly onerous. In fact, there was no federal control on the provinces' levels of spending on universities. As a consequence, federal funding for university education was capped and lumped together with other programs into an unconditional transfer payment to the provinces.

We see that Canada's golden age of government funding of the university system was from the mid-1950s to the early 1990s. Desiring to promote access, governments steadily increased their grants to universities in response to strong growth in the student body, allowing tuition to remain relatively low in comparison with the United States. In most provinces, the contribution of government to university funding exceeded 70 per cent, with the remaining 30 per cent split between tuition (15 per cent to 20 per cent) and other income, including philanthropy (10 per cent to 15 per cent).

This situation was radically altered starting in the mid-1990s. Faced with a budgetary crunch resulting from the economic downturn and a dangerously high national debt, the federal government implemented an austerity plan that included a reduction of transfers to the provinces. The domino effect was not slow in materializing as the provinces slashed university funding. The universities, in turn, well aware of the abysmal state of government finances at both the federal and provincial level, asked the provincial governments to deregulate tuition fees to safeguard the quality of the institutions. While the details varied from one province to the next, all but Quebec agreed to increase and deregulate tuition. These fees gradually begin to rise, but differentially across sectors. During this same period the universities, especially the leading research universities, began looking for other sources of income and intensified their fundraising efforts targeted at alumni, business, and various foundations. These trends in the financing of Canadian universities brought them closer to public US universities, as we shall see below – except, of course, in the case of Quebec.

Mass University Attendance

Developments in how the funding of research and higher education is organized in Canada are of particular interest to anyone seeking to understand the emergence of world-class universities. Government research funding in academia only appeared in Canada after the federal government created the National Research Council (NRC) in 1916. In the absence of university research, it was impossible to have real graduate studies and research-based training as had been created in Germany and was increasingly becoming the norm in US universities. Of course, there was university research in Canada prior to 1920, but it was essentially concentrated in two universities, McGill and the University of Toronto. This research was mostly funded by philanthropy. These private grants, which were neither as large or diverse as in the United States, nonetheless made it possible to not only perform high-quality research in these two institutions, but also – as of the beginning of the twentieth century – laid the groundwork for the creation of PhD programs that mirrored those found in the United States.

These developments were slow in materializing, partially because of research funding scarcity, but also because there was no financial support for students, unlike in the leading US universities (such as Johns Hopkins). Out of a total of 23,418 university students in Canada in 1920–21, only 407 were enrolled in graduate studies. Most of them were at McGill or Toronto, both of which had managed to produce research that was recognized internationally.[5] Throughout the 1920s, in any given year no more than some twenty PhDs were awarded, primarily by these two universities.[6] To compare, research universities in the United States awarded some 12,000 PhDs between 1920 and 1929, and nearly 26,000 between 1930 and 1939.[7]

Aside from some subtle differences, these two pioneering Canadian institutions adopted the US structure for their PhD programs. They more than satisfied the requirements imposed by the Association of American Universities, which was founded in 1920 by leading US universities seeking to standardize PhD programs in the United States. These two Canadian universities adapted so well to the criteria of the

AAU, and the quality of their research was already of such a high standard, that they were both admitted to the Association in 1927. Furthermore, following the lead of US research universities, McGill and the University of Toronto established graduate schools to coordinate graduate education and ensure consistency in its regulation. Though the Canadian university system of that era was by no means comparable to its US counterpart, we can see that it was off to a promising start.

Creation of the NRC changed the lay of the land in terms of university research funding and financial support for students in graduate studies, though it took some time to work itself out. In 1917–18 the NRC only doled out CAN$13,000 for university-based research; in 1927–28 this assistance amounted to CAN$154,000, and by 1937–38 it had reached CAN$214,000.[8]

Since McGill and the University of Toronto already had the research infrastructure and the researchers, they appropriated a very large piece of the pie and consolidated their leadership position in Canada's fledging university system. Enrolment in graduate studies remained modest, with some 3,000 full-time students registered in the mid-1940s, then close to 5,000 at the beginning of the 1950s, and nearly 7,000 by the end of that decade.[9] University research is a prerequisite to graduate studies, hence these two pioneering institutions strengthened their grasp on Canadian graduate studies. So true was this, in fact, that of the seventy-five PhDs awarded by all universities in Canada in 1940, thirty-two were from McGill and thirty-three from the University of Toronto, amounting to 87 per cent of the total. Furthermore, these two institutions contributed significantly to the some 300 PhDs awarded annually by the end of the 1950s.

Just like the First World War, the Second World War had a major impact on university research.[10] The role that research could play in Canada's future and economic development became clear to both the government and the general public. Government funding of university research thus gradually expanded, so that by the end of the 1960s NRC grants in the natural and physical sciences and in engineering represented 80 per cent of the total. The creation of the National Arts Council in 1957 provided additional funding, though modest at first, to the social sciences and humanities. Nonetheless, despite considerable growth in the Canadian university system the institutional concentration of the lion's share of research funding within only a few institutions persisted, owing to an attribution mode that was based on excellence. Thus, in 1965–66 five universities shared 50 per cent of all research funds, and ten universities accounted for 82 per cent.[11]

The war and the associated industrial development clearly had less impact in Canada than in the United States, for three reasons. First, the contribution of university research to the Canadian war effort pales beside the corresponding value in the United States. Next, the Cold War gave a great boost to public support for university research in the United States – we need only think of the space race, and the trauma to the American psyche when the Soviets launched Sputnik – but had little impact in Canada. Finally, the surge in industrial research, which was often indirectly fuelled by university research, barely made a ripple in Canada, a landscape occupied by branches of US firms that conducted their research at home. The university research funding by governments, and especially by the federal government, thus grew at a much less sustained rate in Canada than in its southern neighbour.[12] Nonetheless, over time Canadian universities became a major locus of research activity in Canada, accounting for some 36 per cent of the nation's R&D activities in 2007. This percentage is substantially higher than the OECD average (17 per cent) and even higher than the corresponding value in the United States (14 per cent).[13]

We see, therefore, that research in universities was expanding and the potential demand for PhDs was driven by two obvious factors. First, strong growth in the student body directly implied a corresponding rise in the numbers of academic faculty holding PhDs. Added to this was demand emanating from private, public, and parapublic sectors in the new knowledge economy. In Canada, as in many other OECD member countries, there was a strong growth in the demand for university education during the 1960s. With time this demand took the shape of mass higher education. In fact, it was estimated that university enrolment, which totalled 172,400 in 1963–64, would rise to 417,500 by 1970–71 and 583,400 by 1975–76.[14] This growth not only materialized, but continued afterwards, to the point that by 2010 there were some 1.2 million students attending Canadian universities.

The expansion at the graduate level was just as pronounced: from approximately 13,000 enrolments during the mid-1960s to a little over 40,000 in the early 1970s and then, by the end of that decade, nearly 60,000. Furthermore, this trend persisted to the point that, in the forty years stretching from the end of the 1960s until 2010, enrolments in both master's programs (1968: 23,816 and 2008: 104,079) and PhD programs (1968: 9,604 and 2008: 42,828) more than quadrupled, representing annual growth rates greater than 3.75 per cent in both cases. With respect to the degrees awarded during this same forty-year period, master's degrees increased by a factor of eight (1968: 4,216 and 2008: 36,507) and PhDs by a factor of five (1968: 1,069 and 2008: 5,424).[15]

Such a momentous expansion of university education, and in particular of graduate studies, requires more qualified academic faculty to not only teach, but also participate in the training of researchers. In 1963–67, when the transformation to mass higher education first became apparent and its extension to graduate studies foreseeable, 40 per cent of professors in the natural sciences and engineering, and 67 per cent of professors in the humanities and social sciences, did not have a PhD – this created a major impediment to the growth of Canadian universities. Under these circumstances, maintaining an acceptable student–professor ratio despite the growth in the student body required that academic staff levels increase from 14,600 in 1963–64 to 33,400 in 1970–71, and to 41,900 in 1975–76.[16] At the beginning of the 1960s, and despite a major influx of PhDs from abroad, the state of Canada's university system was a significant drag on its own development, especially in the area of graduate studies.

Today

More than forty years later, and after a strong growth period in output from graduate programs, can this university system rise to the challenges of the future and accommodate another foreseeable surge in demand for PhD holders emanating from within as well as outside of the university milieu? Below we document the very real deficit, in international terms, of Canadian universities in the annual production of PhDs. This is also a finding of the Association of Universities and Colleges of Canada (AUCC), which raised the alarm in 2008, in the wake of the Macdonald Commission. It estimated that Canadian universities would need to hire no fewer than 35,000 new professors in the following decade to replace retirees and accommodate a growing clientèle.[17] Will the Canadian university system accomplish this? We return to this question in a subsequent chapter.

We finally observe that, at the end of the Second World War, despite some progress by Université Laval and Université de Montréal, and the beginnings of a shift toward the North American graduate studies model, francophone institutions in Quebec were still not in the same league as the leading anglophone universities, especially their immediate neighbour, McGill. Fortunately, Quebec's universities received quite a jolt from the Quiet Revolution of the 1960s. As Gingras says: "In fact, the preoccupation of Francophone universities in the 1960s was with the notion of catching up, and the Canadian government became involved with these efforts by providing special financial assistance to allow them to develop their research activities and thus join the ranks of Anglophone universities."[18]

This catching up began with a massive investment in and transformation of Quebec's educational system: reform of the secondary school system; elimination of the classical colleges (which were unique in North America and very exclusive); creation of the system of CEGEPs (Collèges d'enseignement général et professionnel, or general and vocational colleges); expansion of the university network by the creation of the Universités du Québec network and the INRS (Institut national de la recherche scientifique, Quebec's National Institute of Scientific Research); and, finally, the establishment of two granting agencies for university research. As we will see below, current data on students and university research in Quebec clearly reveal that convergence has been achieved and that Canada no longer has a two-tier university system.

Our brief historical overview has revealed the profound influence the US university system had on the emergence and development of the Canadian system. No other system in the world felt this influence so early in its development, or with such an impact. Clearly, geographical proximity played an important role here, but it was mostly the resolve of the emerging Canadian universities to keep the best students in Canada while attracting leading researchers from abroad that conditioned the choices made by McGill and the University of Toronto and the generosity of their early donors as of the late nineteenth century. The influence of the leading universities' academic tradition of excellence in the United Kingdom should not be overlooked, either, because that is where many young professors in the new Canadian universities received their training. Thus, from the beginning the Canadian system was shaped by the two university networks that produced the greatest number of world-class research universities.

Even though the first Canadian universities relied principally on philanthropy and contributions from their students, there was never any question that government funding was essential for their development. Unlike in the United States, there are no strictly private universities in Canada. However, it appears to us that McGill and the University of Toronto have played a role in Canada that is analogous to that played by the leading private universities in the United States, which set the standard of academic excellence for the public universities in that country, and by Cambridge and Oxford, which shaped the evolution of the UK university system.

It is also important to bear in mind that, as of its entrance onto the academic scene, government research funding was based on academic excellence and the ability to carry out peer-assessed research projects that meet internationally recognized scientific standards. This approach prevents government funds from being spread too thin and encourages the rapid development of centres of excellence in a small number of institutions.

Last but not least, Canadian universities competed with each other from the beginning. This applied to the rivalry between McGill and the University of Toronto, but also represented the situation within Ontario, where other universities challenged Toronto's title as the premier university in the province. This competitive environment was not limited to Canada, but extended to the United States, where well-established universities attracted Canada's best and brightest. Thus, it was necessary to rapidly improve the supply of higher education in Canada to stem the potential exodus of that most precious of resources: high-quality grey matter. For a long time French-language universities in Canada existed in a sort of bubble, relatively protected from this outside competition by language and by their isolation from developments in North America.

PRESENT CHARACTERISTICS OF THE SYSTEM

In order to acquire a better understanding of how other organizational features of Canada's university system contribute to the trajectory of its institutions' on an international scale, we need to identify the most current issues relating to the organization of research and its financing within university groupings. We will do the same for the amounts and the sources of their operating revenues, which serve to pay for teaching and the infrastructures it requires. Then we will look at some aspects of the ways and means by which students and professors arrive and evolve before concluding with some brief comments on university governance.

Exactly which Canadian academic institutions will we be looking at? Over the course of its nearly 200-year history, the size and diversity of Canada's university system has evolved greatly. The number of members of the AUCC would suggest that there are over ninety-five institutions in Canada that are considered universities. At the end of the first decade of the twenty-first century, these institutions were serving approximately one million students, three-quarters of whom were full-time and 85 per cent enrolled as undergraduates. Approximately one in ten was an international student, nearly all of whom were full-time. However, as a student population proportion their representation was higher at the doctoral (23 per cent) and master's (18 per cent) level than at the bachelor's level (8 per cent).[19]

As is the case in many other countries, Canada's university system has become very diversified. For quantitative and qualitative data on the organizational characteristics of these Canadian institutions, we will draw on a university categorization into three groups devised for *Maclean's* university rankings. The peak of its pyramid consists of fifteen leading "multi-versities" offering a broad array of programs at all levels and in a vast number of disciplines, including medicine. The next tier consists of some fifteen other universities without a faculty of medicine, but very active in research and that offer a comprehensive slate of studies at all levels and in the professions. They are called "comprehensive universities" in this ranking system. The base of this pyramid consists of some seventy universities and colleges that concentrate on undergraduate studies, with few or no graduate programs and limited research activity. We note, however, that this base is far from homogeneous, since some universities that are ranked here barely fall short of the threshold of being considered "comprehensive universities."

As we observed in the US and UK university systems, in recent years a cluster of institutions that are intensive in research and in advanced training in research has formed in Canada. This group, known as the G-10,[20] was informally cobbled together in 1991. Although membership in this group is based on less rigorous criteria than those used by the Carnegie Foundation to classify US research universities, they are nonetheless great research universities that stand out for the intensity of their scientific endeavours and the way they are integrated into graduate studies, especially at the PhD level. No doubt they would easily satisfy the US criteria for this category of university.

Following a change to the composition of the group in 2006, it was renamed the G-13. The three universities that were added to the original members requested admission on the basis of the criteria that define a research-intensive university: annual investment in research; institutional prioritization of graduate studies; significant contribution to the number of graduate degrees awarded, especially doctoral degrees.[21] More recently, in 2011, membership in this group was again revised upward to fifteen universities as two more satisfied the criteria – thereby rounding out the regional representation in this particular collection of Canadian research universities.[22] How is this group of fifteen Canadian institutions linked to the category of so-called multi-versities we use below? With a single exception, the fifteen institutions in the category of multi-versities are the same as the ones we find in the G-15 group of the most research-intensive universities in Canada. For this reason it is unnecessary to use two different categories to examine the situation within the multi-versities and the institutions belonging to the G-15. We will stick to *Maclean's* group of multi-versities.

In chapter 3 we pointed out that many Canadian universities place in the top 400 of the two most widely used ranking systems. This group of universities also has a few representatives in the top 100, the most prestigious category. As we see in the 2012 editions of the THES and ARWU rankings, four Canadian universities – University of Toronto, University of British Columbia, McGill University, and McMaster University – are solidly ensconced in the top 100. We can add the University of Alberta and Université de Montréal to this list, since they regularly straddle the threshold. Indeed, the point differentials between the lowest positions in the top 100 and the highest positions in the second group of 100 are very small, and it is in this zone that these two Canadian research universities are consistently found.[23]

These six Canadian universities are, of course, members of the G-15 and founding members of the G-10. Furthermore, we observe that they make a major contribution to the output of the Canadian research universities we classify as multi-versities – like the most productive and prestigious universities in the Russell Group in the United Kingdom.

Research Activity

In Canada, independent basic research is highly concentrated in the university sector. In 2009, of the CAN$29.6 billion spent on R&D in Canada, 35 per cent (CAN$10.4 billion) went to universities. This is a very high concentration compared with other OECD major member countries. In fact, at 0.64 per cent of GDP, research that is conducted in Canadian universities appropriates a national income proportion that considerably exceeds the corresponding value for French, UK, and US university research (all below 0.5 per cent).[24]

In table 6.1 we present university research funding sources, i.e., the origins of the CAN$10.4 billion devoted to this activity in Canada.

To begin, we observe that the universities fund 45 per cent of the cost of research from their own resources. With only a handful of exceptions, professors' salaries are fully assumed by the operating budgets of the universities at which they work. They are able to devote up to 50 per cent of their time to research, and the share of their income that corresponds to that activity is imputed to research funding. Researchers generally work on premises that are maintained by the universities. Indirect costs associated with research that are not directly covered by external subsidies are paid by the university from its operating or fixed asset budgets. Finally, the university may dip into its operating budget to subsidize research groups and some of its researchers. In Canada's university system, as in the two others we have already examined, each university exercises direct control over a significant and recurring share of the funding of research performed within its walls.

We further observe in table 6.1 that a significant share (55 per cent) of university research funding is from external sources, primarily the federal and provincial governments. Aside from funds provided by business, monies obtained from other sources – private organizations, international funders – are subject to peer assessment in the vast majority of cases.

In this regard, the federal system for allocating research funds is exemplary. Funds are disbursed to individual researchers or research teams by three arm's-length funding agencies that are completely financed by the federal government: the Canadian Institutes of Health Research, the Natural Sciences and Engineering Research Council of Canada, and the Social Sciences and Humanities Research Council. All funding disbursed by these three agencies is on a competitive basis

Table 6.1
Sources of university R&D funding,
Canada 2009, millions of CAN$

Universities	4,675
Federal government	2,780
Provincial governments	1,058
Business	889
Private organizations	909
Foreign	102

Source: Industry Canada, *State of the Nation 2010*, 2.

and follows a rigorous peer assessment. The period for which funds are allocated rarely exceeds three years, after which researchers must go through the same process to renew their research funding.

The federal government also funds three other major programs: Canada Research Chairs, the Canada Foundation for Innovation, and the Research Indirect Costs Program. The Canada Research Chairs program was created in 2000. Under this program, which is jointly administered by the three research granting agencies, the government of Canada created 2,000 perpetual chairs with a mean annual value of CAN$150,000. A notional distribution of these 2,000 chairs across Canadian universities was based on their research intensity, reflecting their historical success with the three federal granting agencies. However, if a university fails to sustain its output the number of chairs may be adjusted. Moreover, the university must subject the dossier of each candidate for a chair to international assessment by a committee of peers assembled by the three granting agencies. Only if that committee approves the appointment can the university proceed.

The Canada Foundation for Innovation runs an endowment fund provided by the federal government and devotes itself to financing large research infrastructure projects. Each accepted project is funded at a 50 per cent level by provincial governments. Every two years this Foundation issues calls for proposals that are open to universities, either individually or in consortia. Before any grants are disbursed these calls for proposals are also subject to rules of competition and assessment by an international panel of peers in the relevant scientific disciplines as well as by a committee that evaluates the relevance of the major research infrastructure desired.

The federal Research Indirect Costs Program is based on the volume of federal grants received by a university. Thus, it is indirectly affected by the peer assessment rule. The greater professors' success in obtaining merit-based external funding from the federal government, the more their institutions will benefit from institutional funding to support this research activity. In general, provincial research funding programs, which are often complementary to federal programs, are also based on competitions with peer assessment.

Table 6.2 presents the distribution of external funds devoted to research by these institutions, by funding sources, for each of the three categories of university groups.

These data clearly reveal the extent to which research is concentrated in the fifteen Canadian multi-versities. In fact, they receive 78.1 per cent of all university research funding.[25] The six Canadian universities that regularly place among the best research universities in the world account for at least half of all these external funds. The University of Toronto alone takes in 14 per cent of these investments in university-based research.[26]

In the case of the third largest funding source, contributions from business, we observe an even greater concentration, with 87.3 per cent going to the multi-versities. The fact that the biomedical-health sector, which has historically had the closest ties to business, is almost exclusively present in these institutions is the main reason for that trend. We note in passing that, while external sources provide some 55 per cent of all research funding, the contribution of business, even in the case of universities where they have the greatest presence, amounts to less than 10 per cent of university research costs. Thus, if we look at the case of Canadian research universities, the complaints one hears from some quarters that university research is dominated by business appear to have little empirical basis.

Not only does a larger share of research take place in universities in Canada than in the other industrialized countries, but it is highly concentrated in the leading research universities. This is an organizational factor that clearly assists Canadian universities' strategies to place among the best research universities in the world. Not only does external funding make up a large proportion of the resources they are able to devote to research, but these are almost exclusively obtained on the basis of a competitive process involving a rigorous peer assessment. In addition, some funding programs, such as the Canada Research Chairs and even the Research

ble 6.2

ternal research funds by source and category of university, Canada 2007–2008, in thousands
CAN$

roup	Federal	Provincial	Business	Non-Profit	Foreign	Other external revenue	Total
			IN ABSOLUTE TERMS				
ulti-versities	2,167,036	861,210	823,147	43,524	112,554	749,373	4,756,844
Comprehensives"	540,401	190,547	71,894	2,939	11,858	115,870	933,509
ther	221,770	62,277	47,912	890	2,676	65,981	401,506
l universities	2,929,207	1,114,034	942,953	47,353	127,088	931,224	6,091,859
		AS A PERCENTAGE BY SOURCE OF FUNDING					
ulti-versities	45.6	18.1	17.3	0.9	2.4	15.8	100
Comprehensives"	57.9	20.4	7.7	0.3	1.3	12.4	100
ther	55.2	15.5	11.9	0.2	0.7	16.4	100
l universities	48.1	18.3	15.5	0.8	2.1	15.3	100
		AS A PERCENTAGE BY CATEGORY OF UNIVERSITY					
ulti-versities	74.0	77.3	87.3	91.9	88.6	80.5	78.1
Comprehensives"	18.4	17.1	7.6	6.2	9.3	12.4	15.3
ther	7.6	5.6	5.1	1.9	2.1	7.1	6.6
l universities	100	100	100	100	100	100	100

urce: Computed from Canadian Association of University Business Officers (CAUBO) online data, www.caubo.ca.

Indirect Costs Program, measure performance at the level of the institution and its academic faculty.

Canadian research universities also benefit from a broad diversity in their sources of external research funding, of which over 40 per cent is from non-governmental funders. This diversity gives rise to distinctions between institutions. For example, in reference to the aforementioned group of six universities, we find that McGill and the University of Toronto receive at least half of their research revenues from the federal government and draw less on other external sources, whereas McMaster University obtains 70 per cent of its research funding from non-federal sources. The University of Alberta, in turn, relies more heavily than the others on funding from the provincial government.[27]

While research funding in the Quebec university system and the rest of Canada shares the same features, the former has been remarkably successful in bringing its research activity up to the same standards over the past forty years, as we see in table 6.3.

We observe in this table that during the period 2000–08 Quebec universities received, on average, a large 27 per cent of all of the funds devoted to university-based research, exceeding Quebec's population share (around 23 per cent) within Canada. Moreover, during this same period these universities managed to acquire 27.7 per cent of federal funding for universities. In light of the fact that these funds are subject to the stiffest competition and the most rigorous peer assessments, we may conclude that, in this regard, their catch-up growth has exceeded all expectations.

Sources of Operating Funds

Operating expenditures generally include the compensation paid to teaching and other staff as well as non-wage costs incurred by other services such as libraries, IT, communications, housekeeping, security, etc. In table 6.4 we present operating expenditures by our three broad categories of universities. These numbers are for 2007–08, the last year for which we have complete data. However, we see the stability of the inter-university distribution of these data in the averages for the period 2000–08.

Even though they only represent 15 per cent of the total number of universities in Canada, these multi-versities, that is, the leading research universities – counting all faculties, including medicine – account for 54.2 per cent of Canadian universities' operating expenditures. This percentage is considerably higher than their share of the total full-time university student body in Canada (48.2 per cent). We will look at this in more detail below. On their own, the six Canadian research universities that regularly appear in the top 100 of the best universities in the world (Group of Six) receive nearly one-third of the resources made available to pay for university operations. Once again, the University of Toronto stands out for the volume of funding it can count on.[28]

Three main factors explain the income disparity across institutions and the position occupied by the multi-versities. First, multi-versities have the most expensive disciplines in the university system, such as medicine, dentistry, veterinary medicine, pharmacy, etc. Next, as we shall see, they have a significantly higher proportion of their students in graduate studies than the two other university categories and graduate education is more expensive than undergraduate

Table 6.3
External research funds by source, region, and annual mean, Canada 2000–2008,
in thousands of CAN$

Region	Federal	Provincial	Business	Non-Profit	Foreign	Other external revenue	Total
IN ABSOLUTE TERMS							
Quebec	630,419	265,124	163,753	54,529	23,002	179,392	1,316,219
Rest of Canada	1,643,088	677,325	522,734	204,891	94,909	416,477	3,559,423
All	2,273,508	942,448	686,487	259,420	117,911	595,868	4,875,641.75
AS A PERCENTAGE BY SOURCE OF FUNDING							
Quebec	47.9	20.1	12.4	4.1	1.7	13.6	100
Rest of Canada	46.2	19.0	14.7	5.8	2.7	11.7	100
All	46.6	19.3	14.1	5.3	2.4	12.2	100
AS A PERCENTAGE BY REGION							
Quebec	27.7	28.1	23.9	21.0	19.5	30.1	27.0
Rest of Canada	72.3	71.9	76.1	79.0	80.5	69.9	73.0
All	100	100	100	100	100	100	100

Notes: "All" includes all universities in the CAUBO database (110 universities).
Source: CAUBO database compiled by CREPUQ (See table 6.2).

education. Finally, as we have seen, university-based research in Canada is highly concentrated in these fifteen multi-versities, which has ramifications for their operating costs.

Table 6.5 below itemizes operating fund sources for the three broad categories of university we have been using and reveals their wide diversity. Our data are for the year 2007–08, but once again we see the stability of the distribution of these values over the period 2000–08.

Universities in Canada are supported by four major funders. The first, and generally largest, is the provincial government. Despite being public institutions, 45 per cent of Canadian universities' operating funds are from sources other than government, as the table reveals. We will see below that, when the influence of Quebec is removed, this percentage is even higher for the rest of Canada.

Provincial funding of universities is governed by complicated formulae that differ from one province to the next. They account for

Table 6.4
Operating expenditures by category of university, Canada, 2007–2008,
in thousands of CAN$

Group	Expenditures	% of total
Multi-versities	9,005,849	54.2
Comprehensives	4,652,685	28.0
Other	2,962,826	17.8
All universities	16,621,360	100

Source: Computed from CAUBO data.

variations in costs associated with the number of students enrolled, their disciplines, and the level of study. Indeed, the annual cost of educating a student in veterinary medicine can be five or six times as high as for an undergraduate in French studies. Taken together, these rules and provisions constitute an annual budget given to universities by provincial governments. As a rule, they are then free to spend these monies as they see fit as a function of their priorities for training programs and the required infrastructure.

These government grants are complemented by tuition and ancillary fees paid by the students. All of these fees vary from one province to the next, sometimes between universities and, in many provinces, across disciplines and levels of study. Observe, however, that at 31.8 per cent of total operating revenues, tuition constitutes the second highest operating fund source for Canadian universities.

Revenue from other sources, representing 10.3 per cent of all resources for university operating expenditures, round out this breakdown. These include income from philanthropic organizations and capitalized endowment funds constituted from individual, business, and foundations' donations. While Canadian universities undeniably rely on philanthropy to fund specific projects, the contribution of this source of income to overall operating funds is marginal. A large share of philanthropic donations are devoted to funding new buildings, research activities, and providing scholarships to students. Revenue from other sources also includes a diverse category of smaller incomes that contribute to the funding of operating costs. These may include profits from auxiliary businesses, income from licenses and patents, etc.

This current distribution of total funding by source also illustrates developments in Canadian academia in the past twenty years very

Table 6.5
Funding of operating expenditures by source and category of university, 2007–2008, in thousands CAN$

Group	Govt. grants	Tuition	Philanthropy	Other income	Total
	IN ABSOLUTE TERMS				
Multi-versities	5,135,343	2,642,275	279,223	1,112,108	9,168,949
Comprehensives	2,492,122	1,736,359	91,773	411,861	4,732,115
Other	1,716,280	983,927	74,420	207,814	2,982,441
All universities	9,343,745	5,362,561	445,416	1,731,783	16,883,505
	AS A PERCENTAGE BY SOURCE OF FUNDING				
Multi-versities	56.0	28.8	3.0	12.1	100
Comprehensives	52.7	36.7	1.9	8.7	100
Other	57.5	33.0	2.5	7.0	100
All universities	55.3	31.8	2.6	10.3	100
	AS A PERCENTAGE BY CATEGORY OF UNIVERSITY				
Multi-versities	55.0	49.3	62.7	64.2	54.3
Comprehensives	26.7	32.4	20.6	23.8	28.0
Other	18.4	18.3	16.7	12.0	17.7
All universities	100	100	100	100	100

Source: Computed from CAUBO data.

well. During this period, in fact, the government's share of operations funding declined by some twenty percentage points – a phenomenon we have already observed in the United States and the United Kingdom.

The data in table 6.6 make it clear to what extent Quebec stands out in the Canadian context in that tuition fees were frozen for a long time. However, since this freeze was only partially compensated by a corresponding increase in funding from the government of Quebec, the universities in this province are now underfunded by at least CAN$600 million annually.[29] One finding is unavoidable: the greater the diversity of funding sources that universities in a given group can draw on, the more resources they have at their disposal.

The composition of university funding is very different in Quebec than elsewhere in Canada. This difference has two primary components: government grants and tuition fees (including ancillary fees). Though the government contributes 66.9 per cent of university funding in Quebec, the corresponding value in the rest of Canada is

Table 6.6
Funding of operating expenditures by source and region, Canada–Quebec, 2007–2008, in thousands of CAN$

Region	Govt. grants	Tuition fees	Philanthropy	Other income	Total
	IN ABSOLUTE TERMS				
Quebec	2,230,410	646,275	85,413	370,175	3,332,273
Rest of Canada	7,113,335	4,716,286	360,003	1,361,608	13,551,232
Total	9,343,745	5,362,561	445,416	1,731,783	16,883,505
	AS A PERCENTAGE BY SOURCE OF FUNDING				
Quebec	66.9	19.4	2.6	11.1	100
Rest of Canada	52.5	34.8	2.7	10.0	100
Total	55.3	31.8	2.6	10.3	100
	AS A PERCENTAGE BY REGION				
Quebec	23.9	12.1	19.2	21.4	19.7
Rest of Canada	76.1	87.9	80.8	78.6	80.3
Total	100	100	100	100	100

Source: Computed from CAUBO data.

only 52.5 per cent. Conversely, there is an equally great disparity in the contribution that tuition fees make to funding the operating costs of universities. In the rest of Canada these rates, being higher and more variable across disciplines, account for 34.8 per cent of total revenues, whereas in Quebec they only amount to 19.4 per cent of the total resources available to universities. The two other sources, philanthropy and other income, contribute in comparable amounts in these two regional groupings.

As is the case with the funding devoted to research, the resources that support the operations of Canadian universities are highly diversified and, for the most part, acquired in a competitive environment, as we saw in the United States. A dominant characteristic of the Canadian university system, this diversity naturally carries over to the operating funds of the Group of Six, and especially to the lead institution in that club, the University of Toronto. We also note that this diversity takes different forms in each university. This reflects the particular configuration of the Canadian system by province, but also the entrepreneurship demonstrated by the universities with regard to tuition fees, incomes from auxiliary businesses, philanthropy, etc., contributing in no small way to the standing of Canadian research universities among world-class universities.[30]

Human Resources

STUDENTS

At the beginning of this century, Canadian universities in all three categories collectively had approximately one million students. Table 6.7 shows the distribution of this student body in 2007–08 among the three categories of universities; these numbers have since increased somewhat. We point out that the values in this table differ from those presented earlier because they are for full-time equivalent students.[31]

These data clearly reveal that the multi-versities dominate graduate education in Canada. Though they only represent 15 per cent of Canadian universities, they are responsible for the education of 68.2 per cent of PhD students and 54.6 per cent of master's and other graduate students. This strong focus on graduate studies is not at the expense of undergraduate studies, where they have 46.4 per cent of the total student body. Overall, these fifteen multi-versities dominate university education in Canada at all levels and in all disciplines.

The data in table 6.7 also indicate that the distribution of students by level differs with university categories. Thus, 17.3 per cent of the students in multi-versities are in graduate programs, versus 11.8 per cent of students in comprehensive universities and 10.3 per cent in the remaining schools. This differential across institutions in terms of the proportion of students registered in graduate studies is even more pronounced at the PhD level. This group makes up 6.2 per cent of the student population of multi-versities, 3.3 per cent in the comprehensive universities, and only 1.6 per cent in the remaining universities. These are broad averages, and there are considerable variations from one institution to the next within each of these categories.

Nearly half of the students enrolled in a Canadian university attend a multi-versity. Of this contingent, the Group of Six accounts for a good half (26 per cent of the total). The dominance of these multi-versities at the graduate level is also reflected in the contribution of these six universities to doctoral (42.1 per cent) and master's (30 per cent) studies. The multi-versity nature of these institutions is borne out by the fact that their undergraduate programs are sufficiently well developed to attract 24.7 per cent of students at that level. Clearly, by virtue of its 65,000 full-time equivalent students, the University of Toronto has a special status among Canada's leading

Table 6.7
Distribution of full-time equivalent students, by level of studies and category
of university, Canada, 2007–2008

Group	Bachelor's and other first level degrees	Master's and other second level degrees	PhD	Total
	IN ABSOLUTE TERMS			
Multi-versities	341,155	45,840	25,743	412,738
Comprehensives	258,801	24,966	9,626	293,393
Other	135,402	13,155	2,379	150,936
All	735,358	83,961	37,748	857,067
	AS A PERCENTAGE BY LEVEL OF STUDIES			
Multi-versities	82.7	11.1	6.2	100
Comprehensives	88.2	8.5	3.3	100
Other	89.7	8.7	1.6	100
All	85.8	9.8	4.4	100
	AS A PERCENTAGE BY CATEGORY OF UNIVERSITY			
Multi-versities	46.4	54.6	68.2	48.2
Comprehensives	35.2	29.7	25.5	34.2
Other	18.4	15.7	6.3	17.6
All	100	100	100	100

Notes: Computed from Statistics Canada and CAUBO data. For "All" we only used the intersection
of the universities in both the CAUBO and Statistics Canada datasets (86 universities).

universities. While these elite universities cannot, in general, be characterized as mega-universities – aside from the University of Toronto
they have fewer than 40,000 students on average – the sizes of their
student bodies are, in general, comparable to those of the universities in the United States, above all the public ones, that make up over
50 per cent of the top research universities in the world.

Table 6.8 compares the situation in Quebec with that of the rest
of Canada in terms of university student distribution by level of
studies.

University students in Quebec only make up 22.7 per cent of total
attendance in Canadian universities, because the bachelor's degree
only requires three years in Quebec, versus four in the rest of Canada
– the instruction given in CEGEP is equivalent to first year university in the rest of Canada. We also note the overrepresentation of
Quebec students in total enrolment in graduate studies in Canada:

Table 6.8
Distribution of full-time equivalent students, by region and level of studies,
Canada–Quebec, 2007–2008

Group	Bachelor's and other first level degrees	Master's and other second level degrees	PhD	Total
	IN ABSOLUTE TERMS			
Quebec	155,819	26,861	12,254	194,934
Rest of Canada	579,539	57,100	25,494	662,133
All	735,358	83,961	37,748	857,067
	AS A PERCENTAGE BY LEVEL OF STUDIES			
Quebec	79.9	13.8	6.3	100
Rest of Canada	87.5	8.6	3.9	100
All	85.8	9.8	4.4	100
	AS A PERCENTAGE BY REGION			
Quebec	21.2	32.0	32.5	22.7
Rest of Canada	78.8	68.0	67.5	77.3
All	100	100	100	100

Note: Same sources as table 6.7

32 per cent at the master's level and other graduate diplomas and 32.5 per cent in PhD programs. This is another very clear indication of the fact that Quebec universities have caught up to the rest of the country in terms of both graduate education and university-based research.

Admission criteria are the responsibility of each institution. The number and quality of students admitted into each university program result from internal decisions. In some cases the provincial government might cap admissions into certain professional branches, such as medicine, but these are exceptions. Since a large part of university operating budgets depends on the number of students, it will be clear that there is a certain degree of competition between Canadian universities to attract students in terms of both quantity and quality, especially at the graduate level.

In general, Canadian universities, in particular research universities, have a long tradition of selectivity in their student recruitment. These practices safeguard the quality and the reputation of institutions, which are key factors in their positioning within university ranking systems and, in turn, reinforce the tradition of selectivity.

At the graduate level, a similar interaction between enrolled student selection and institutional reputation is of capital importance.

Other dimensions of how students are received into university are just as important: the quality of teaching, infrastructure, and supervision. These elements are not easily quantifiable, but there is one measure that is clearly of the essence: Investing an adequate volume of resources per full-time student helps maintain good teaching programs and create high-quality academic environments and infrastructures.

Table 6.9 below details university operating costs per full-time equivalent student for our three categories of university and by region. These data reveal that it is in the sector of multi-versities that we observe the highest investments per full-time student. Comprehensive universities rank lowest in this regard. Many factors can have an impact on this variable: the distribution of students by program and level of study, specificities of a campus and its challenges with maintenance, or simply under-funding of a given university in comparison to another. In this matter, however, the multi-versity category mirrors the pattern of the Group of Six. Most of them have higher costs per full-time student than the average costs in the multi-versities.

We note, however, that spending levels in Quebec universities are not comparable to those in other Canadian universities. This marked differential is largely explained by the unique structure of university funding in Quebec that creates chronic underfunding.

The very first Canadian institutions that set out to become research universities opted early on to adopt the US graduate school model to provide an adequate environment to their graduate students, especially doctoral students. For many years now virtually all Canadian multi-versities have implemented this academic structure – it is an essential component of the vertical division of academic labour between undergraduate and graduate studies in North American research universities. From the recruitment and admission of students to their graduation, graduate schools provide support and leadership while promoting institutional priorities and overseeing quality control in graduate studies. In fact, academic achievements, the quality of teaching, student supervision, and training programs are central to their interventions.

This Canadian implementation of these academic structures is every bit as effective as its US counterpart. Canadian graduate schools have

Table 6.9
Operating costs per student, by group
and by region, Canada, 2007–2008

Group	Cost per student
Multi-versities	$21,820
Comprehensives	$15,858
Other	$16,258
All	$18,800

Region	Cost per student
Quebec	$17,091
Rest of Canada	$19,302
All	$18,800

Notes: In the case of "All" we have only used
the intersection of the CAUBO and Statistics
Canada datasets (86 universities).
Source: Statistics Canada database compiled
by CRÉPUQ.

contributed significantly to improved pedagogical and financial
support for students by means of internal fellowships and paid TA
and RA positions, consolidation of best practices among professors
and program directors, development of interdisciplinary programs,
and the imposition of high standards in graduate studies.[32]

We have already noted that the quality of a university's graduate
programs, advanced training in research, and scientific output are
contingent on recruiting the best academic faculty. Especially in the
case of research universities, research grants awarded to their professors by committees of peers make all the difference. These levels of
success speak eloquently to the quality of the academic faculty and
also ensure the quality of the scientific output and the creation of a
nurturing environment conducive to advanced training in research.
Our data reveal considerable differentials across the university categories in terms of external research funding – not only per professor, but also per graduate student.

Table 6.10 reveals that Canadian multi-versities, just like US
research universities, recruit professors who not only excel in
research, but also work in a diversity of disciplines with highly
unequal research costs. Income per professor is thus much higher in

Table 6.10
Research income from external sources, by professor and by full-time equivalent student, in CAN$, Canada, 2007–2008

BY GROUP			
Group	Per professor	Per graduate student	Per PhD student
Multi-versities	282,339	103,771	184,782
Comprehensives	81,352	37,391	96,981
Other	53,642	29,152	161,198
All	171,229	72,341	160,906
BY REGION			
Region	Per professor	Per graduate student	Per PhD student
Quebec	179,813	55,930	122,600
Rest of Canada	169,249	80,377	180,026
All	171,737	72,556	161,384

Notes: In the case of "All" we have only used the intersection of the CAUBO and Statistics Canada datasets (86 universities).
Source: Data on students from Statistics Canada database compiled by CRÉPUQ. Data on professors from University and College Academic Staff Survey, Statistics Canada, 2011. Computed from a CAUBO database compiled by CRÉPUQ.

multi-versities. At the other extreme, each professor in the best Canadian undergraduate universities has one-tenth as much research funding. No doubt about it, the Canadian university system consists of university groups with very different missions – but not as the result of some master plan. The competitive modes of research fund allocation, among other factors, have had their effect.

More external research funds per professor also means more resources for the supervision of each student in graduate and doctoral programs. The paradoxical results for research funds per doctoral student in other universities can be attributed to their very small numbers in these institutions. This is corroborated by the minute level of research funds per graduate student we observe in these universities.

Of course, there are differences in this respect across the multi-versities, which are very well illustrated by disparities within the Group of Six. Thus, the University of Toronto shares a prominent position with McMaster University which, as we have already seen, receives a large proportion of its external research funding from non-government sources. These two institutions lead this university group, acceding to research resources per professor that are one-quarter greater. But overall, these six institutions place at the top of the multi-versities with higher mean research income per professor.[33]

We also observe in table 6.10 that research funding per professor in Quebec universities is comparable, or even slightly higher, than in the rest of Canada. Here again, we find evidence that Quebec's university system has been catching up. That being said, the very large number of students in graduate studies in Quebec, combined with the underfunding of Quebec universities – which limits their ability to hire professors – means that the availability of research funds per student is considerably lower than elsewhere in Canada. This may be one of the most serious ramifications of the current university underfunding in Quebec.

FACULTY MEMBERS

In Canada, a university will decide how many professors it can hire in any given year as a function of its needs and budgetary constraints. Appeals for candidates to fill these positions may be national or international in scope. The evaluation of dossiers and the choice of candidate is performed by peers within the academic units into which the new professor is to be integrated. An institution may choose to require that the candidate have prior academic experience. Job offers and the associated working conditions are prepared by the university. Nonetheless, this institution is acting in a specific competitive environment that will be a function of its mission, the size and quality of the academic market for professors into which it can tap, its specialization fields and centres of excellence, and the current state of the socio-economic cycle.

The career of the professor will unfold in accordance with the hiring institution's rules. These rules deal with the components of the assigned tasks (teaching, research, supervision of students, collective management) tenure, terms of promotion, provisions for retirement, etc. This set of rules varies from one university to the next. The ability of a university's administration, as well as that of its subordinate units (faculties, schools, and departments), to oversee and manage professors' careers will be more or less circumscribed – depending on whether they are unionized. But here again, the union is local and the collective agreement specific to the institution, precluding any significant intervention from the provincial bodies responsible for universities. In summary, each Canadian university is an independent employer of its academic faculty, with all the associated powers and responsibilities.

With regard to the hiring and career management of other categories of employees the situation is somewhat similar, though generally less complicated. The employee numbers vary with the size and mission of the institution, but Canada's biggest universities can have more than ten thousand employees, when professors, managers and professionals, technicians, support staff, etc. are included. The terms governing hiring, the working conditions, and the careers of each of these employees is the individual university's responsibility, and may vary from one to the next.

University Governance

Governance modes of Canadian universities are not identical across the ten provinces, but despite some marginal differences, there is a great deal of consistency in the broad principles. As public institutions, Canada's universities are all under the aegis of a provincial government that has granted them a Charter of Incorporation or, in the case of the oldest ones, has simply recognized them. The governance modes of universities are generally determined by an act of the provincial legislature or by an institutional charter that has been accepted by the provincial government and cannot be amended without its consent.

As a rule, Canadian universities have all the rights and powers of a corporation and may perform any actions that are compatible with their missions. Thus, they can award degrees, create programs, and establish faculties and institutes while receiving, obtaining, employing, and administering all financial, material, and human resources required to fulfill their mission. In practice, however, the creation of new programs is subject to certain constraints imposed by provincial departments of education or associations of universities. The purpose of these controls is to ensure the quality and relevance of any new program established in a university.

In most Canadian universities two bodies share the prerogatives and powers of the institution: the board of directors and the university senate (or university assembly).[34] In addition to having the last word on the broad orientation of the institution, its budget, and the administrative processes, the board of directors appoints the head of the university (called the president, rector, or vice-chancellor), usually on the basis of the recommendation of a search committee and after consultation with the university senate. In the Canadian system this is the most important decision made by the board of directors. In fact, in light of the broad autonomy of Canadian universities, presidents and their management teams have the ability, with the cooperation of the board and the university senate, to change the direction of a university.

The university senate is a consultative body that essentially deals with academic issues and policies, including teaching programs, research, academic structures, the statutes of the academic faculty, and disciplinary issues.

This governance structure is characteristic of a university bicameral functioning. In principle, the board of directors and the university senate play complementary roles: the former primarily deals with financial and administrative issues, and the latter with academic issues and policies. In practice, the boundaries between the respective roles of these bodies are generally porous, and there are few universities that experience no tension within these complementary relationships.

With respect to this, Canada was not immune to the changes that affected university governance during the 1960s and 1970s. The rise of student movements and the expanding unionization of university employees, including professors and frequently even students (especially at the graduate level), had a significant impact on the composition of these two major bodies.

First, boards of directors, which had mostly consisted of outsiders representing the interests of the broader society, gradually had to make room for delegations of students, professors, other employees, and alumni. Today, university boards of directors in Canada have an average of twenty-seven members. External members remain in the majority, but professors account for 17 per cent of the total and students for another 9 per cent.[35] Furthermore, these three groups are complemented by representatives of the alumni, support staff, affiliated schools or colleges, etc. Despite these considerable changes, Canadian universities' boards of directors have retained their responsibilities and powers.

Next, the university senate, which had mainly consisted of professors and academic professionals, was also opened to representation from the student body and other employees. Today, the average size of this body in Canada is fifty-eight members. Virtually all of them are internal (92.5 per cent) and, in consideration of its role, professors (44 per cent) and students (17 per cent) occupy most of the seats.[36]

The long-term ramifications of these changes are clear and sometimes problematic: The boundaries between these traditional bicameral governance bodies, which were already porous, became more so. What is more, in some instances entities that had been characterized by collegiality were transformed into arenas in which power struggles between unions and management were played out. However, the impact of this transformation varied from one institution to the next. Over time the university itself became more of a social and economic actor in a diversity of roles and its governance increasingly supplemented the traditional bicameral governance model, relying on professionals and managers who assumed responsibility for dossiers and portfolios of ever greater complexity.

More and more managerial and professional staff with strong qualifications and skills now occupy positions within universities as allies of the leaders and administrators in terms of both classic university administration – the officers of the university and its intermediate structures, faculties, and academic departments – and collegial bodies such as the senate, departmental assembly, and faculty council. These are objective allies with whom power, authority, and freedom to act and decide must be coordinated. From this standpoint also, traditional bicameral governance must also adapt, which cannot always occur without tension.

CONCLUSION

An examination of current data, both quantitative and qualitative, on the operating characteristics of Canadian universities has given us a better understanding of why so many of them place among the best research universities in the ARWU and THES international rankings. We see how six Canadian multi-versities manage to place among the top 100 world-class universities year after year.

Canada's university system is decentralized. This decentralization can be attributed to the fact that these universities are under the exclusive jurisdiction of each of Canada's ten provinces. They receive transfer payments from the federal government that are designed to ensure theoretically comparable provision of government services but leave a great deal of leeway in how they are allocated. Over time a healthy competition has arisen between the provinces over the quality of their universities. Clearly, Ontario and Quebec started out in the lead, though the less populous provinces have been able to establish exceptional undergraduate universities that attract students from all over the country.

Universities in Ontario, in particular, quickly adapted to the North American context by comparing their performances with those of US universities. Their various funding sources thus gradually adapted to alleviate the growing discrepancy between the funds available to universities in Ontario and to public universities in the United States. Leading universities in the other provinces soon pressured their respective governments for more funding to strengthen their competitive position vis-à-vis universities in Ontario. Even today, Quebec universities' underfunding is typically expressed in terms of comparisons with the situation in Ontario and the other provinces. Quebec universities regularly complain of increasing difficulty competing with universities in the rest of Canada when trying to recruit the best professors and the most gifted students, compelling the provincial government to find new ways to make resources available to them.

Overall, this interprovincial competition has forced governments in each province to consider not only the Canadian context, but also the broader North American setting that is more relevant to leading research universities. In our opinion, the decentralized structure of the Canadian university system has been beneficial in terms of the total amount of resources it receives. It is probably the same for the leading public universities in the United States, which have to compete not only amongst themselves, but with the leading private universities as well. The states are also under strong pressure to increase their contributions to the funding of universities within their jurisdictions.

The high concentration in universities, especially in multi-versities, of government-funded basic research confers upon them a key role in performing research while also providing them with significant resources. But Canadian universities operate in an environment that is characterized by stiff competition for the large amounts of resources required for the functioning of a research university. This competition is primarily over research funding, which is allocated to members of the academic faculty on the basis of merit, but also over a considerable portion of the institutional funds that universities invest in research.

Access to resources in a competitive environment also extends to recruiting the best students and hiring and retaining the most productive professors. Competition is also over funds donated from charities and government. This environment is critical for the emergence of world-class universities because it creates a series of incentives that are often mutually reinforcing and promote the pursuit of excellence at both the individual and institutional level.

In passing, we note that the Canadian university system is also characterized by a diversity in the sources from which it acquires the funds required for its operations and research activities. Diversity of funding sources implies greater flexibility in their disposition and, by extension, more growth potential. This diversity also buffers research universities from the vagaries of the political market in which decision-makers ply their trade in the matter of government financing of universities, and whose support cannot be taken for granted.

Canadian universities, in general, benefit from great autonomy, supported by the responsible governmental bodies. Thus, just as Clark observed in the case of US research universities, they have the scope to become entrepreneurial and attract visionary, innovative, and highly performing leaders – accountable only to the board of directors that appoints and evaluates them – to all levels of academic administration. These institutions have the capacity to increase their income by targeted efforts, to focus their spending as a function of objectives that are clear and accepted by the university community, and to organize operation modes, hiring, compensation, and recognition so as to foster performance and innovation.

It should not come as a surprise that great leaders from the academic world have agreed to take charge of Canada's multi-versities and to surround themselves with managers who share their vision. Consider, for example, the impact Dawson and his successors had on the emergence of McGill University; the contributions made by James Loudon and, more recently, Robert Prichard to the development of the University of Toronto; David Strangway guiding the University of British Columbia (UBC) into its great research mission, and Martha Piper fostering its internationalization; the foundational role played by Roger Gaudry in solidifying the identity of the Université de Montréal as a great research university thriving in a context that is both public and secular.

The history of each of these Canadian universities is wrapped up with its visionary leaders. If these leaders were able to steer the course of events in Canada's leading institutions, it is because they had the authority to match their responsibilities and were fully accountable to their respective boards of directors and university senates. These institutions would never have been able to attract this calibre of individual if their roles had been limited to refereeing internal conflicts resulting from the distribution of a predetermined budget allocated by the state.

But a leading research university is not built in a day. Excellence develops over time, because the practices and structures of a vibrant institutional culture do not become entrenched overnight. Persistence over time in the provision of innovative leadership to Canada's world-class research universities has been key to their success. It should not come as a surprise to see that McGill University, the University of Toronto, and the University of British Columbia have emerged and made such a splash as great world-class universities. They are caught in a virtuous circle, where past performance and established reputation give them the means to shape their own future.

APPENDIX

Table A-6.1
External research funds by source, Group of Six, Canada, 2007–2008, in thousands of CAN$

Universities	Federal	Provincial	Business	Non-Profit	Foreign	Other external revenue	Total
IN ABSOLUTE TERMS							
University of Toronto	422,210	114,749	192,674	8,383	27,104	79,469	844,589
University of British Columbia	194,943	85,849	128,606	(247)	9,713	51,282	470,146
McGill University	251,696	56,128	43,764	8,578	8,611	49,777	418,554
McMaster University	109,789	32,951	17,061	9,063	18,373	186,305	373,542
University of Alberta	165,440	211,508	43,032	3,261	10,580	57,921	491,742
Université de Montréal (HEC and Polytechnique)	227,074	93,919	62,476	–	6,023	79,237	468,729
Total for the Group of Six	1,371,152	595,104	487,613	29,038	80,404	503,991	3,067,302
All universities	2,929,207	1,114,034	942,953	7,353	127,088	931,224	6,091,859
AS A PERCENTAGE BY SOURCE OF FUNDING							
University of Toronto	50.0	13.6	22.8	1.0	3.2	9.4	100
University of British Columbia	41.5	18.3	27.4	–0.1	2.1	10.9	100
McGill University	60.1	13.4	10.5	2.0	2.1	11.9	100
McMaster University	29.4	8.8	4.6	2.4	4.9	49.9	100
University of Alberta	33.6	43.0	8.8	0.7	2.2	11.8	100
Université de Montréal (HEC and Polytechnique)	48.4	20.0	13.3	0.0	1.3	16.9	100
Total for the Group of Six	44.7	19.4	15.9	0.9	2.6	16.4	100
All universities	48.1	18.3	15.5	0.8	2.1	15.3	100

Table A-6.1 Cont.

Universities	Federal	Provincial	Business	Non-Profit	Foreign	Other external revenue	Total
	AS A PERCENTAGE BY UNIVERSITY						
University of Toronto	14.4	10.3	20.4	17.7	21.3	8.5	13.9
University of British Columbia	6.7	7.7	13.6	−0.5	7.6	5.5	7.7
McGill University	8.6	5.0	4.6	18.1	6.8	5.3	6.9
McMaster University	3.7	3.0	1.8	19.1	14.5	20.0	6.1
University of Alberta	5.6	19.0	4.6	6.9	8.3	6.2	8.1
Université de Montréal (HEC and Polytechnique)	7.8	8.4	6.6	0.0	4.7	8.5	7.7
Total for the Group of Six	46.8	53.4	51.7	61.3	63.3	54.1	50.4
All universities	100	100	100	100	100	100	100

Notes: "All" includes all universities in the CAUBO database (110 universities).
Source: Computed from a CAUBO database compiled by CRÉPUQ.

Table A-6.2
Operating expenditures, Group of Six, Canada, 2007–2008, in thousands of CAN$

Universities	Expenditures	% of the six	% of total
University of Toronto	1,316,977	25.7	7.9
University of British Columbia	1,020,685	19.9	6.1
McGill University	647,747	12.6	3.9
McMaster University	505,740	9.9	3.0
University of Alberta	875,597	17.1	5.3
Université de Montréal (HEC and Polytechnique)	766,975	14.9	4.6
Total for the Group of Six	5,133,721	100	30.9
All universities	16,621,360	323.8	100

Source: Same as table A-6.1.

Table A-6.3

Funding of operating expenditures by source, Group of Six, Canada, 2007–2008, in thousands of CAN$

Universities	Govt. grants	Tuition fees	Philanthropy	Other income	Total
IN ABSOLUTE TERMS					
University of Toronto	611,360	639,381	41,812	115,910	1,408,463
University of British Columbia	608,096	302,574	6,061	154,465	1,071,196
McGill University	300,814	160,354	64,490	86,230	611,888
McMaster University	237,035	149,396	37,059	104, 807	528,297
University of Alberta	549,350	197,348	10,395	78,048	835,141
Université de Montréal (HEC and Polytechnique)	524,545	126,358	10,217	84,572	745,692
Total for the Group of Six	2,831,200	1,575,411	170,034	624,032	5,200,677
All universities	9,343,745	5,362,561	445,416	1,731,783	16 883 505
AS A PERCENTAGE BY SOURCE OF FUNDING					
University of Toronto	43.4	45.4	3.0	8.2	100
University of British Columbia	56.8	28.2	0.6	14.4	100
McGill University	49.2	26.2	10.5	14.1	100
McMaster University	44.9	28.3	7.0	19.8	100
University of Alberta	65.8	23.6	1.2	9.3	100
Université de Montréal (HEC and Polytechnique)	70.3	16.9	1.4	11.3	100
Total for the Group of Six	54.4	30.3	3.3	12.0	100
All universities	55.3	31.8	2.6	10.3	100
AS A PERCENTAGE BY UNIVERSITY					
University of Toronto	6.5	11.9	9.4	6.7	8.3
University of British Columbia	6.5	5.6	1.4	8.9	6.3
McGill University	3.2	3.0	14.5	5.0	3.6
McMaster University	2.5	2.8	8.3	6.1	3.1
University of Alberta	5.9	3.7	2.3	4.5	4.9
Université de Montréal (HEC and Polytechnique)	5.6	2.4	2.3	4.9	4.4
Total for the Group of Six	30.3	29.4	38.2	36.0	30.8
All universities	100	100	100	100	100

Source: Same as table A-6.1.

Table A-6.4

Research income from external sources, by professor and by full-time equivalent
student, in CAN$, Canada, Group of Six, 2007–2008

Universities	Per professor	Per graduate student	Per PhD student
University of Toronto	414,014	136,180	195,779
University of British Columbia	258,606	106,779	177,548
McGill University	286,485	128,707	162,925
McMaster University	502,073	209,737	335,015
University of Alberta	364,253	160,805	207,925
Université de Montréal (HEC and Polytechnique)	267,539	65,630	142,644
Total for the Group of Six	334,676	118,713	188,213

Source: Data on students from Statistics Canada database compiled by CRÉPUQ. Data on professors
from University and College Academic Staff Survey, Statistics Canada, 2011. Computed from a
CAUBO database compiled by CRÉPUQ.

7

THE UNIVERSITY SYSTEM IN FRANCE

The history and characteristics of France's university system – which play such an important role in determining the positioning of French research universities in the leading international rankings, ARWU and THES – are quite unique. Recall that, from the perspective of the macroeconomic indicators we presented in chapter 3, there are quite a few French universities in these rankings, but most striking is the underperformance of these French universities in the highest categories of the top 200, top 100, and top 50 world-class institutions, regardless of which ranking system is used.

As we did for the other university systems, we will review historical developments, the principal institutional arrangements, and the most current operating modes of the French system. We will focus in particular on the milieu in which French academic institutions, especially research universities, function, to gain a better understanding of their performance in international rankings. We begin by reviewing the main features of the French university system, especially as of the latter half of the nineteenth century, when the research university as a specific type of academic institution specialized in teaching and research first appeared in the systems we have examined.

Next we will look at the French university in the second half of the twentieth century – a pivotal era characterized by important developments in French research that coincided with an upheaval in university structures, particularly in the aftermath of May 1968. More recent changes in the global governance of French universities will also be examined. We will see how their history illustrates the difficulties faced by the universities in this country – the pool from which leading world-class research universities could emerge. There is one fundamental question: Are more recent reform attempts addressing the entrenched patterns that are shaping the future of French universities? Do they exacerbate the operating constraints or foster an environment that is more conducive to a strong positioning of French research universities on the international scene?

A BIT OF HISTORY

In France, as in other large European countries, the earliest universities were founded starting in the thirteenth century, including Toulouse (1229), Montpellier (1289), and Grenoble (1339), plus several in Paris and in various other regions of France. It is estimated that by the end of the *Ancien Régime*, there were some twenty universities in France. These were all closed down by the French Revolution and replaced by lycées (upper secondary schools) and écoles (post-secondary schools).

The university was to reappear under the First French (Napoleonic) Empire in the guise of the Imperial University of France. However, under this system France was covered by faculties directly overseen by the single Imperial University, rather than by a collection of universities, strictly speaking. Situated in various regions of France, they were grouped into academies and were ultimately under the aegis of the Ministère de l'Instruction publique (National Ministry of Public Instruction).[1]

These faculties – divided into five disciplinary families: medicine, law, science, literature, and theology – were patterned on a uniform and centralized higher education that was administered by the supervisory ministry. This feature is well documented, as is the fact that these faculties and their professors, especially in the sciences and humanities, spent a lot of time supervising the instruction provided by upper secondary schools and certifying the bachelor's degrees they conferred.

Another dimension to this Napoleonic Jacobinism was just as formative in the history of French universities: As noted by Musselin, it took a corporatist approach to establishing centralized bodies for managing the careers of university professors. Appointed by the ministry, academic representatives from different disciplines were assembled into ministerial agencies and tasked with drawing up and enforcing internal regulations governing professors in every major disciplinary family. Management of academic faculty was, thus, removed from the Imperial University's faculties.[2]

At the end of nineteenth century a sweeping reform movement refocused the efforts of the Third Republic on higher education. Under the leadership of Louis Liard, the reformers of that era embraced the German concept of the research university as advocated by Humboldt. Faculties of the French university were encouraged to recruit full-time students and structure their educational offerings. Also, from now on the hiring mechanisms for academic faculty were expected to give much more consideration to candidates' research capabilities.

The faculties of the newly created universities of the late nineteenth century had thus been endowed with greater powers. As was the case in many other national university systems, university faculties had already put down roots in the cities and regions of France by that time.[3] Overall, however, the ambitious reform of universities undertaken by the Third Republic failed. As Musselin emphasizes, referring in particular to the work of C. Charle,[4] research in universities was completely trumped by a focus on supervising degrees to be granted and providing instruction. Humboldt's vision of the university played no unifying role in bringing university faculties together.[5]

The universities that were reconstituted in 1896 proved to be much more nominal than real. They were under the aegis of two authorities. One was the supervisory ministry, which exercised final decision-making power in its capacity as the administrative apparatus of a centralizing government. Many of the operating conditions of university faculties – such as student admissions, the formal design and accreditation of curricula and training programs, the awarding of nationally recognized degrees, and funding – were dictated by Paris. The ministry thus ensured that higher education was uniform, centralized, and dispensed on an egalitarian basis by the faculties that were assembled in the nation's universities. Furthermore, the reforms of the Third Republic did not alter the centralized and discipline-based management of careers in French universities. This domain remained solidly ensconced in central commissions related to the supervisory ministry that were in the hands of the broad disciplinary families within university faculties.

Thus, though revamped in theory, universities remained unable to assert themselves over the prerogatives of the previously established faculties. Against this backdrop, faculty deans played the role of key intermediaries with regard to both the ministry for their general operating conditions and their peers' disciplinary commissions for the management of university professors' careers.

The era that Musselin describes as the Republic of Faculties, which was to last until the passage of the Faure Act in 1968, was characterized by a co-management that simultaneously consolidated two major features of the French university: centralized and bureaucratic management of the establishments by the supervisory ministry, and a corporatist management, also centralized though structured along scientific disciplines, of professors' careers. The universities and their administrators were practically shut out of the process.[6]

This historical snapshot has examined the university branch of higher education in France. There is another, the so-called Grandes Écoles, which consists of highly specialized vocational schools. Created during the eighteenth century, they are primarily responsible for educating bureaucrats and government professionals: they include École des ponts et chaussées (1747), École de génie militaire de Mézières (1748), École des mines (1783), École polytechnique (1794), and École normale supérieure (1794), among others. These are highly selective institutions that recruit the cream of the crop among post-secondary students and have access to vast resources to achieve their missions. Initially, they had no mandate or inclination to conduct research, though much later some of them were challenged to reconsider this aspect of their mission and show a greater openness to it.

The mere existence within the French higher education system of the Grandes Écoles shows that, from the beginning and through to today, universities proper have been crowded out from above. Less selective and less endowed, they are not tasked with educating the elites of French society, even if they do make a significant contribution to the traditional liberal professions of law and medicine, for which they continue to be responsible.

However, in a curious turn of events, during the nineteenth century French universities were also crowded out from below. The very prestigious Grandes Écoles mentioned above are only one part of a complex set of more diversified schools and institutes. Early participants in the French system of higher education, specialized schools are deeply committed to education in applied sciences. The initial phases of the industrial revolution, which came to France and many other European countries during the nineteenth century, required a labour force with stronger qualifications in applied science, especially engineering. Despite their prestige, the Grandes Écoles, such as the École polytechnique, École des ponts et chaussées, and École des mines were not sufficient.

Indeed, it was somewhat in opposition to them that a new group of institutions began to spread, such as École centrale de Paris (1829), or institutes specialized in applied science, such as schools of engineering. Connected to various government ministries or other public agencies or, more rarely, the private sector, these institutions began to appear as of the end of the nineteenth century – especially the schools of engineering. They were highly selective, even seeking to tap into the same pool of candidates as the Grandes Écoles.

However, these institutions share another characteristic: They are not, in general, part of the university system. They directly provide education in applied sciences and confer state-recognized degrees in engineering. A large number of French schools of engineering thus thrived outside of the university system. As of 1934 engineers could only be qualified by and accountable to a national board that accredits these establishments to provide this training and safeguards the integrity of the nationally certified title of engineer conferred by the degree. It was not until the middle of the twentieth century that Écoles nationales supérieures d'ingénierie (ENSI) (National Engineering Superior Schools) gave some visibility to university training of engineers. However, these only amount to a small fraction of the institutions tasked with education in the various fields of engineering and applied sciences. We observe that during the nineteenth century and for a long time thereafter, the potential spur of specialized engineering training that was well-integrated into their specific programs was withheld from universities.

At the time during the nineteenth century when research universities in Germany, the United States, and Canada were flourishing, France was still either under the Imperial University regime or struggling to rebuild its system. These institutions, which had the least selective admission criteria and were being crowded out from above and below, were the weakest link in France's higher education system. Formally legal entities, these universities did not have any real academic power, limited as they were in their autonomy by a ubiquitous ministry and the powers that their faculties wielded, acting also as a guardian of their management.

One finding, which summarizes the viewpoint expressed by numerous observers, is incontrovertible. Throughout the nineteenth and into the early twentieth centuries, the soil of the French university system was inhospitable to the germination and growth of research universities in the German mould.

Despite the fact that the university reformers of the Third Republic might have been influenced by this vision, French national universities, as such, did not absorb an approach that placed a high value on the spirit of discovery and research. There was no model university to provide the others with a template for missions central to science, culture, and the future of French society. As Alain Renaut observed: "If the policies of the Third Republic did not truly succeed in embedding the idea of the university in the national mould, this is exactly mirrored in the fact that the renaissance of the university could only follow a flowering of cultural and intellectual life outside of this university setting ... The renewing of the traditional disciplines, not to mention the development of new ones, largely occurred outside of universities."[7]

The Mid-Twentieth Century

In the interwar period, France joined many other countries in striving to intensify its research efforts. This provided the backdrop against which the government saw fit to establish yet another public service:[8] institutions that paralleled universities. These were funded from the public purse, and tasked with conducting research, in particular basic research. With little involvement in research, universities were not given this mission.

First, the Centre National de la Recherche Scientifique, or CNRS (National Centre for Scientific Research), which was founded in 1939, came into its own after the Second World War. Other public research agencies were subsequently established in various sectors that reflected the preoccupations of the government: health and biomedical sciences (Institut national de la santé et de la recherche médicale, or INSERM); agronomy (Institut national de la recherche agronomique, or INRA); and aerospace, ONERA (Office national d'études et de recherches aérospatiales) etc., placing a wedge between universities and the key actors in basic research in France, and confirming the secondary status of French universities in research activity. This depreciation proved to be laden with consequences.

It should be clear, indeed, that it created a structural dissociation between teaching and research in the case of universities – even between graduate studies, still largely situated in universities, the core of which are normally made up of advanced training in research and the practices of experimentation and discovery that never really took root within them.

Thus, the French university was not in charge of the activity of discovery that would have conferred upon it a basic research mission for training the next generation of scientists. It could not, therefore, exercise the decision-making power that would allow it to acquire resources, build the infrastructure required for research and, by extension, play a central role in the development of scientific culture, activity, and innovation – all critical to French society's socioeconomic development.

Like many other industrialized countries, though with a slight lag, post-war France resolutely turned toward mass higher education. In ten years, from the late 1950s to the late 1960s, enrolment in higher education tripled from 250,000 to 750,000. Subsequently, from 1970 to the end of the 1980s, this value rose by a further two-thirds. The decade between the mid-1980s and the mid-1990s saw a second expansion of mass university education, with enrolment reaching nearly 1.5 million students. At the beginning of the 1990s, the higher education attendance rate was 30 per cent for the relevant age group.[9]

Several French higher education establishments were called on to absorb this rapid growth in the student body, universities in particular.[10] Traditionally less selective, they had to handle a surge in demand, largely from candidates who were ineligible for other institutions. They confronted many challenges to the quality of teaching resulting from excessively high student-to-faculty ratios – at least thirty students per professor, more in the social sciences and humanities – and impressive hordes of undergraduate students.[11]

The University at the End of the 1960s

At a time when mass higher education was creating structural upheaval in universities and in the wake of the events of May 1968, French academia was the scene of another important structural change. The Faure Act strove to provide universities with a stronger identity and greater decision-making power. One of the key steps it took to that end was to target the unlimited power of the faculties, which were undermining the autonomy of universities' central administration. To put an end to what Musselin called the "Republic of Faculties," they were abolished. The university was then endowed with centralized decision-making bodies. These included a board of governors and a scientific council, with representation from academic and administrative staffs, students, and community members. Its president was a member of the academic faculty who was elected to a five-year term.

Abolition of the faculties and their replacement by teaching and research units (UER: Unités d'enseignement et de recherche) was intended to pave the way for more multidisciplinary education supported by the universities' various UERs. These new official teaching and research units – which shared some features with the disciplinary departments of Anglo-Saxon and North American universities – were encouraged to link up with other, related university-based units to form new groupings whose boundaries could be subject to review. In the politically charged climate that followed May 1968, this change had the unfortunate consequence of creating a systemic fragmentation of many French universities. These new teaching and research clusters did not necessarily reflect a broad academic vision. Rather, they also represented considerations that were more ideological in nature and, in some cases, a more or less openly avowed political desire to restore peace on campuses deeply divided by sociopolitical turmoil. Even afterwards, new universities continued to be founded with a mere handful of disciplinary fields. So much so, in fact, that it was estimated in 1980 that only sixteen of the sixty-seven existing universities could be classified as multidisciplinary, ten partially multidisciplinary, and forty-one with only one or two broad disciplines.[12]

Institutional emphasis on quasi-disciplinary units and their combinations corresponded to the proliferation of curricula resulting from the rapid expansion of a mass higher education system.[13] The emergence of new training programs, even when they were not created by existing teaching and research units – the French name was changed by the Savary Act of 1984 from unités d'enseignement et de recherche to unités de formation et de recherche (UFR) – had the long-term effect of undermining the uniformity of training programs and the pedagogical management of curricula and degree certification by the ministry.

The rapid expansion of mass education that characterized French higher education in the second half of the twentieth century was thus accompanied by the introduction of new disciplines and subjects and a review of training program levels and degrees conferred. In fact, the impact of what had become mass university education gave rise to irresistible pressures toward an institutional diversification of curricula. The centralized management mode characterized by educational uniformity and egalitarianism that culminates in the conferring of state degrees is still struggling to come to terms with this diversity.[14]

After expanding to a size representative of mass higher education, the French system has become a shattered mosaic of highly diversified institutions. A segment of this mosaic – made up among other things of the most distinguished Grandes Écoles – accounts for a relatively small proportion of the individuals in higher education. But this segment also comprises other schools whose number is inflated by the proliferation of institutions of architecture, applied arts, business, communications, and, especially, engineering and applied sciences. These have experienced sustained growth and harbour large contingents of students. And they share a common characteristic: they are all a segment of the higher education system that generally practises candidate selection and parallels universities, though with a better reputation.

The other major segment, universities, is growing at a remarkable pace, though not without having experienced significant upheavals. Their secular values of uniformity, egalitarianism, and centralized management have been shaken by trends toward differentiated curricula and training programs. But overall, this segment, which is still officially unable to select its own undergraduate and master's students, remains at the bottom of the French higher education system. This fact contributes to an image problem for French universities.

Shortcomings and Reforms

A complex mosaic representing higher education in France, in which the university plays a secondary role, has emerged from frequent reform attempts. A detailed examination of these attempts, even the most recent ones, would detract from our objectives. As Neave emphasizes, there has not been a minister of higher education in

France who has not been associated with a reform of this institution, frequently with very limited success.[15]

We can cut to the chase by pointing out that these reforms were designed to mitigate the well-known limitations of the French university, such as the gulf between one sector that is very selective and another in which there is no selectivity in admissions. The first, as we have pointed out, consists mostly of the Grandes Écoles – joined by ENAP (École nationale d'administration publique, or National School of Public Administration) in 1945 – but also many others, offering training in applied sciences and engineering for example, which have greatly expanded that official but eclectic sector of the Grandes Écoles. With regard to the legislative framework that governs higher education, these institutions have been granted some exemptions that give them greater flexibility in their operations.

The second sector is universities. This sector has been the target of the most sustained and ambitious reform attempts over time. It represents a large proportion of the pool from which research universities would emerge. Two potential paths toward strengthening the operations of a system that has been swamped by the influx created by mass university education and whose operating costs are an increasing drain on government finances were rejected out of hand: Introducing some selectivity into admission criteria for undergraduate studies and forcefully diversifying funding sources by raising tuition to a level closer to the actual costs of education.[16]

Another weakness that needs to be addressed is the coexistence of universities and government institutions of a scientific and technological character that are devoted to basic research and funded from the public purse. This situation creates paradoxes. In fact, to fulfill their mandates, CNRS and many other public scientific and technological establishments draw on the services not only of their own research units, but also of affiliated units that are often based on university campuses. Since the mid-1960s, for example, CNRS has been using an increasing number of affiliated research units. One form of affiliation that has proved to be popular and persistent – combining the resources and staffs of CNRS with those of participating universities – is university mixed research units.

CNRS participates in financing these mixed research units, lending them staff and scientific teams and investing in their infrastructure and equipment. It is believed that the research units associated with universities and other French institutions of higher education have gradually become a clear majority of all research units affiliated with CNRS and other public scientific and technological establishments. This has been true to such an extent, in fact, that a large share of French research resources, including basic research of course, were localized in the university itself. However, since they do not control many vital strategic assets and resources devoted to research conducted on their premises, are the universities truly able to transform strategies for research and the sustained integration of research activity performed within their walls into advanced training in research? We will have the opportunity to return to this, but for the moment we note that the schism between research and university creates many structural difficulties for the latter.

There have been efforts to fix another weakness: the general lack of university decision-making autonomy. Over time, many stakeholders have clearly identified this as one of the critical determinants of universities' future. The Faure Act summarized many earlier contributions by emphasizing the collective identity and autonomy of universities. This effort was bolstered by the Savary Act of 1984, which increased the number and size of university governing bodies. There is every reason to believe that these attempts, which enabled universities to stand up to the faculties, failed to achieve their ultimate goal. Musselin is unambiguous in this matter: These efforts were unable to dislodge the odd duality of governmental and corporatist co-management, centralized at the same time in the supervisory ministry and structured by scientific disciplines. This dual centralized co-management hamstrings presidents and severely limits the power of universities in their areas of governance.[17]

Only in the last decade of the twentieth century did things begin to change. Again we turn to Musselin for insight into these developments. The turning point came with the proposal by the supervisory ministry, made during the late 1980s, to sign four-year contracts with each establishment that would commit them to setting institutional goals in the areas of teaching and the development of academic and administrative staffs, even of their buildings and equipment. On acceptance of the contract, an institution could be granted supplementary credits equivalent to a certain percentage (5 per cent initially and then 10 per cent) of its operating funds. This tool, which was soon to cover strategic research planning – under a similar agreement since the early 1980s – affirms the authority of university presidents and encourages modernization.

In this fashion the supervisory ministry gives greater recognition to the presidents and the main governing bodies of the institutions with which they work, for their decisions regarding university operations. This trend is gradually gaining ground, though again in fits and starts, in the area of managing the careers of academic faculty. Filling job vacancies and recruiting professors is, in fact, beginning to shift from centralized corporatist commissions to local boards composed of disciplinary experts and to presidents and their management teams who oversee them.[18]

Today

At the beginning of the twenty-first century, the need to decentralize decision-making power to the universities remains on the agenda. The government and a number of stakeholders are openly questioning whether French research universities are capable of competing internationally against the backdrop of the globalization of knowledge-based societies.

In tandem with the devolution of decision-making powers, there is also a drive to more directly restructure the academic foundations of universities. This is a matter of expanding the range of disciplines, both in teaching and research, so as to create institutional entities that provide a broader coverage of knowledge and training, as in the international research multi-versities. Thus, a two-pronged operation was launched in the mid-2000s.

The goal of the first part was to modify certain characteristics of the university system to increase institutional autonomy, efficiency, and (it was hoped) performance. The second sought to foster associations of universities and other institutional entities, such as the Grandes Écoles. The Programme des investissements d'avenir, or PIA (Future Investment Program), was then set up to equip ten leading research universities to compete with the best world-class universities.

The 2007 Loi relative aux libertés et responsabilités des universités, or LRU (University Freedom and Responsibility Act), is a focal point of these operations. It strives to give greater autonomy to universities and more power to their presidents and boards of governors. In a document that was released by the government of the day, the following passage explicitly explains the rationale for this law: "Currently, governance is simultaneously characterized by a lack of leadership, a lack of transparency, and a lack of openness. Thus, university presidents who are elected by a joint decision of three university councils waste their time in mediation rather than action."[19]

This reform thus has implications for the role and responsibilities of the board of governors, the Scientific Council, and the Education and Academic Life Council, all of which were established by the Faure and Savary Acts. The institution's board of governors is henceforth the only deliberative body, as the Scientific Council, and the Education and Academic Life Council have been reduced to consultative roles. This reform also redefined and reinforced the role and responsibilities of the university president. Finally, it sought to increase both budgetary autonomy and independent human resource management in these institutions. The universities that so desired could even assume ownership of their buildings. In principle, these reforms were to be implemented in all universities by 2013.

The universities' strategic development plans were simultaneously challenged by incentives prepared by the government and targeted at groups of institutions. The loi de programme pour la recherche (Research Planning Act) of 2006 had already proposed the creation of pôles de recherche et d'enseignement, or PRES (research and training clusters), bringing together universities, mixed research units, and, potentially, other components of higher education, such as the Grandes Écoles. The pooling of teaching and research capacities and students, especially at the graduate level, from several disciplinary fields makes it possible to create larger academic collectives that are able to provide a multidisciplinary coverage of knowledge and training. It is generally thought that, in one way or another, most French universities participate in a PRES. There are twenty-four of them with the status of établissement public de coopération scientifique, or EPCS (public institutions of scientific cooperation).[20] The LRU, adopted in 2007, consolidates the legislative efforts to bring together higher education institutions. It confers on an institution's board of governors the right to request affiliation with a new or existing establishment.

The schemes for research and training clusters and for public establishments fostering scientific cooperation were ultimately meant to pave the way for Plan Campus (or Opération campus). This is a plan to create ten world-class university campuses by means of substantial investments in transforming and clustering existing universities and schools. The intent is to increase the intensity of the battle against the harmful fragmentation of many French universities. These clusters are to be converted into institutions that are active in many different fields of knowledge by giving them a critical mass of professors and researchers and the teaching and research infrastructure to make them into true multi-versities. This operation's ultimate goal is very clear, and has been explicitly stated by the former president himself: Increase the number of French universities that can place in the highest categories in international rankings. These campuses are starting to take shape in both Paris and the major regions of France.

The changes and tentative reforms that characterized the turn of the century will undoubtedly prove pivotal in the history of the French university system. They are more or less promising steps in the right direction. It remains to be seen whether their first results will be able to hoist these research universities into the top ranks internationally. This is a question that we will examine in much more detail in the following pages.

It is indisputable that contracting practices, the LRU, and efforts to consolidate academic institutions will take a long time – at least another five or ten years – to solidly establish the international positioning of French universities. In fact, France's current international position in terms of the quality of its research university system stems from its operating mode over the past several decades. However, the specific and targeted improvements the latest reforms, such as the LRU, intend to implement add to our understanding of how French universities function.

PRESENT CHARACTERISTICS OF THE SYSTEM

For some time, the mosaic of the French higher education system has included a weak link: public universities. These have a long history of struggling against structural shortcomings that impair their functioning. They are still grappling with management and governance modes that have long deprived them of real decision-making autonomy, and they have been beset by the fragmentation of disciplines and lacked the critical mass of professors and researchers to form the backbone of a research university as an organizationally integrated actor.

Nonetheless, French public universities remain the most natural source from which research universities with international visibility can emerge. Results from the 2012 ARWU and THES rankings confirm this: Most of the French establishments they feature are universities. Consequently, it seems clear that the difficulties of public universities undermine the number of research universities that can place in international rankings, especially in the more selective categories of world-class research universities.

The Grandes Écoles are subject to their own fragmentation dynamics. Only a fraction of these many diversified institutions attain a very high level of teaching excellence. Nor do they all reach great heights in the area of research or advanced training in research.[21] We have emphasized in passing that higher education in France saw the emergence, both before and during the transition to mass higher education, of uncountable numbers of architectural, art, business, communications, and especially engineering schools that swelled the Grandes Écoles sector's institutional ranks. The Ministère de l'enseignement supérieur et de la recherche (Ministry of Higher Education and Research) provides the following description of the some 450 institutions that this group currently contains: "The name Grandes Écoles covers institutions like schools of engineering, Écoles normale supérieure, and business and veterinary medicine schools. These Grandes Écoles are characterized by the excellence of their degrees and their stringent admission criteria."

On the website of the Conférence des Grandes Écoles it is emphasized that Grandes Écoles do not only provide vocational education, but that, in fact "in 2011 they were responsible for nearly one-half of all research in science and approximately 46% of doctoral degrees in science."[22]

In a North American university setting we would expect developments in applied science, engineering, and business to occur within universities.

In the following pages we will be looking at French public universities as the principal source of leading research universities. These eighty universities, some of which include university technological institutes (Instituts universitaires de technologie), are under the aegis of the Higher Education and Research Ministry. In 2009–10 they had 1,445,317 students, or nearly 60 per cent of the approximately

2.5 million students enrolled in all institutions of higher education in France. We also note that there appear to be a suboptimal number of public universities compared with what would prevail in a less splintered system.

We will use this population of universities to examine their principal operating characteristics, just as we have done in the case of the United Kingdom, the United States, and Canada. We will find it useful to draw on more specific data, both quantitative and institutional, with regard to operating resources, the delivery of research, some characteristic ways and means by which students and professors arrive and evolve, and governance modes. All in all, do these organizational arrangements impede the ability of French research universities to make a mark on the international scene?

Choosing universities as the population for our study has ramifications. In so doing, we exclude nearly 40 per cent of the French higher education system previously described. This is because a very large number of institutions in the Grandes Écoles segment simply do not have the characteristics that would allow them to be classified with the leading universities, especially the research multiversities that make their mark on the international scene. Some French institutions that are not, strictly speaking, universities, nonetheless have the reputation and research accomplishments to allow them to place in the international rankings. While there can be no doubt that this is a remarkable achievement, it involves only a minute number of small institutions that cannot, on their own, override the primary features and operating conditions that characterize French universities. There is no attempt here to pass judgment on the quality of these schools and institutes in terms of their own mission. It is, rather, an observation.

In our analysis of specific university systems in the three previous chapters we have generally been able to identify university subgroups that are particularly research-intense for purposes of comparison, such as the members of the Russell Group in the United Kingdom and the fifteen research-intensive universities in Canada. The purpose of subdividing the population of institutions this way is to see whether the most research-intensive universities differ in their characteristics from the pool from which they are drawn. Since, to our knowledge, there is no comparable subgroup in France, we have created one using the sixteen French universities that appear in the 2010 edition of the ARWU ranking. The choice of the year 2010 was dictated by the fact that we only have quantitative data on French universities for 2009–10.[23] This is, needless to say, an arbitrary choice. However, we believe we will be able to differentiate this subgroup from the remaining French universities.

Research Activity

We begin by examining various aspects of research as practised in French universities. We will be interested in whether recent data bear out some of the constraints on the conduct of basic research that were identified in the preceding pages or whether those data show that universities have real opportunities to stand out for their level of investment in research.

We must admit that we were forced to abandon any hope of finding disaggregated data at the level of the institution. The coexistence of universities with public research organizations that are also funded by the government and largely operate on university premises complicates the issue of university research funding in France. In the absence of clear, detailed, and easily accessible data on research in universities we were obliged to fall back on OECD data. These are, obviously, less disaggregated than the data on university research we compiled for the three other countries examined in the previous chapters.

Data from the OECD, which are compiled to facilitate international comparisons as much as possible, allow us to address three issues that may affect how research is conducted in French universities. We first examine the amount of resources devoted to this activity; we then comment on the diversity of sources of research funding; and, finally, we look at how the university community in France accesses the resources it invests in research.

In 2009, France devoted no less than 2.26 per cent of GDP, or US\$762 per capita, to research and development – placing it among the top industrialized countries in terms of research intensity. It surpasses Canada and the United Kingdom, and lags only slightly behind the United States. Conversely, the proportion of this remarkable national research effort that is conducted in higher education institutions, 20.6 per cent or US\$10.2 billion, stands in stark contrast to both the domestic research intensity and observations from other countries. This is not attributable to a greater presence of the private sector in gross domestic R&D expenditure, but rather to the predominance of the government as a research-performing sector. At 16.4 per cent, its share is greater than that observed in the other countries examined.[24]

These OECD data cover all resources committed to research in French universities, including those made available to mixed research units operating in universities. We conclude that these numbers bear out the historical trend observed at the beginning of this chapter with regard to the split of government-funded research between higher education institutions and public scientific and technological establishments. The coexistence of public establishments and higher education institutions as parallel hubs of research, both funded by the government, continues to prevent universities from playing the central role in research they enjoy elsewhere.

These data do not, however, shed much light on the exact proportion of research performed in universities proper. Recall that universities only account for 60 per cent of the higher education sector, whereas Grandes Écoles claim that they are responsible for half of all research performed in the natural sciences. What impact does this fragmentation of the higher education system in France have on the amount of resources devoted to research and on the degree to which this activity is concentrated in the universities proper?

In the absence of detailed and reliable data we propose the following hypothesis. Assuming that nearly 70 per cent of total intramural research in France's higher education system consists of university-only research activities, we arrive at approximately US$7 billion (70 per cent of US$10,184 billion) in 2009. In international terms, this figure does not reflect very well on French universities. There is every indication that, despite a high research intensity in France, French universities are at a considerable disadvantage in terms of the resources available to them to fund their research activities.

In previous chapters we have emphasized the benefits that accrue to universities from having diversified revenue sources to fund their operations. This diversity not only allows for an increase in the amount and stability of available resources, but also provides flexibility in spending that makes it possible to seize the opportunities that constantly arise in a world of ever-evolving knowledge. France stands out in that the government funds 90.1 per cent of gross domestic research conducted in institutions of higher education.[25]

France is also unique in how funding for the research conducted in universities is appropriated. In general, the universities fund approximately half of their research from their own funds, which are mainly contributed by the government. These are disbursed according to a formula based on specific criteria that provide little incentive for performance.

External funds account for the other half of research activity. We know that, for several decades now, public scientific establishments in France, such as CNRS and INSERM (Institut national de la santé et de la recherche médicale, or Institute of Health and Medical Research), have had a strong commitment to mixed research units, which link them to teams of professors in universities. The resources of these mixed research units thus account for a large share of the external funding available to universities.

As several observers have pointed out, CNRS and INSERM are the senior partners in this institutional arrangement: they contribute large research budgets, high-level scientific personnel and technological staffs, and they may tend to foist their own planning and research agendas onto the universities. Furthermore, the contribution of resources to mixed research units by public scientific establishments is not reported in university budgets, but rather in the budgets of these establishments – Établissements publics à caractère scientifique et technologique (EPST) (public scientific and technological establishments).

Contractual agreements with the supervisory ministry have begun changing this since the 1980s. Thanks to greater delegation of management to the universities they were expected to exercise more control over the research performed on their premises, in consideration of their own critical masses and of what they can gain from their participation in mixed research units.

Though they are indisputably a step in the right direction, these establishment-level contracts appear to have had limited impact, according to the Commission sénatoriale de d'application des lois (Senate Committee for the Control of Law Enforcement). It is, in fact, no easy matter for a university to design a research strategy when it depends on other authorities and agencies for a significant share of the resources required by such a strategy. On the other hand, the contracts and even their associated assessments do not seem to have had any real impact on the funds provided to an institution by the ministry. We also observe that the research strategies developed by universities, especially when they are open to forming associations of institutions in PRES, frequently encounter resistance from public scientific establishments. Marginalized from PRES and sceptical about their actual roles, they have approached this strategy with some caution.[26]

What is striking here is the virtual absence of any mechanism for obtaining external research funding on a competitive and recurring basis following a rigorous peer assessment. The Higher Education and Research Ministry was not totally oblivious to this shortcoming, so in 2005 it created the Agence nationale de la recherche (ANR) (National Research Agency), which doles out research grants on a competitive basis following peer assessment. There can be no doubt that, from the government's point of view, one of the goals of this policy was to bolster the practice of university research and create greater research incentives for professors.

At the international level, ANR's contribution of €629 million in 2010 was quite modest in comparison to the amounts advanced by similar agencies in other countries. This is particularly true in light of the fact that only 18.9 per cent of this amount went to universities, versus 30.3 per cent to CNRS and 7.8 per cent to INSERM. It appears likely that a considerable amount of the funding obtained by public scientific establishments ended up in university-based mixed research units, which tend to be under the control of those establishments.

Overall, the most recent research practices in French universities appear to be conditioned by structures that are unable to counteract or lessen the impacts of the constraints built into the French higher education system. France's universities are clearly compromised by the low level of resources available to support university-based research, by the government's virtual monopoly over funding and, finally, by resource appropriation modes that create little or no incentive for performance. This has a corollary effect of reducing the concentration of research in the leading universities. The schism between research and university thus continues to cause harm.

Sources of Operating Funds

And what can we say about operating revenues, which are used to fund teaching and the supporting infrastructure? Data disaggregated at the institution level provide an overview for both the eighty French public universities and for the subgroup that we created from the 2010 ARWU ranking. Will the trends that emerge from these data alleviate some of the constraints on French universities, or can they dilute their impact? It should come as no surprise if here, once again, the issue is both the volume of resources available to universities and the diversity of their sources.

With regard to this, let us see what table 7.1 reveals about the situation of the French universities we have chosen.

Two features clearly stand out in these data. At nearly 91 per cent of the funding, the government assumes the lion's share of university operating costs.[27] Contributions from other sources are proportionally much smaller. The difference with the trends that our data revealed in the case of UK, US, and Canadian universities is pronounced. This can be mostly attributed to the much larger share of their operating revenues that they receive from tuition fees, but also from other sources.

The second characteristic relates to the structure of the funding of these two university groups, which clearly stands out in this table. We first observe that the sixteen research universities receive over one-third of this funding, though they only account for one institution in five. As for the rest, the structure of their operating funding is a carbon copy of that applicable to all French universities. Is there a comparable uniformity in the structure of operating revenues made available to the Grandes Écoles? As we have noted, the latter benefit from a few exemptions from the legislative framework that governs higher education in France – but do these exemptions extend to providing them with a greater diversity of funding sources?

Until quite recently, this funding, which was almost exclusively from the government, was allocated by the supervisory ministry using results from the SANREMO model. A brief description of this model's characteristics reveals the absence of budgetary flexibility in each of these institutions: "The purpose of the SANREMO model (a criteria-based model for allocating resources to universities) is to provide an objective measure of universities' requirements for credits to cover operations and staffing (professors and administrators) … Estimates of staffing needs are derived from a fine grid (over 40 classes of training), with each training class allocated a theoretical endowment of professors based on the values in effect in 1994, revised on a case-by-case basis since then."

After the introduction of the LRU in 2007 this model was revised and then replaced by the SYMPA model, reflecting the desire of the government to grant greater autonomy to universities in the

Table 7.1
Funding of operating expenditures by source and category of university, France, 2009, in thousands of US$

Groups	Govt. grants	Tuition	Business	Other income	Total
IN ABSOLUTE TERMS					
Group of 16	4,042,890	168,319	32,927	201,937	4,446,074
Other	7,186,503	368,299	62,976	250,407	7,868,185
All universities	11,229,393	536,619	95,903	452,344	12,314,259
AS A PERCENTAGE BY SOURCE OF FUNDING					
Group of 16	90.9	3.8	0.7	4.5	100
Other	91.3	4.7	0.8	3.2	100
All universities	91.2	4.4	0.8	3.7	100
AS A PERCENTAGE BY CATEGORY OF UNIVERSITY					
Group of 16	36.0	31.4	34.3	44.6	36.1
Other	64.0	68.6	65.7	55.4	63.9
All universities	100	100	100	100	100

Notes: Government grants include cover operating expenditures and the wages of staff on the government payroll. These values converted into US$ using PPP based on 2009 OECD GDP numbers. Source: Government endowments to universities 2009, Ministry of Higher Education and Research, preliminary data.

management of their operating budgets.[28] We will have occasion to return to the impact of that law, but for now we note that it has not altered the fact that the government has a virtual monopoly on funding higher education in France. However, it should be pointed out that this law explicitly acknowledges this constraint and encourages universities to work on diversifying their sources of revenues, though they are not allowed to tamper with tuition. Various avenues have been opened to them: establishing ties with the private sector, creating foundations, expanding donations, acquiring equity positions or establishing subsidiaries, generating income by offering continuing education, etc.[29] The efforts made by some institutions to raise funds from these complementary sources in the face of the obstacles raised by an entrenched institutional and social hostility have not met with much success.[30]

Against a backdrop of onerous financial constraints and various requirements involving the government, the almost exclusively public funding of higher education in France is the primary cause of its underfunding. In fact, as a percentage of GDP, the government of France (1.25 per cent) spends nearly as much as the United States (1.26 per cent) on higher education, but a severely limited recourse to other funding sources dramatically reduces the level of funds available to French universities. On top of government funding, tuition only amounts to the equivalent of 0.35 per cent of GDP in France versus 1.68 per cent of GDP in the United States.

What are we to conclude? French research universities, like all universities in that country, are subject to severe funding constraints. But compared with countries with whom they enjoy a relationship of emulation and competition on the international scene, these institutions are much more captive to a single decision-maker who is beholden to the vagaries of the political market and government finances. They are still shackled by rigid budgetary rules established and enforced by the supervisory ministry. Under these circumstances, we see that French research universities wishing to make their mark as world-class institutions struggle to compete with foreign rivals that are better equipped in terms of decision-making autonomy in the area of operating resources.

Human Resources

We will quickly look at some aspects of the ways and means by which students and professors arrive and evolve in French universities. We will then identify the features and issues involved in their governance. We seek to highlight which of their operating modes and conditions mitigate or exacerbate the impact the aforementioned constraints have on the trajectory of French universities, to better understand the position of French research universities on the international scale.

Table 7.2 presents a statistic we have already mentioned: in 2009–10 French public universities were educating over 1.4 million students. They are distributed as follows: two-thirds in undergraduate studies (65.1 per cent), a little less than one-third at the master's level (30.5 per cent), and 4.4 per cent in doctoral studies. In international terms, the student body distribution in French universities is characterized by a greater number of students in graduate studies. The difference appears to be mostly reflected at the level of master's programs. We cannot preclude the possibility that this is attributable to how student enrolments are counted in light of the harmonization

Table 7.2

Distribution of full- and part-time students, by level of studies and category
of university, France, 2009–2010

Groups	First level	Second level and other graduate	Doctoral	Total
		IN ABSOLUTE TERMS		
Group of 16	236,846	126,847	23,627	387,320
Other	704,029	314,001	39,967	1,057,997
All universities	940,875	440,848	63,594	1,445,317
	AS A PERCENTAGE BY LEVEL OF STUDIES			
Group of 16	61.1	32.7	6.1	100
Other	66.5	29.7	3.8	100
All universities	65.1	30.5	4.4	100
	AS A PERCENTAGE BY CATEGORY OF UNIVERSITY			
Group of 16	25.2	28.8	37.2	26.8
Other	74.8	71.2	62.8	73.2
All universities	100	100	100	100

Sources: Number of students in *licence* programmes (equal to undergraduate), number of students
in master's programmes, number of students in doctoral programmes. Student population: various
tables; Statistical tables 2010, *Direction de l'évaluation, de la prospective et de la performance*
(Evaluation, Forecasting and Performance Directorate) available on the Extranet "Pléiade" of the
Ministry of Education.

of French university education with the requirements of the European
Union's Bologna Agreement.

Taken together, these universities account for nearly 64,000 doctoral students who are preparing to assume the mantle of France's
scientific succession. The sixteen research universities in our subgroup are more focused than the others on graduate studies, in particular the doctoral students who make up nearly 6 per cent of
universities' total student population. As we saw in the other university systems, these research universities account for a large proportion (nearly 38 per cent) of the doctoral students in the eighty French
universities in our sample. This trend resembles what we have seen
elsewhere, but has some differences. In the systems examined in previous chapters, the concentration of doctoral students in the most
research-intensive institutions was much more pronounced: nearly
70 per cent in Canada's fifteen research-intensive universities, and
even more concentrated in the United States.

STUDENTS

What resources are these institutions able to make available to their students? We have established that the government of France devotes a significant share of its GDP (equivalent to that of the United States) to higher education. However, owing to the dearth of ancillary funding, per-student expenditures of US$16,145 in France are not in the same league as, for example, the corresponding values for the United States (US$30,147).[31] In fact, they are 88 per cent higher in the United States than in France.

Our data on the operating expenditures of French universities corroborate these international disparities. In US dollars, the operating resources of French universities – a little more than US$8,000 – correspond to somewhat less than 50 per cent of the per-student funding in Canadian and UK universities. At US$11,000 per student, the institution operating revenues in our subgroup of sixteen French research universities exceed those of the other universities.

However, in the case of these universities, whose higher research costs explain the differential with other institutions in the same system, international comparisons reveal an equally, if not even more, dire situation. If, on a per-student basis, these French research universities have approximately half the resources available to equivalent Canadian institutions (US$21,820), the gap is much greater with universities in the United Kingdom (US$26,986) and even greater with US public research universities (US$31,836). When differentials of that magnitude are combined with a lack of incentives, even practices centred on efficiency have their limitations. How could these funding differences not affect education quality?[32]

The most selective higher education institutions in France, such as the Grandes Écoles and university technological institutes, clearly prove, by their stellar reputations and high number of candidates, the powerful attraction of the high-quality education they offer, as attested by their very selective admission policies. While there are students enrolled in universities with outstanding academic records, it remains the case that for many of them this is a fall-back position because they were not admitted into the more selective institutions. A less fragmented higher-education system in this respect would allow universities to better base their reputation on the quality of students admitted and support them in their quest for excellence. For leading research universities that compete with the corresponding French institutions, this dimension of the quality of the student population, at all training levels, is vital to the extent that it contributes to their overall quality and visibility.

It may also be true that tuition levels provide an incentive, both to institutions charging them and students paying them, to excel in the quality of the education offered. Provided they are well integrated into a system of loans and fellowships to mitigate their potential to undermine access, tuition levels that are closer to the real costs of education could give students a greater incentive to care about the quality of the courses, seminars, infrastructure, and general supervision they receive. Similarly, the university that receives a large share of its revenues from tuition fees paid by students will have an interest, not only in having a solid reputation to be able to attract them, but also in retaining them by an appropriate provision of services. Unfortunately, neither of these incentives comes into play at French universities.

We note that admission criteria are more selective at the doctoral level, especially when the candidates, in natural or biomedical sciences or in some sectors of the social sciences, must fulfill the requirements associated with being a student researcher on a good research team, frequently as part of a mixed research unit. There can be no doubt that the creation of doctoral schools in the early 1990s has improved the quality of the environments in which students in advanced training in research receive training and supervision. This is particularly the case when these doctoral schools can help to alleviate problems resulting from limitations in a number of disciplines, or in the critical masses of professors and students in some universities, by regrouping in a doctoral school professors of several academic institutions and mixed research units. Accredited and financed by the supervisory ministry of higher education and research after a national assessment, they are often bolstered by the presence in the university setting of a significant number of mixed research units and research partnerships involving the universities and public scientific and technological establishments (EPST). Doctoral schools are under the leadership of scientific directors and councils who ensure their academic achievements and seek to optimize their results by a better integration of research to doctoral education.

Selective in the area of admitting students and accrediting professors, doctoral schools are, at a strictly academic level, a major step toward providing advanced training in research that is both of higher quality and better supervised. It remains to be seen whether they will integrate into the dynamics and organizational identity specific to each university, and succeed in influencing the impact of research activities, not only as they relate to the mission of doctoral education, but also to other levels of university programs.

FACULTY MEMBERS

The quality of these doctoral schools and, more generally, the teaching and research units that make up a university, depend in large measure on the quality of the academic faculty. Universities, especially research universities, are thus attentive to and careful in recruiting faculty members and supporting them by contributing, to the best of their ability, to a competent and stimulating management of professors' careers.

First we note a very specific characteristic of the professors who work in French institutions, be they universities or Grandes Écoles. The academic faculty in these institutions are civil servants. They are "permanent civil servants appointed to a position in a public establishment of higher education and research. University professors are recruited by means of an open competition by the establishment. They must first be included on a list of accredited university professor candidates maintained by the Conseil national des universités (CNU) (National Council of Universities)."[33]

For regular faculty members, lecturers (maîtres de conférence), and professors, the supervisory ministry determines how many positions a university may claim. They are employees of the government, which sets their wages and their hiring and promotion conditions. Thus, it is the supervisory ministry that manages all the organizational issues surrounding the positions given to a specific institution.

The selection of candidates to occupy the positions is ensured by specialists in the discipline. In the context of the dual centralization, governmental and corporatist, of the operation of French universities, a key role is played by disciplinary commissions of experts. These are specialists, two-thirds of whom are elected by their peers and one-third appointed by the supervisory ministry. They are agencies of the National Council of Universities, which the supervisory ministry appoints and regulates.

The role assigned to the CNU and its disciplinary sections provides that experts certify an individual's qualifications for a regular teaching position as a lecturer or professor in a university. In addition to holding a PhD in research, the CNU requires accreditation by a disciplinary CNU section to work as a lecturer or a professor in a university. However, in the case of professors, candidates cannot obtain a green light from a CNU commission until they have been accredited as research directors. This accreditation is conferred by universities after a review of the file by referees, who in turn report to a jury that summons the candidates to defend their scientific achievements and research program. Once the CNU has granted its own accreditation for a position in a university, the candidates submit their applications for any position they desire that the university has been authorized by the ministry to fill.[34]

Experts assembled into commissions of specialists – some national, who directly answer to the CNU, others local, and active in candidate selection for a specific institution – also intervene in the selection of individuals seeking positions that have been duly opened and posted in a given university. The commissions create a hierarchical list of candidates out of the pool of individuals with recognized qualifications who have expressed an interest in the position, a list that is automatically accepted by the supervisory ministry. Selected on the basis of their ranking on the list of potential candidates, those who accept the job offers automatically become civil servants, appointed by the president of the Republic, and receive corresponding compensation and working conditions. This procedure makes it practically impossible for an establishment to somehow "sweeten the pot" to ensure that a specific candidate who has received several offers chooses that one. Once the nomination has been made, the lecturer (*maître de conférence*), for example, will normally be tenured after eighteen months.

In recent years some changes to the process of hiring academic faculty by French universities have been made, giving the establishments more leeway. Today, still with regard to positions it has been assigned, the university assembles its own hiring committees for each position as it deems necessary on the basis of the selected field or disciplinary speciality. The composition of these committees, half of whom are external experts, must be approved by the university president. The list of candidates prepared by the selection committees is submitted to the board of governors. The institution president retains a veto over all these decisions.[35]

Universities assume responsibility for managing the part of their budget related to their regular academic faculty without, however, becoming their employers – they remain civil servants. The institutions have the option of hiring individuals on limited-duration contracts who are not government employees. Similarly, they are authorized to pay premiums for specific mandates in teaching, research, or administration.

It should be noted that in recent years it has become easier to hire foreign professors, since they can be exempted from the requirement to be accredited by the CNU on the basis of their demonstrated qualifications. Clearly, the recruiting academic unit must convince the university scientific council of the merit of passing over the long list of French candidates that are accredited for the function in question.[36] Once this stage has been passed, the candidacy is submitted to the local hiring committee, which must prefer it to all the others before a job offer, reflecting the conditions offered in the French civil service, can be made to the foreign candidate. Anyone with experience of the processes and negotiations that characterize the international academic market for the most eminent professors will understand that these procedures severely impair the competitiveness of French institutions.

But there is more. In Canada, the United States, and the United Kingdom, a university seeking to enhance the excellence of a teaching or research-specific sector can target a group of professors in other universities, either domestic or foreign, and attempt to poach them by offering them better work, research, and teaching conditions. Within a given university system this competition makes it possible for exceptional concentrations of research and training to emerge in graduate studies. These critical masses are the principal constituents of world-class research universities. Again, we find that French institutions have limited resources for attracting professors, whether domestic or foreign.[37]

Local selection committees and the boards of governors and their presidents now ensure greater autonomy in the recruitment of professors for French universities. We should note, however, that the university presidents rarely exercise their powers in this area. Since they are unable to challenge the assessment of the scientific, pedagogical, or professional qualifications of the candidates proposed by the selection committees, any potential opposition to a candidacy can only be justified, to the board of governors, on the basis of criteria reflecting their institutions' strategic plans or administrative considerations. Between 2007 and 2011, of the some 15,000 candidates recruited, it appears that only forty-seven (0.25 per cent) of the choices of selection committees were vetoed by the university president.[38] However, they may have used other means of influencing candidate selection processes. Universities and their presidents appear to have considerably more leeway in the area of hiring contract staff.

With regard to the transfer of payroll management to the institutions under the provisions of the LRU, serious difficulties must be acknowledged. This transfer is subject to compliance by the participating institution with the applicable ceilings: a cap on compensation expenditures for staff that reflects the total number of jobs that the establishment may have on the payroll on the one hand, and the specific number of jobs that the government agrees to fund from the establishment's authorized budget on the other. Loopholes in these rules allow institutions a certain amount of room to manoeuvre in the management of their academic faculty, including topping up compensation packages to attract professors from abroad. However, it should be noted that, for now, these are the exceptions.

This is particularly true in that the supervisory ministry retains decision-making power in the matter of civil servant wage scales, pensions, etc. Thus, from one year to the next, the funds available for payroll but administered by the universities vary. It appears that the ramifications of this policy of transferring payroll administration to the universities were not adequately examined before the measure was implemented. This reality does nothing to reduce the complexity and severity of budgetary regulations imposed on universities.

Too often, the universities do not adequately master the sophisticated accounting practices required to manage a budget of this size, with the unfortunate effect that many presidents have been compelled to request that the Higher Education and Research Ministry resume administering their payrolls.[39]

A further issue is the creation of incentives to universities to reward outstanding performance, the implementation of which is entrusted to the boards of governors. They can make use of the new scientific excellence premiums or design and implement incentive schemes targeting various aspects of professors and researchers' responsibilities. However, we observe that few academic institutions manage to take this path. Deterrents include complicated regulations that apply to their operating budgets and difficulties with managing the payroll.[40]

Those university presidents who have asked the ministry to continue administering the payroll lament that they were not given the basic tools to exercise their functions as employers, in particular with regard to professors and researchers, who have the status of civil servants.[41] They are constrained by the interventionism of the government – with its many decrees, regulations, and procedures that hamstring their management of the careers of university professors and researchers. Though they have acquired a little latitude in the hiring process, the culture of French universities remains impervious to active involvement by their academic administrators in the management of professors' careers – a vital dimension of a research university's development and reputation.

Also, the aspect of governmental co-management that is, strictly speaking, more corporatist, continues to have far-reaching ramifications. The working conditions and relationships that shape professors' careers play out within the walls of universities whose administrators are still not key players in these matters. Too often, power struggles characterize the relationship between the government and professors, united by their disciplinary and union affiliations. Thus, we find that university administrators are marginalized in several areas related to faculty members' resources and academic careers.

Academic Governance

The relatively autonomous boards of governors within Canadian, UK, and US universities exercise the power to appoint the high officers – usually following recommendations from a search committee – who assume the mantle of leadership and, supported by a team that they have typically assembled themselves, have a significant impact on the performance of their institutions. This is why leading North American research universities, for example, are careful to recruit top-notch academic leaders, frequently from outside, who can guide their institutions to new heights.

The president of a French university, on the other hand, is elected by an absolute majority of the members, themselves elected – aside from the external members – from the board of governors. The management team he or she assembles will rely on bodies (board of governors, Scientific Council, and Education and Academic Life Council) whose roles and functions have been reviewed and, generally, expanded – at least in the case of the board of governors. We will recall that since the beginning of the 1990s university presidents have been encouraged to collaborate with the board of governors in creating an institutional strategic plan that encompasses all of its educational activities and programs and research strategy. On the basis of this plan, establishment-level contracts covering a five-year period are signed with the ministry of higher education and research.

Achieving this plan requires that the affected institutions demonstrate organizational dynamism and a great capacity for governance. This is a necessary step toward greater institutional autonomy, even if the dual centralization of governmental and corporatist co-management continues to regulate the functioning of the institutions and the management of careers within the university setting. This organizational arrangement is certainly evolving, but its impact on establishments is nonetheless making itself felt.

The strategic planning exercises of recent decades have prepared French universities to better define their objectives and orientations as institutions, but they have not yet endowed them as agencies equipped with organizational means. Their new budgetary freedom remains constrained by the rules and procedures of the supervisory ministry. The universities are still far from having ready access to a broad array of performance incentives that would allow them to prosper in a competitive environment in the same way as other university systems.

Overall, national university systems provide for improvements in the quality of their teaching and research by selecting the desired number of students with excellent academic records and by recruiting the best professors who, thanks to their success in obtaining funds disbursed on the basis of peer assessment, contribute to funding for research activities. This approach facilitates three important activities: the creation of centres of excellence on an international scale that assemble critical masses of researchers and students; raising funds from philanthropic organizations; and lobbying governments to appropriate a concentration of resources that is, if not optimal, at the very least adequate for funding the development of the institution.

Stymied in their efforts to behave as agencies equipped with means, French universities today are confronted with two conflicting organizational principles that render their governance particularly complex: a vertical organization of the university that ties its management and central administrative entities to its various teaching and research units.

This structure implies certain tensions for presidents and the boards of governors, because the conditions under which these teaching and research units operate and bring together professors and students are very open to the outside and exposed to centrifugal forces that ultimately weaken the institution. The principle of this vertical organization is still defined by the constraints stemming from the dual centralization of governmental and corporatist co-management in universities

Since the creation of Agence pour l'évaluation de la recherche et de l'enseignement supérieur (AÉRES) (Evaluation Agency for Research and Higher Education), academic institutions can be evaluated based on their educational and research objectives, as spelled out in their respective institutional plans and contracts. In theory, these exercises play a role in allocating some of the recurring funding disbursed by the ministry, but in practice a substantial discrepancy persists between the results of the assessments of contractual agreements and the allocation of recurring funding to the teaching and research missions of the establishments.[42]

The principle of vertical management lays the establishments open to centrifugal forces that have a significant impact on their organizational dynamics. The centralizing power of the government, which is based on the persistence of the corporatist management of careers in academia, neutralizes the decision-making capacity of the institutions. This in turn diminishes the scope for initiative not only of the administration, but also of the academic faculty.

This vertical principle is intersected by a horizontal organizational principle. Most French universities, including research universities, consist of a variety of entities. Although these are, in fact, rooted in the institution, they are often beholden to authorities that lie outside of the organization's perimeter, such as the mixed research units described above.

Even doctoral schools, academic units that are critical for the quality of advanced training in research, are not immune to this trend. They are active in the training, the research units, and the supervisory activities of doctoral students in a given university, but they also extend outward to many other institutions. They have their own management structures, the focal point of which may, in fact, be external. As a result, with regard to such a central component of the offerings of a research university as advanced training in research, the administration of an establishment may have to contend with a doctoral education management that is largely based outside of its own premises and thus far from its other degree programs, which would normally be influenced by its own research activities.

This horizontal management principle is now further complicated by recent changes that have resulted in integrating outside establishments into the universities and in missions entrusted to agglomerations of universities. We have already noted, for example, that universities have been required to absorb university technological institutes, though these remain relatively autonomous and keep their own central administration.

Today, this horizontal management principle is experiencing an even greater extension. Academic institutions are being challenged, by means of aggregations of universities and other institutions of higher education, to structure sites and spaces that assemble a greater concentration of resources and course offerings, training programs, and strategies and infrastructures for research. As we have seen, the creation of PRES, the LRU, and Plan Campus are all recent measures designed to encourage the creation of institutional centres of excellence fit to raise themselves into the ranks of the best world-class research universities.

The French university is thus confronted by severe tensions arising from its dual management principle. Just as the stage has been set to give presidents and boards of governors greater powers and autonomy, they are now actively encouraged to join agglomerations of institutions that are similar to those they currently lead. This type of restructuring implies, of course, that they will have to surrender some of the additional autonomy they have just received. While the PRES have been rather well received, the fact is that mergers of establishments are still rare: To date, there have only been three.[43]

The job of university president in France is not easy; it requires great strengths. Owing to the constraints on university administration the job consists more of mediation than of action. Although the presidents are no longer merely "firsts among equals," the organizational principles that shape their establishments continue to complicate their jobs as leaders.

The daunting challenges confronting these establishments – which have been in the throes of major organizational transformations since the turn of the century – are enough to deter any individual who sincerely desires to innovate. Also, a board of governors that has signed a multi-year contract faces the dilemma of being account-able for it, knowing that the elected president and his or her manage-ment team strive to act on the commitments undertaken in these documents while leading an institution that can hardly behave as an agency equipped with the powers of ways and means. So how can the inertia and debilitating tensions, as well as the contradictions inherent in two almost irreconcilable management principles, be overcome? We are far removed from the type of administrative autonomy that is conducive to innovative leadership. Overall, these conditions render the idea of a university as a strong and integrated organizational actor impossible.

The initiatives taken by the supervisory authority to implement establishment-level contracts are certainly a major step in the right direction for consolidating the beachhead of university autonomy. The LRU also sets the stage for a promising development that will, over time, have a positive effect on the performance of French uni-versities and allow more of them to take their place among the top ranks of world-class research universities. However, as we learned from a recent report (26 March 2013) from the Senate Committee for the Control of Law Enforcement to the senate leadership, the road to real autonomy for the universities will be long, arduous, and rocky.

This report mentions the scorecard created in 2011 by the European University Association to assess the quality of the auton-omy of twenty-nine European higher education systems. Overall, five years after the LRU, France is in the bottom third of this rank-ing. With regard to the issues of financial independence and the management of human resources, French universities place in twenty-third and twenty-eighth position, respectively. They are sev-enteenth in terms of organizational autonomy, and dead last in aca-demic independence.[44]

As we write these words, a new president and a new higher educa-tion and research minister have assumed power and introduced legislation covering higher education. In July 2013 the Loi de l'enseignement supérieur et de la recherche (Higher Education and Research Act) was passed, amending some aspects of undergraduate studies – the introduction of English, for example – and providing supervision practices to improve the condition of students, especially those in, and recently graduated from, doctoral programs. However, student selection at admission to universities is not covered. This Act also makes changes to the bodies that administer universities, expanding the composition of boards of governors and increasing academic and administrative staff and student representation. The Scientific Council and Education and Academic Life Council, transformed into Research and Education Commissions, respectively, have been merged into a new body: the academic council, which has been given some specific spheres of responsibility in addition to its consultative role. Moreover, a council of university academic administrators, which is headed by its president, has now been included in the law.

The incentives to promote association, coordination, and even mergers between higher education institutions and universities proper have been maintained. However, they take a different path from that laid out by the 2006 Act: The PRES, which were subject to serious criticism even while they had their defenders, have been abolished. The desired coordination can now be achieved by merging institutions or by integrating a public scientific, cultural, and vocational educational institution. It might also take the form of a territorial community of universities and institutions with its own governing bodies: board of governors, Academic Council, and Council of Members, and a single, comprehensive contract with the supervisory ministry. Finally, a Haut Conseil de l'évaluation de la recherche et de l'enseignement supérieur (High Council for the Evaluation of Research and Education) was created, which takes the place of AÉRES in the assessment of establishments, research units, and training programs.

One tradition persists: Each new government undertakes its own reform of higher education in France. Most of the time it is the university sector that is targeted by legislative intervention. It remains to be seen how this somewhat piecemeal reform will change the operating conditions of French universities, especially of those that can legitimately aspire to international prominence among the leading research universities.

CONCLUSION

The history of French universities is long, but riddled with events that have hobbled their development. These events have limited their ability to engage and perform as key actors in the scientific and academic world of the twentieth century, a world that has been in the throes of a profound transformation. They share this feature with several other countries in continental Europe that were scientific powerhouses in the nineteenth and early twentieth century. One of the legacies of this history is that, over time, the development of the French higher education system has occurred under operating conditions that too often took the shape of constraints. This is particularly true of universities, whose problematic antecedents did not prepare the fertile soil that would have easily allowed a contingent of French research universities to flourish as leading world-class institutions.

Our data have revealed that the most current characteristics of French university operating conditions fail to undo the many constraints that are deeply rooted in their history. Overall, modern trends in the organization and funding of research in universities, the means by which operating revenues are accessed, and the ways and means by which students and professors arrive and evolve are more likely to entrench, when they don't exacerbate, the principal historical constraints of the French system. Major steps have been taken to open university governance to the challenges of greater autonomy and decision-making authority, but recent findings clearly demonstrate that the complicated structures that shape French universities have thwarted attempts to leverage true autonomy to address these difficulties and contradictions.

The words of Aghion and Cohen on the subject of French universities are still timely: "there is no competition between research centres or between the CNRS and universities, whether French or foreign. There are no monetary or non-monetary incentives to reward good basic research within a university ... and there is no inter-university competition to attract the best elements. Nor are there sound systems for assessing research performance, whether individual or collective, and there is no credible equivalent to the NSF [National Science Foundation] system to assess and fund the best projects."[45]

The report written by the Senate Committee for the Control of Law Enforcement stated that "the university is still struggling to assert itself as a path to educational excellence."[46] We see that – despite the many advantages conferred by the size of the population, the level of development and relative wealth of the economy, and the high national research intensity – the history and current operating characteristics of the university system are intimately linked to the difficulties French universities face in their attempts to penetrate the top tiers of the best research universities' international rankings.

8

A BROADER ANALYTICAL FRAMEWORK

An initial examination of how international rankings have distributed leading research universities across countries reveals the limitations of our analytical model, which fails to fully explain this dispersal. Therefore, we will significantly deepen and broaden our analytical approach.

We will also draw more systematic and comprehensive conclusions from data we have already collected. Using various descriptive attributes of the four university systems examined above, we propose an expanded analytical framework for explaining the factors and conditions that allow the research universities of any given system to place among the best in the world. We will also strive to shed some light on the international distribution of these institutions by filling in some of the gaps in our initial analysis.

Recall that, at the end of chapter 3, we were forced to conclude that our analytical model, which was mainly based on macroeconomic variables for the various countries, was unable to fully explain the international distribution of the research universities featured in the ARWU and THES rankings. What are the principal characteristics of this international distribution of research universities listed in the ranking systems that are used?

First, the US university system is in a league of its own in terms of its ability to produce a remarkable number of leading world-class research universities. This characteristic stands out even more at the top end of the two rankings. Because of this striking performance, we are using this university system as a benchmark.

The UK university system also merits special attention. At all levels in the two ranking systems we are using, UK universities far outdo the predictions of our first analytical model, which was based on a series of macroeconomic variables. Though less impressive than their UK counterparts, the results for Canadian research universities are nonetheless surprising. In our comparative context, they do relatively well considering Canada's small population base.

As for French research universities, their performance is difficult to reconcile with the results of our analytical model, considering both the economic density and the research intensity of modern France. It appears from our comparative analysis that the French university system is underperforming, particularly in the highest categories of international rankings.

To better understand the international position of US, UK, and Canadian research universities, as well as their considerable lead over their French counterparts, we will need to broaden our perspective. Recall that, for each of the selected university systems, we have described some organizational and institutional features that might have an effect on their ability to place well internationally. We draw both on pre-existing studies and the quantitative and institutional data that we collected to validate, qualify, complete, and sometimes amend the principal conclusions of earlier analyses.

In the following pages we will seek to complete and reach beyond our macroeconomic model by focusing on factors and operating conditions that determine the development of university systems. We must acknowledge the key figures – Burton R. Clark, Joseph Ben-David, Roger Geiger, and Philippe Aghion, for example – who have accompanied us so far. Their work suggests a more general and comprehensive approach to an analysis of the functioning of comparable institutions. While their starting point may be different, these broader and more comparative studies ask questions that are similar to ours. They also strive to explain the differential performance of institutions in various higher education systems. We will dialogue with some of these authors to identify similarities and differences in our points of view.

INSTITUTIONAL SELF-GOVERNANCE, GOVERNMENT REGULATION, AND MARKET INFLUENCES

According to Burton R. Clark, we can model the operating modes of national higher education systems – including, of course, the research universities to which he devoted much of his work – using a three-dimensional analytical space. The three axes are: the establishment's real ability to exercise institutional control over its destiny; the government regulation or control to which it is subject; and its operating conditions, which are largely shaped by various market influences. To describe the organizational characteristic of universities or, more generally, higher education systems, these axes must be combined. Also, the particular integration of a university is reflected in the specific configuration among potential combinations that corresponds to the dominance of any given axis over the other two – thus considered subordinate axes.[1]

The conclusions we draw from our own case studies will largely follow this line of reasoning. However, we must express some reservations with regard to the axes and their combinations. While the government's regulatory role is an inescapable part of most higher education systems today, this fact cloaks another central dimension of the effect of modern governments on university education: its partially public funding. This dimension, though not completely dissociated from government regulation, differs from it because it deals with another aspect of university education and how it is delivered in contemporary societies.

The university is unique in being the locus of a high concentration of a nation's basic research covering all fields of human knowledge. On top of its role in generating new knowledge, university-based research is essential for providing the right environment for training the new generations of scientists in all areas of knowledge. Moreover, to be accredited as a true contribution to knowledge, a university's scientific output must be recognized by peers and made public, accessible to all. Thus, in today's academic reality virtually the entire output of university-based research and its links to training are public goods, and funding for the processes by which they are created must mostly originate from government or philanthropy. This dovetails with our findings, even in the case of the leading private US research universities.

There is another element of higher education that justifies government involvement in its funding – its potential for generating externalities, in the economic sense of the term. Indeed, a university education can yield benefits that are greater than those received by the graduate alone. These might include its impact on economic growth, creativity in any number of fields, the lower level of criminal activity, and the richness of democratic life. Moreover, a university

has a role in transmitting knowledge and scholarship across generations, constituting essential cultural and socio-economic capital for
the development and democratic well-being of societies. It is unfortunate that this distinction between the government as a regulator
and as the funder of a public good is not made clearer by Clark. This
is particularly relevant because the delicate balance between public
and private funding of university systems is a key issue today.

However interventionist the government's regulation of its university system, the issue of its contribution to funding the university as
a producer of public goods and externalities cannot be ignored.
There is, in fact, no university system that can entirely avoid government funding and its associated constraints.

We will also look at another dimension of university organizational dynamics that appears to have eluded Clark. The three-
dimensional space defined above does not help us understand how
research universities manage to stand out in international rankings,
except in those cases in which the dominant axis is institutional
self-governance.

Even in that case, it is vital to clearly identify the role played by the
subordinate axis of government regulation or control. We believe
that it is very possible for the axis of government regulation to crowd
out the potential dominance of institutional self-governance to the
point of completely neutralizing it. Henceforth, a key element of
the combination of axes in a system of institutional self-governance
is the specific path taken by government regulation. In this case it
becomes important to distinguish between the role played by government regulation, on the one hand, and the balance between government and private funding of university education, on the other.

We also differ with Clark on another, closely related, point. Developing the conclusions of our analysis of higher education systems
further, we see that the three-dimensional analytical space also loses
its explanatory power in the case of institutions or university systems whose organizational integration is dominated by strong regulation and government control.

In this case, we observe that government control is often strengthened by the fact that its contribution to funding is so pivotal that
private funding is virtually absent. However, on the other hand, very
interventionist regulation by the government has the effect that
the roles played by the other axes – institutional self-governance
and operating conditions guided by market influences, which are

identified as subordinate – are eroded to a point that they carry little weight. Confronted by strong government regulation, the subordinate axes are unable to shape the organizational integration characterizing the institutions or the higher education system to which they belong.

RESEARCH UNIVERSITIES WITH INSTITUTIONAL SELF-GOVERNANCE

We begin by observing that universities in higher education systems that are based on the institutional self-governance principle generally develop in an environment in which there are no parallel dominant institutions conducting basic research and funded by the government.

Government funding of university-based research is a universal feature, but significant differences between countries can be observed in how basic research is distributed across institutions that are supported from the public purse. In keeping with our own findings, Clark and Ben-David emphasize that the research universities that are most successful in combining basic research with advanced training in research operate in countries in which basic research is intensively concentrated in universities. We know that, over time, the trend in France and Germany (among others) has been to confer a large share of basic research on public institutes that are parallel to the university system.

In countries where that has not occurred, research universities play a central role in the production of new knowledge. The data we have presented on the proportion of the national budgets that three of the countries in our study (the United States, the United Kingdom, and Canada) invest in university-based research confirm this observation. The research universities in these countries find vital resources and strong incentives that contribute to their standing on the international scene as the result of their central role as the primary engine of basic research.

Since state-of-the-art research activities in a university setting are expensive and require outstanding, but scarce, talent, there are generally not very many research universities that provide them. In fact, it is not possible for every university to have the size, the scope in its disciplinary offerings, or the accumulations of significant critical masses of professors and students in advanced training in research to consistently stand out for their high quality. US, UK, and Canadian research universities that regularly appear in the top categories of the ARWU and THES international rankings must heed these factors to remain at the top. They represent a minority of the institutions in their home countries with research university missions.

Another characteristic of institutions whose predominant organizational principle is self-governance has been observed by several of the authors we mention and has also been corroborated by our recent data. These institutions benefit from diversified sources of funding for their teaching mission and the associated infrastructures. To have the desired effect on institutional self-governance, this diversity must not only include several different funding sources, but their relative contribution must be balanced.

In general, four main funding sources cover the operating budgets of research universities, but with intensities that vary from one institution to the next: tuition fees, government grants, returns to endowment funds supported by public fundraising campaigns (among other sources), and profits from ancillary businesses. The era in which the operating budgets of higher education systems in the United States, the United Kingdom, and Canada were mostly supported by private sources is now very much a thing of the past. Starting in the interwar period, governments gradually became the primary funders of universities as they recognized the externalities to society generated by higher education. Their initial tendency was to provide relatively large public investments over long periods of time.

Today, while still a reality, government grants are no longer as dominant. In recent years, their maximum contribution has amounted to approximately 50 per cent of the budgets for many of the university groups we have been examining. For reasons that vary from one case to the next, we have underlined the extent to which governments have had to reduce their contributions to the costs of university education following recent downturns in the economic cycle.

A university's diversity of funding sources gives it significant advantages by fostering its institutional self-governance and its ability to make a mark by the excellence of its output. Aside from the flexibility, this makes it possible to increase total funding. When government grants are cut because of a budget crunch or a shift in the political climate against investments in higher education, the university with institutional self-governance has the option of turning toward other funding sources. This conjunction of events, in which government authorities partially retreat from their funding role, raises the issue of the optimal balance between public and private funding of university systems. This has been the subject of innumerable debates, which are still ongoing and to which we will return in the last chapter.

Self-Governance, Market Relationships, and Organizational Incentives

The means by which institutions appropriate resources is another important aspect of self-governance. We agree with the conclusions of other analysts: Universities that practise institutional self-governance acquire a large share of their resources and means of action through market-type interactions. These are even more important if they relate to the essential operating conditions.

Indeed, at the domestic and international level, research universities are in competition with each other for vital and scarce strategic resources. Each institution must, for example, attract a sufficient number of students, including international students, to pay the tuition fees it needs to ensure the required diversity in its operating funds. Its student population must also contain enough high achievers to drive its programs of advanced training in research and consolidate its institutional reputation.

Clearly, the same is true of academic faculty members of a research university with institutional self-governance. As we have emphasized, high-quality professors attract students of the same calibre. Moreover, by their successful applications for research grants and their scientific publications, such professors consolidate the performance of the institutions that recruit them. Obtaining a high-quality academic faculty is an essential aspect of the competitive relationships between research universities. Naturally, this competition extends beyond national borders: very good professors and promising graduate students are increasingly mobile internationally.

Research universities also receive funding from other sources that are indispensable to them and subject to national and international competition because of their scarcity: funds and budgets for university research – obtained directly by the universities themselves or by their professors – and public fundraising campaigns.

Another factor in the success of research universities that is strongly affected by market influences needs to be considered. Indeed, in this world of national and international rankings and quality assessments and assurance exercises, an institution's reputation is created, demonstrated, and transmitted in a space that is structured very much like a market. Our analyses, which have largely dealt with universities characterized by institutional self-governance in the US, UK, and Canadian context, corroborate this point.

Using historical information and statistical data we have described all the resources and the means of action that the best-performing universities succeed in amassing by their position on the market of institutions with excellent reputations. Reputation is the most precious capital for any research university wishing to make a mark on the domestic, and then the international, scene.

We might even go so far as to claim that the position that an institution on the market for reputation occupies will directly determine its ability to control the rest of its operating conditions – which are largely shaped by the various influences stemming from the differentiated markets we have been examining. The best students and professors, who are the most mobile nationally and internationally, are very sensitive to the overall reputation of the leading research universities. Also, an institution's reputation carries a lot of weight with decision-makers in both the public and private sector. This reputation conveys a lot of information about its characteristics and performance that interested parties will consider when deciding whether to attend, join, or be associated with the institution.

Therefore, research universities striving to consolidate and improve their reputations engage in a positive feedback loop: desiring the validation provided by these distinctions and recognitions and the results of assessment and ranking exercises. At the same time, these accumulated distinctions and recognitions extend beyond the boundaries of the organization and signal to their environment the precious visibility they have acquired – which only enhances their reputations. Clearly, the market for academic reputation supersedes national boundaries, but not without generating a feedback effect that provides exceptional validation locally to an institution that has acquired world-wide recognition.

Research universities thus operate in a highly competitive environment that binds them in relations of emulation and competition. A direct implication of this fact is that the way in which they appropriate resources and means of action creates incentives for themselves and their principal actors.

Philippe Aghion, a French economist who spent his working life in the United States, examined this issue of incentives in the context of studies dealing with the organizational principles of universities. From an *a contrario* standpoint, so to speak, he and his collaborators took a look at the shortcomings of university systems in Europe, in particular France – especially in terms of resource appropriation modes that were too insulated from institutional and personal incentives.[2]

The example that best illustrates the concerns voiced by Aghion is that of US research universities. They provide a prime illustration of organizations whose incentive structures include the key influences of competition and emulation between institutions and academic faculty, all of which are framed by resource appropriation modes that are responsive to market influences. In the chapter devoted to the US university system we noted the very large amounts of research funding that professors bring to both public and private universities. We might be inclined to believe, incorrectly, that this is merely a matter of scale – that US universities are dipping into a larger pool of intramural research funds, made up of their own and external contributions. This would be a mistake, since the per-capita amounts of intramural university research funding available in the United States are comparable to those in the United Kingdom and scarcely more than in France.[3]

The very intense competition for research funding between professors in US universities – as well as between them and academics in other elements of the university system – has the effect of strongly concentrating all the basic research and scientific publication activity in a limited number of institutions, as we have seen. Also, in endeavouring to fulfill their multiple missions, US research universities succeed in assembling levels of resources per graduate student and per professor that are higher than anything we have observed for comparable institutions elsewhere in the world.

This mode of resource appropriation, so fundamental to any research university, has the effect of consolidating the dynamics of their institutional self-governance. In the case of public US research universities, we must further bear in mind that they are operating in a broader organizational milieu in which private universities exert strong pressures, particularly in terms of competition between institutions and academic faculty. Recall that, in keeping with the findings of the National Research Council Committee on Research Universities, our own data have documented the key contributions and very promising advances made by these institutions. Overall, public universities more than hold their own in the US system of research universities.

In both their public and private incarnations US research universities greatly benefit from the dynamics of institutional self-governance. However, from the perspective of the proposed three-dimensional analytical space that purports to provide an adequate explanation of modern university operations, these dynamics tie in with an axis of government regulation, which is an incontrovertible dimension of modern university organizational integration.

Market Relationships and Government Regulation

Thus, the research university with institutional self-governance primarily accesses resources through market relationships. We must also consider that in the vast majority of cases these market relationships are mediated by government regulation. We accept this proposal, derived from the three-dimensional analytical space discussed by Clark, which aptly delineates the conditions under which modern universities, and specifically research universities, operate. As we know, government intervention in university education involves more than regulation. Research universities that depend on generous public contributions to finance their research activities will be affected by the government's scientific and technological innovation policies, which frame the programs and interventions of funding agencies responsible for allocating the share of GDP earmarked for university research.

Though theoretically distinct, government regulation also ties in with government funding of the operating and infrastructure costs of university teaching. This second dimension contributes significantly to the weight of government regulation.

However, this regulation is by no means limited to the direct participation of the government in university funding. In addition to the direct funding it may provide, the government also tends to mediate the modes by which universities practising institutional self-governance appropriate some categories of their operating resources

– which they access through market relationships. This government regulation may not cover all markets or all categories of resources required for the effective functioning of the research universities we have examined. However, certain key markets, on which resources coveted by research universities are available and contested, cannot escape this government mediation.

This is, in general, the case for at least two or three categories of operating funds that are useful for the institutionally self-governing research universities we have observed. The most common target of government regulation is tuition fees, or the magnitude of tuition differentials, charged to different categories of university students (local, domestic, or international; undergraduate or graduate). In addition to tuition fees proper, similar government regulation may, for example, control and channel recruitment and selection practices for the students that the universities in our study seek to attract. Quotas or other quantitative measures may apply to contingents of local, domestic, or international students actively recruited by institutions.

To a lesser extent, our observations suggest that another dimension of government regulation is its impact on some aspects of access to the faculty resources desired by these institutions – the precedence given to domestic, even local, candidates, immigration policies and rules, etc. Nonetheless, the institutionally self-governing university is where the finest expression of professional collegiality is found among teaching and research faculty members who are assembled into base units (departments) by academic discipline. This collegiality is open to the world of science, but is no less defined by its relations with the institution's administration. Professional collegiality and the autonomous administration of the university generally combine to counteract the impact of government regulation on academic careers.

This regulation also has ramifications for funding provided by governments: the central government in the United Kingdom, state or provincial governments in the United States and Canada, respectively. These funds are intended to partially cover expenditures on teaching and on university research indirect costs and infrastructure. Like all resources, they are scarce and limited, and so universities must compete for them.[4]

As we saw in our data, government authorities in the American states and the Canadian provinces, as well as the national government of the United Kingdom, have all devised mechanisms and policies that have, over the years and with (sometimes sweeping) amendments, regulated the modes by which research universities appropriate these resources.

But let us return to the three-dimensional space. We clearly see, in particular in the case of these institutionally self-governing research universities, how this dominant axis is linked, on the one hand, to the operating environment of these institutions largely characterized by the influences exercised by assorted markets and, on the other, to the government control and regulation to which they are subject.

Our data on the role played by the axis of government intervention in the organizational integration of self-governing institutions require more clarification. This government regulation varies in intensity and scope from one country to the next, even as the influence of this axis always operates within a three-dimensional space in which it is clearly unable to dominate.

However, the essence of the role played by government regulation in an institutionally self-governing research university remains to be specified. If this institution type is to remain self-governing, then government regulation must not undermine its capacity for autonomous decision-making.

Most of the public US research university operating funds are provided by state governments. Thus, in the matter of government support for university education, they have to contend with rules that vary from one state to the next. However, the net impact of private US research universities, the competitors that are most shielded from this reality, is to contain this government regulation and its potential effects. The broad diversity and the remarkable size of the US university system relative to the population, as well as the concentration of research universities' missions in a very small number of institutions, also contribute to shaping the form of this government regulation.

Against this backdrop of incentives and emulation, government regulation does not appear to impede institutional self-governance dynamics, which remains the dominant axis of public US research universities as integrated organizational actors. Indeed, if a government threat looms large over their present and future, this is largely because of government funding belt-tightening which can be attributed to recent economic conditions.

We find the data and analyses presented on the subject of UK universities more helpful for identifying the role that government regulation can play. Government regulation of UK research universities, though sweeping and extensive, does not fundamentally undermine their institutional self-governance. This finding contradicts Clark's results on UK research universities, though his work used older data. Certainly, the government regulations that British research universities must contend with appear, in general, to be more interventionist than those imposed by US states on the research universities in their jurisdictions. The same could be said for Canada's provincial governments and their research universities. But the crucial point remains that the British government regulation does not crowd out the competitive modes of appropriation by which UK universities access their operating resources.

Recall that UK universities overperform in international rankings according to the model we presented in chapter 3. We know that this cannot be attributed to the level of intramural university research funding to which they have access, as it is virtually the same as in the United States. The funds made available to UK universities for research, in particular to pay for research indirect costs and infrastructure, depend on their individual performance in the RAEs periodically conducted by the Higher Education Funding Council for England (HEFCE). The output of their professors on a competitive basis also affects the resources available to them for investing in research. In addition, the funding council will only provide additional resources for the supervision of students in advanced training in research and post-doctoral fellows if the institution's comparative assessment results are relatively strong. In fact, these additional funds are also contingent on the university's position after an assessment of its preview performance.

The situation of student recruitment is comparable. In the case of English universities only, we have observed that the responsible funding council sets an institutional quota of undergraduates for which it will provide funding, depending on the discipline chosen by the students. To stimulate competition and emulation between institutions, this council has amended the rule by adding a clause allowing universities to exceed their quota of duly funded students, without incurring a penalty, if they are able to attract students classified as the best and brightest candidates in their cohorts. There is no government control over the tuition fees a university can charge international students.

In fact, the government regulation to which British research universities are subject in no way replaces (quite the opposite, actually) the competitive relations between them and the market influences they need to master. The handful of elements we have just mentioned illustrate this trend well, and we could have added other processes – such as the impact of the activities undertaken in the context of the Quality Assurance Agency for Higher Education.

In short, government regulation for UK research universities generally helps to spur them on to greater heights. By means of rigorous interventionist policies and practices, the government ultimately harnesses, modifies, and even stimulates, more than it weakens, the predominant model of organizational integration for these institutions, that is, institutional self-governance. This does not extend to the universities of Scotland, Wales, or Northern Ireland. However, in the case of UK research universities situated in England, we can confirm that government regulation does not unduly impair their capacity for institutional self-governance. They are mainly free to make their own choices and set their institutional priorities, administering the incentives that determine the resource appropriation modes by which they take their place in international rankings.

Canadian research universities are also organizations with institutional self-governance. We see that the universe in which they operate resembles that of UK and US universities, though in the case of the United States they are most like public research universities.

As we have seen, Canadian research universities, like their US counterparts, must deal with regulations imposed by provincial governments that mediate their access to a significant share of their operating resources. But in the Canadian global environment, the absence of the prestigious US private research universities tends to cause government regulation to have a stronger influence on the future of universities. In addition, one could argue that the UK model, in which regulation encouraging emulation between institutions notably emanates from the central government, has not found many adherents in the provincial jurisdictions of Canada.

Canadian research universities face competition from the United States, in particular from private US research universities, owing to the strength of the North American academic market's integration. It is nonetheless true that the Canadian academic environment is less intensely competitive than that of the United States. Nor should we ignore the extent to which recent strategies of substantial tuition hikes implemented by private US universities, to which we will return in the next chapter, have heightened competition between the institutions. This trend has not been replicated in Canada, in all likelihood because – aside from the regulatory role played by governments – provincial and federal authorities have striven for a different balance between public and private funding of universities.

To place well in the international ARWU and THES rankings, Canadian research universities fully exploit their decision-making autonomy. In this competitive environment, they need to assemble their operating conditions through market relationships in which the output of their faculty members, supported by the incentives that guide their career paths, can play a major role.

The potential effect of a less intense level of competition between research universities in Canada than in the United States would be considerably greater if the government contributed less to university-based research. As we have observed, by international standards Canada stands out for the very high proportion of its gross domestic product devoted to university research, which is proportionally higher than in the United States.[5] Per-student in advanced training in research and per-professor resources devoted to Canadian and US public universities are thus very similar. This does not mean that the current situation of doctoral studies in Canada is without its challenges. This is an issue we will return to in the next chapter. For now, we need to look at another type of university institution – one under strong government regulation.

RESEARCH UNIVERSITIES UNDER GOVERNMENT REGULATION

We have seen that, on the basis of the high research intensity of France and the per-capita resources devoted to research as a consequence, a large number of French research universities should place in international rankings. But although some French institutions do appear in these rankings, this high research intensity does not have the anticipated impact on the university segment of the French higher education system.

This is because, in France, the schism between research and university continues to undermine the functioning of universities. The French university shares the task of basic research with research institutes, centres, and teams that are funded from the public purse and are parallel organizational and decision-making entities to the universities proper. This coexistence is not consequence-free: French universities are not central to the nation's efforts in basic research. US, UK, and Canadian universities play more of a key role in basic research. As a result, a greater number of them place in the international rankings and rise to their highest categories.

What is the link between this basic research organization and the structure of universities under a dominant government regulation? First, we need to distinguish between the government's spending powers on research and higher education and government regulation as the dominant organizational principle of an institution. Government funding of higher education in France is especially pronounced with regard to the costs of teaching and infrastructure: It is the source of nearly 90 per cent of university operating funds, which are disbursed by the supervisory ministry. In international terms, French establishments thus have a more limited amount of room to manoeuvre to expand the global base of resources to invest in their operations.

French establishments are also confronted with the risk of experiencing long periods of chronic underfunding, since they are more vulnerable to crises in government finances and to swings in the moods and ideologies of the government of the day. Efforts have recently been made to provide more leeway to French universities in the area of funding sources, but their impact has been marginal. Of course, *ceteris paribus*, it remains a universal and inalienable principle that the funding of higher education must be largely governmental – as the other university systems in our study have illustrated. However, in the case of France, and looking beyond the government's function of public funder, regulation of the university system has unique features of its own.

Dominant Government Regulation and Deregulation of Market Influences

When government regulation is joined with preponderant, even quasi-exclusive, public funding of universities, its influence is much more constraining and ubiquitous, with serious strategic fallout.

On the one hand, the management practices of universities will be focused around the rules and conditions imposed by the supervisory ministry, the source of nearly all its operating resources. Many rules, conventions, and requirements govern the delivery of training programs, the admission of students, and the disposition of both basic grants and infrastructure budgets. A system that is so centralized normally goes hand in hand with mountains of red tape that determine not only the resource allocation, but also the administration's exercise of decision-making power and the flourishing of initiative within that governance.

We documented many efforts by governments over the past twenty years – ranging from management-by-contract initiatives to legislation – that were designed to give French universities greater leeway and decision-making autonomy in these areas. But even quite recently, a senate committee reviewing the implementation of the key 2007 Act on university liberties and responsibilities noted the extent to which they remain beholden to bureaucratic models of resource distribution that hobble their decision-making capacity.

On the other hand, government regulation has a particular impact on the access universities have to resources and operating conditions that are shaped by various market influences. This applies to the recruitment and hiring of academic faculty members. In fact, a dual centralization (governmental and corporatist) – strongly supported by the responsible ministry and government authority – continues to characterize the functioning of French universities and, despite some changes designed to render it more flexible, the management of careers. Government regulation consolidates corporatist management of all elements of professors' careers by representatives of the various disciplines. This dual centralization continues to prop up a university co-management that is largely governmental–corporatist.

The virtual absence of a domestic academic market for university professors in France, combined with its tepid attempt to open up to the international market for the best professors, does not foster emulation and competition among French universities, where each of them would benefit from competitive access to these scarce resources. Their institutional culture mostly continues to fall short in terms of practices for managing professors' careers that can build and consolidate, within their campus and under their leadership, the critical masses of quality they would need to be able to offer their country and their student populations substantial and productive centres for the conduct of basic research and peerless settings for training in and through research.

Similarly, the way undergraduate students are recruited, selected, and admitted does not show any real competitive relationship between universities seeking to attract the best candidates to university studies, with the exception of a few of their components, such as university technological institutes, which have recently opened up a breach in this area. Furthermore, we know that universities do not, in general, receive any significant additional revenue for efforts to increase the size of their student bodies.

Overall, when it is dominant, government regulation tends to derail the impact of market influences and the critical relationships of emulation and competition between institutions. This is precisely the effect desired by some who advocate that government regulation should be the dominant integrating principle of university organization. However, the marginalization of incentives ultimately undermines the lifeblood strength and innovative capacities of the affected research universities. We will recall that this was the finding of Aghion and his colleagues in the case of French universities.

An institution for which the dominant axis is government regulation is not well modelled by Clark's proposed three-dimensional analytical space for explaining university organizational dynamics. In this case, the combination of three axes with effects that are distinct and differentiated but jointly influence the organizational integration of institutions is not appropriate.

Rather, we have a simpler model that makes no provision for combining several axes. Thus, for two complementary reasons, dominant government regulation becomes the principal explanatory factor of institution organizational dynamics captured by it. On the one hand, it severely constrains the decision-making self-governance of the affected institutions. On the other hand, rather than mediating universities' access to operating conditions in the shape of market relations, dominant government regulation is more likely to wipe out the impact of these factors.

THE RESEARCH UNIVERSITY
AS AN ORGANIZATIONAL ACTOR

A number of factors can either foster or impede the potential of research universities to stand out on the international scene.

These factors range from a strong involvement of research universities in the national basic research mission to a highly diversified funding of their teaching and research missions. They also include competitive modes of human and financial resource appropriation, including those resources that depend on the merit of their faculty members as recognized by their peers. Against this backdrop, the institution's reputation and prestige prove essential to its operations. Largely exposed to market influences, institutional reputation tends to carry a very determining weight in shaping appropriation modes for all other resources that a university will use to improve its performance and potentially rise to the top ranks of the best world-class universities.

Furthermore, we have observed that research universities whose organizational integration is dominated by the principle of institutional self-governance increase their likelihood of attaining greater output. Let us take a closer look at what is meant by this notion of organizational integration. This describes the capacity of a research university to act as an integrated unit. Notwithstanding the potential benefit from identifying and appending, in one form or another, organization-specific factors and the competitive appropriation of resources or prestige, what matters to a university is that it see itself and act as an integrated organizational actor. This is the most fundamental driving force of a research university.

In a very competitive academic environment, research universities tend to become key organizational actors that pursue many complex missions with strong societal externalities. This forces them to clearly define their objectives, to articulate strategic plans, and to make institutional choices. Their decision-making structures are thus at the service of these missions and objectives against the background of today's competitive environment.

These decision-making structures are subject to a dual rationale and legitimization. On the one hand, there is professional collegiality. This primarily finds expression in the basic academic units under the leadership of groups of professors and researchers from various scientific disciplines. On the other hand, there is pedagogical and administrative management at various institutional levels ranging from the central administration to the management of the base units, including the faculty administrations. Representatives from the central administration and the various disciplines jointly make up the ranks of the bodies in which the broad pedagogical, academic, scientific directions, as well as administrative issues, are debated.

Just like the university's missions, these decision-making structures must evolve. This not only concerns trends toward new and enhanced complementarity linking the academic administration's centres of power and leadership with institutional instances in which the professional collegiality of the university's key stakeholders, especially faculty members, finds expression. In today's academic world, in which the roles played by research universities are decisive and, to some extent, new, these two traditional centres of academic power and authority need to confront serious challenges regarding their missions and governance.

It is also necessary for the research universities' decision-making structures to successfully accommodate effective collaboration between these two centres of academic authority and management professionals. Present in greater numbers than ever before, these new professional groups make a significant contribution to the management of staff, buildings, libraries, computer centres and virtual data banks, centres of scientific and technological knowledge transfer, and large-scale public fundraising campaigns.[6]

As an integrated organizational actor, the modern university must be able to stimulate and support groups of students and academic faculty. It must constantly review the management of its many infrastructures that support them. Moreover, we know that successfully introducing appropriate forms of academic labour division between undergraduate and graduate studies, especially advanced training in research, is crucial. This type of academic labour division allows organizational actors that rely on it to be more successful in their tasks of combining teaching, research, and the supervision of students enrolled in advanced training in research.

Aside from the handful of elements that we have enumerated, for example, there are unavoidable elements of governance that contribute to shaping research universities into strong and integrated organizational actors. Thus, we have seen how academics who are already recognized by their peers in their fields of expertise have a tendency to become important leaders of their institutions. Their personal credibility and their insightful understanding of the internal operations of research universities allow them to make a mark on their development.

This type of influence is all the more likely to contribute to structuring a research university as an organizational actor in that it relies on innovative and visionary leaders at all levels of the institution. Strong leadership ability forms the strand of transmission and mobilization binding together members of the teaching and research base units, intermediate faculty structures, and central administration bodies. This is the context, in fact, in which organizational actors not only access the means to innovate and develop, but also build on the flexibility to make changes and offer their key stakeholders and groups of actors modes of gratification that encourage innovation.

A high-quality research university, which is an organizationally well-consolidated and integrated academic actor, is not created overnight – even if, in the case of Canada, Australia, the United States, and even some emerging countries, we have seen that the time frame may be closer to decades than centuries.[7] It requires persistence from visionary leadership, adequate decision-making structures, and innovative academic units that are well-suited for promoting at all levels the most effective use of the available resources for attaining the goals of excellence shared by the university community.

Sometimes in the history of these research universities we see that the leadership, especially stemming from the central administration, has been less affirmed. Under these circumstances, the institutional culture and collective will that has already become embedded at all levels of the institution will continue to foster the pursuit of quality and excellence and mitigate the potentially negative effects of a weaker and less informed leadership. As our data have revealed, these universities will continue to develop, and those that succeed in making their mark internationally often have a long history of pursuing excellence.

Further, there are long traditions of higher education and university systems that have not always favoured the emergence and consolidation of universities, especially research universities, as organizational actors. It is a safe bet that the distinctions we have made, drawing on Clark's model for the dominant principle of the organizational integration of university systems, especially in terms of whether they are characterized by institutional self-governance or government regulation, are of some relevance here.

It seems that the trend among European universities to assert themselves as organizational actors is quite recent. It should be considered a key element of the current upheaval in European higher education systems.[8] Nonetheless, the situation in Europe is less clear-cut.

It appears self-evident to us that the UK higher education system and its leading research universities have been asserting themselves as integrated organizational actors for some time. Moreover, as we have shown, they are developing in an academic environment that is exposed to robust government regulation. The dominant principle of their organizational integration, institutional self-governance, corresponds closely with their self-assertion as organizational actors able to effectively control their missions, objectives, and resources in a competitive academic environment.

As for French universities, we have seen the extent to which they are subject to reform projects designed to increasingly render them integrated organizational actors. But, as we have also seen, the dual principle – vertical (the relationship of teaching and research units with a central administration) and horizontal (the relationship of confederal administration with relatively autonomous components of the institution) – that characterizes the governance of French research universities creates pitfalls on their path toward well-anchored status as integrated organizational actors.

When its tradition as a well-integrated organizational actor is deeply entrenched, a research university can act in its environment in light of its mission and goals. In its own sphere of activity – the numerous and complex missions of quality education and basic research – it is equipped to manage and control the influences of various markets that shape its operations and the resource appropriation modes required for achieving its objectives. Drawing on work by Lindblom, Clark rightly reminds us that markets have no goals and do not pursue strategies.[9] It is the research universities as organizational actors, as well as their driving forces – professors, researchers, students, academic administrators, and specialized support services professionals – that pursue goals and develop a culture of innovation and the collective will to strive for high-quality success.

For any research university that has established itself as a well-integrated organizational actor, dealing with the various aspects of its operating conditions, which are largely marked by the influences of different markets, is neither the only nor perhaps even the main path over which it can open itself to emulation and competition. The scientific world of knowledge creation and the spirit of scientific discovery and experimentation that give research universities their raison d'être and structure their missions and objectives are already strongly characterized by emulation and competition.

There is no spirit of discovery and experimentation, and no knowledge creation, if there is no competition and debate in the search for theoretical frameworks, strategies and methodological tools, and experimental fields and technological infrastructure which become more capable of producing and transmitting new knowledge that is often validated by means of lively and intense debate. For a research university, managing on its own turf the highly competitive conditions under which it will autonomously accomplish its complex missions requires, in some respects, that it maintain a strong connection to its founding principle: the universe of emulation in scientific research.

9

CONCLUSION:
THE FUTURE OF RESEARCH UNIVERSITIES

We conclude this analysis with a look at some of the major challenges that will undeniably shape the immediate future of research universities. The situation in the United States – which has served as our benchmark – and in Canada, with which we are most familiar, will provide us with points of reference. However, many of the challenges discussed below extend beyond the boundaries of the US and Canadian university systems as they confront the missions of research universities within contemporary knowledge-based societies.

Research universities do not develop in isolation and they are not the only higher education institutions that matter. Rather, their destiny is inextricably linked to broader trends in the university tertiary education sector. Thus, we begin by exploring some of the characteristics of this sector's educational institutions, which provide the pool from which research universities emerge.

Next we will briefly examine some of the critical issues affecting the integration of research and teaching in the university setting. The research function of contemporary universities is, in fact, increasingly under fire – raising questions about the very raison d'être of research universities.

The issue of privatizing university teaching, or even the missions of research universities, has been the subject of impassioned debates. We will briefly look at this trend, in its application to both teaching and research, to see more clearly the challenges that research universities, in particular, must confront today.

Since their very inception, research universities have been associated with PhD-level training programs. A highly skilled labour force, especially one that includes the less common but essential beneficiaries of doctoral training in advanced research, is a vital component of any knowledge-based economy. We end this chapter with a few trends in doctoral education in US and Canadian research universities, in terms of both its importance today and the challenges it will have to confront.

COMPLEMENTARY MISSIONS AND UNIVERSITIES

A specific type of university has been the subject of this book: the research university. Of several different definitions, we mainly used the most publicized one proposed by the Carnegie Foundation to pin down our subject matter.[1]

Also, following the lead of this Foundation, we have emphasized that only a limited number of establishments belonging to a university system are, strictly speaking, research universities.

We can debate the value and relevance of the definitions of a research university. Some institutions, though they don't yet have critical masses of professors and graduate students in a wide variety of disciplinary and interdisciplinary fields, can nonetheless be home to important centres of excellence with the ability to show leadership, effectiveness, and potential in research. These institutions may even be well on their way to acquiring the status of research university in the strict sense of the term.[2] Even if we concede that a somewhat expanded use of the definition of a research university might make sense, especially in the case of certain institutions in many countries that already have strong assets in research and teaching, one fact remains.

Although no self-respecting university can be cavalier about one basic principle – the spirit of discovery and culture of research that have laid the groundwork for the missions of modern universities for over a century – not all institutions need to be considered research universities in the strictest sense of the term. No knowledge-based society can flourish and grow by relying only on research universities. And whatever their spheres of activity and principal roles, they cannot single-handedly meet all of a modern society's requirements for education and specialized knowledge. As we have observed in passing, the United States has established great universities that are not considered research universities, but without which it would be unable to stand out for its achievements in scientific, cultural, and social innovation.

Diversified branches of higher education, or even of university education proper, thus jointly cover a set of missions that are all essential to the future of knowledge-based societies. The challenge to these institutions is for each of them to attain a high level of quality within the parameters established by their specific missions. Their unique contribution enriches the fabric of society and creates a much-needed chain of resources, the means to put specialized knowledge into action, and a well-endowed labour force.

These features of a generally outstanding university system are so constraining that we easily understand the dilemmas confronted by the United States. First, as we observe from table 3.4 (chapter 3), at the beginning of the twenty-first century the proportion of the US labour force (aged 25–64 years) with a university tertiary A education gave that country an enviable edge. Indeed, among all the OECD member countries we have examined, the United States ranks first in tertiary university education.

However, necessary distinctions between stocks and flows indicate other dynamics that are both more complicated and troubling. For too long, the United States has suffered from a severe erosion in the annual graduation rates in both the tertiary A and B sectors of university education.[3] Once the world leader in university attendance among the relevant age groups, the United States today is near the mid-point of OECD member nations in terms of both graduation and admission levels (approximately twelfth). This is both reported and deplored by the Spellings Commission appointed by the secretary of the Department of Education.[4]

Recovery measures and strategies are on the political agenda of state and federal governments.[5] The Obama administration is no exception, having announced measures to promote attendance in community colleges which, for the most part, belong to the tertiary B sector of university education. In the short term, these policies are also intended to encourage higher transfer rates of students and graduates from this sector to the longer programs in the tertiary A sector: bachelor's degrees and higher. These measures, which address the distinctive academic functions of various institutions, are designed to shore up the missions of all US universities anew. The intent is to re-examine their foundations and strengthen a diversified higher education system without which research universities would be unable to excel.

But what of Canada's university tertiary education? The Canadian labour force (aged 25–64 years) with a post-secondary degree or, more specifically, a tertiary degree, stands out internationally for its large size. Canada is first among OECD members in the number of individuals with a tertiary A or B education. However, distinguishing between these sectors reveals that globally Canada's advantage in terms of the qualifications of its population principally lies in the contingent that has completed tertiary B. Again referring to table 3.4, we see that Canada does not perform as well in degrees awarded in the tertiary A sector.

These data reflect the stock of individuals with a tertiary education, but what of annual changes in the number of tertiary students and graduates? We see that, in general, Canada does very well at the tertiary B level. In this segment of university education, its yield exceeds the OECD average by a healthy margin. In fact, it places in the top ranks. The situation is quite different for tertiary A university education, where Canada's annual flows hardly attain the average of OECD countries, even fall a little below. More often than not, Canada finds itself in the bottom half of the thirty-some OECD member countries.

The university-level academic foundation on which Canadian research universities can build appears quite brittle. These international comparisons argue for higher university attendance at the tertiary A level. Canada would benefit greatly from this and from more graduates completing this level of university education in a reasonable time frame. This is all the more true in that, unlike the United States which needs to correct a situation that has begun to deteriorate in recent years, Canada must make up for long-standing deficiencies. Recall that, even today, as a proportion of its population, Canada has one-third fewer research PhDs than the United States. Canada's university system is facing the monumental challenge of moving its students and graduates from the tertiary B sector, which is operating at full capacity, to the tertiary A system.

In short, in the absence of a tertiary university education sector comprising a sufficient number of institutions with varying missions, Canadian research universities will struggle to stand out internationally, or even to sustain their current performance. High-quality, large universities with diversified missions are essential to economic and social development, democratic well-being, and the culture of a knowledge-based society. Research universities must coexist with other first-rate universities that assume different, but essential, roles. In particular, a more dynamic and more developed university tertiary A education sector would attract a greater number of students and see more of them through to graduation, providing better direction for an evolving knowledge-based society.

RESEARCH ... RESEARCH AGAIN?

As we have mentioned several times, contrary to popular belief, throughout the long history of universities the integration of research into teaching has not always been self-evident. With the advent of the modern research university, especially in countries that have focused basic research in universities and not in parallel publicly funded institutions, the integration of research has gradually been written into the history of university teaching.

This history has been in fits and starts, as key observers of the evolution of the modern university have noted, and the current period is not immune to these vagaries. Many critics lament the emphasis that contemporary research universities, in particular, place on research at the expense of teaching, for example.

In our discussion of the evolution of US research universities, we highlighted the central role played by professors in these institutions, especially after the Second World War. They espoused the specific standards of a successful career in which research played a role as decisive as the ability to shape the future of scientific knowledge. This "academic revolution" was characterized by a model that gradually made professors' scientific output, which was thoroughly rooted in the research universities themselves, the incontrovertible measure of professional success, as was well documented by Jencks and Riesman.

This single standard encompassed many universities with different missions. It reflects the normative metric and the valuation of research that lies at the very heart of the vision of a modern university. Such a sweeping application of a single standard of professional success is, however, counterproductive. It has the effect of masking the very real issues, challenges, and objectives that affect high-quality academic careers in institutions that, while not tasked with the mission of research universities, nonetheless need to excel in fulfilling their own mandates. Also, within the research universities themselves this focus tends to devalue other elements of professors' tasks, such as teaching.

As might be expected when much, even too much, attention is paid to the value of research and the importance of shaping the future of one's discipline as a condition of professional success, strong tensions and even significant conflict soon spread through North American academia.[6] In a reaction to the excessive weight given to research, and even to advanced training in research, critics stressed the importance of the tasks and responsibilities of university teaching, even of teaching at the undergraduate level. Steven Brint reports on two broad movements that have emerged during the past quarter century that strove to shift the emphasis back onto teaching and learning in the US system of higher education.[7]

The first, which is primarily supported by leading foundations active in higher education and also rooted in the development within academia of pedagogy and learning service centres as well as the production of a number of teaching guides, has appropriated the mantle of neo-progressivism in higher education, as Brint explains. According to this philosophy, university education must value the active learning experience and a general education that covers the most basic elements of knowledge while challenging the undue emphasis placed on research and academic standards. Higher education should be expressly engaged with current issues that are relevant to citizenship and cultural and ethnic diversity.

This movement, which advocates a better liberal education, has often clashed with a student culture that is very sensitive to the labour market's increasing demands for professional training that more directly and adequately prepares students for a plethora of well-paid jobs. Universities are increasingly expected to provide a high-quality education whose orientation is more applied and vocational. According to Brint, for some student populations the challenges of an education that, while relevant, is also embedded in a broader academic and scientific culture is less appealing than more technical, and immediately applicable, knowledge, for which they are prepared to pay.

The other movement that contributed to refocusing attention on teaching in a university setting resulted from the attempts of many states and the federal government to promote and reward an academic administration more responsive to the tangible contributions made by institutions: notably, by basing its orientations and organizational choices on quantitative and comparative measures of output. This fleshes out the obligation to demonstrate the results of teaching and learning by means of external assessments of the skills acquired by students. Institutions must also provide proof of their graduates' successful integration into the labour market. These benchmarks thus provide some indication of the scope of the tasks and responsibilities specific to teaching that faculty members must assume.

It is clear that the tensions and criticisms surrounding the metamorphosis of the professorial career induced by what Riesman and Jencks call the academic revolution bore fruit with, among other things, a renewed and more systematic focus on teaching and teaching skills during the recruitment and selection of professors in US universities, including research universities. These universities have also deployed systematic efforts to ensure that the advanced training in research provided to doctoral students is permeated by the obligation to master the skills and aptitudes required for university-level teaching. In many ways, these trends are mirrored in Canadian research universities.

However, we must take note of a concern expressed as early as 1995 by no less an astute observer of the functioning of US research universities than B.R. Clark, that movements focusing on teaching at the undergraduate level too often interfere with the requirements of research and advanced training in research. Ultimately, their impact will be to undermine the mission of research universities in the area of basic research linked to advanced training in research. This issue is all the more pressing in that, fifteen years later, Steven Brint in turn expressed his concern about distressing trends in the career paths of professors in US research universities.

First, drawing on recent surveys of the academic faculty of universities, he finds a significant decline (10 per cent) in the proportion of professors in US public research universities who express a desire to become recognized authorities in their respective disciplines. He expresses dismay at the gulf that has opened between two extremes: academic milieus that primarily value teaching versus those that emphasize research. On the one hand, the importance of university-based research and its increasing centrality in the economy undoubtedly contributes to creating a wedge between research and undergraduate teaching. On the other hand, the so-called progressive movement in higher education is an expression of the myopia of students, who rebuff a university education that places high demands on them.

Brint reaffirms that the calling of the professor is not to advocate active learning or civic engagement, but rather to defend the disciplinary requirements of rigorous intellectual and scientific work. He argues that the academic community in the United States might have to turn the tide and restore the pre-eminence of research in very short order, as occurred during the era of the academic revolution described by Riesman and Jencks.[8]

A few other findings that are exclusive to the offerings of research universities and are the direct upshot of their complex status as multi-versities also merit our attention. The hundred or so public and private US research universities that serve as a reference sample for R.L. Geiger in his 2004 book are by no means limited to research and advanced training in research. We recall that they award 28 per cent of US bachelor's degrees and 34 per cent of first professional degrees. They are also responsible for 68 per cent of all PhDs awarded by US universities, while performing nearly 75 per cent of all university-based research.[9]

The contribution Canadian research universities make to society mirrors that of their US counterparts. In 2007–08, the fifteen research-intensive universities in Canada had 46.4 per cent of full-time equivalent bachelor's and other undergraduate student enrolment and 54.6 per cent of students in master's and equivalent programs. These same institutions accounted for 68 per cent of all students enrolled in doctoral programs, and in 2008, they awarded 76.2 per cent of all PhDs granted by Canadian universities.[10] On average, they absorb approximately 80 per cent of all the external research funding received by Canadian universities.

It is abundantly clear to what extent research activity enjoys close and productive ties with graduate education, in particular at the doctoral level. We too easily forget that doctoral education – which sprouts in the greenhouse of active university-based research and the work done by professors, teams, groups, and research centres – is at the very heart of the vital and strategic task of teaching, while the linkage between research and teaching also extends to the master's level. In view of this, we cannot claim that teaching is too isolated from active participation in research.

Nonetheless, the remarkable flourishing of university-based research during the second half of the twentieth century has caused considerable upheaval in US and Canadian universities. In the midst of these changes, university-based research collaborated with enterprises and service organizations by means of scientific partnerships and training in research. But today it plays a more direct economic role, notably in that the products of basic research give rise to patent applications.

Against a backdrop in which the research university is at the heart of the knowledge-based society, the supervision and training of student-researchers in certain graduate programs can sometimes create tensions with undesirable fallout. This is an issue that universities must take seriously, in particular by acting on measures advocated by their graduate schools. They must constantly juggle the challenges that confront the research university – which is so central to today's society. Their task is to generate basic research that can foment a renewal of knowledge and support the innovation that our knowledge-based economies greatly need. But they must, for now and forever, channel university-based research into training in research, especially at the PhD level.

And what of links between research and undergraduate teaching? The research university must contend with a tendency among its academic faculty to eschew undergraduate teaching. Its professors have an obligation to contribute to its strength in that arena. At all levels of teaching and in all training branches, the missions of the multiversity must be permeated by a vibrant research culture. To accomplish this, the best researchers and teachers on the faculty must also put their shoulder to the wheel for undergraduate studies.

What we see is that, because of underfunding, research universities have taken to hiring supplementary teaching specialists and contractual junior lecturers to provide regular undergraduate teaching. With the current financial situation of some research universities, it would be virtually impossible to completely eliminate these supplementary lecturers. However, meticulously monitoring the quality of the teaching provided requires that these resources be supervised and controlled in a way that is compatible with the mission of a research university.

The structural accretion process described by N.J. Smelser, which is mostly relevant to research universities and which we have already mentioned, has its own requirements. A research university will be unable to accommodate additional roles and functions, while keeping alive its basic foundational mission, unless it has a vision, a culture, and a very specific ideology that concretely encompasses the core academic tasks of its groups of teachers and researchers, spurring their involvement in providing teaching and research at all levels of education. For those who share this vision, it must nourish and guide very concrete practices to inform the careers of professors and thereby contribute to the quality and sustainability of leading research universities.

THE HIGHS AND LOWS OF RESEARCH PRIVATIZATION

To some observers, it is simply a matter of course that research universities will show a net trend toward privatization of research in terms of both its funding and orientation. So pronounced is this trend that university-based research is substantially shifting into the sphere of the private sector. This is a strong statement, but can it be verified? Let us begin with a few definitions, since several terms are used (privatization, commercialization, orientation of university research, etc.) to show the extent to which the idealized research university is in peril.

The central issue is whether and how funders, private or public, can alienate the freedom of university-based research and thus divert it from its primary goal, which is the advancement of knowledge in a context of training the next generation of scientists.

Industry funding of university-based research is the first aspect targeted. In principle, it not only dictates the subject of the research but it further privatizes its main findings to profit from the exclusivity of new products, production processes, or service developments. This privatization generally takes the shape of reducing, or completely blocking, publication of the scientific results, thus removing their public nature. We can see how this could affect the university's ability to execute its primary mission, and might severely compromise the quality of its research and training through research.

In addition to these partnerships between academia and business, the university might decide to privatize some portion of the fruits of research conducted within its walls, on its own behalf. It can do this by taking out patents or licences on results that have commercial viability. In this way, the dissemination of scientific results is delayed and an attempt is made to block access to them by other university researchers who could use them to advance their own research activities. In so doing, the goal of the university is clearly to increase its funding and thus meet its various needs. It is also easy to see how the government could be in favour of this, because of the dual advantage of reducing universities' demand for government funds while fostering development of the local economy.

Has the situation deteriorated to the point that the primary mission of the research university is threatened? First, we must bear in mind that output with commercial potential is limited to a few subsectors of research conducted in universities. The humanities and arts are, for the most part, excluded from this trend, as are most specializations within the social sciences. The same is true for many sectors of the natural sciences. This is why, incidentally, as our own data show, external funding of research in US universities provided by business remains a very small proportion of total resources dedicated to university-based research. In 2008–09 this share was larger in public (between 8 per cent and 9 per cent of total external funding), than in private (between 6 per cent and 7 per cent), research universities. Since external sources account for less than half of university-based research funding, it follows that industry only contributes approximately 4 per cent of the total.

We also note that US research universities, notably riding a wave of intense activity in biomedical sciences, dramatically increased their patent applications on the basis of their research activities. These rose from 250 per year in 1980 to over 3,600 in 2003.[11] However, as Geiger points out, by the turn of the century over half of these applications were from research universities that stood out for their research intensity and had no strong links with business.[12]

In Canadian universities the situation is somewhat different. According to our data, between 2000 and 2008, universities received an average of 14 per cent of their external research funding from business. Once again, we need to emphasize that external sources only amount to 50 per cent of total research funding, so the contribution of industry to research in Canadian universities accounts for less than 8 per cent of the total. In light of the high concentration of Canadian research in universities, this difference from the situation in the United States is of no consequence.

Another limiting factor for the privatization of university-based research is that those researchers who chose to satisfy their passion for research in academia instead of in the private sector place a high premium on their freedom, orienting their careers by their desire to advance knowledge in a context of training the next generation of scientists. They would refuse to allow the institution that employs them to restrict their room to manoeuvre and repudiate the vision, culture, and belief system that gives meaning to their academic careers. If needed, they know how to remind their institution and its administrators that this vision is at the heart of the university's missions in contemporary society.

It is, however, undeniable that the increased economic role played by university-based research has created pressure for more commercialization of its products. Some believed – erroneously, we think – that they had found the goose that laid the golden egg, which would solve universities' financial problems. Notwithstanding a few resounding success stories, in both the United States and Canada, this will not prove to be a panacea. Research-intensive universities have, however, seen fit to adopt intellectual property policies to manage the knowledge and discoveries produced by professors in their teaching and research units.

Governments and their university research granting agencies have circumscribed this trend with appropriate laws and mechanisms. For the institutions in question, the stake was to protect the rights and responsibilities not only of professor- and student-researchers (even if, generally, few professors were involved), but also those of the universities themselves, bolstering their core missions of experimentation and discovering new knowledge for the community and teaching in many branches of knowledge, regardless of their commercial viability.

The greatest threat to North American research universities rests in the behaviour and choices of their governments in the matter of funding universities and university-based research. Three factors come into play: the volume of resources, which sectors receive the funding, and the requirement for short-term results. We have seen that, notwithstanding a cyclical element, there has been a strong upward trend in government funding of university-based research since the Second World War. Both in Canada and the United States it clearly predominates as the source of funding for university-level basic research, demonstrating that the government continues to provide significant support.

A sectorial orientation of this funding persists, but is not nearly as pronounced as it was, at least in the United States during the Second World War and the subsequent Cold War, in particular as it played itself out in the space race. In Canada, the criteria of relevance were introduced into some new university research funding programs, reducing the number of eligible sectors and projects. Generalized application of these modes, which make research funding conditional on certain criteria of relevance, could seriously threaten the mission and quality of research universities. Indeed, how is the relevance of a basic research project to be assessed, and what is the appropriate time frame? In the case of basic research, if scientists knew what they would discover before beginning the experiments the research would be superfluous. This makes it difficult to establish relevance criteria that are not purely arbitrary.

To counter this trend, researchers, universities, and groups of universities must continually inform the public of the importance of basic research to the fundamental mission of universities, especially research universities. It will be the general public, as it buys into the grandeur and the vital nature of this primary mission of universities, that will ultimately curb the short-term ambitions of governments too hasty to cash in on the investments made in universities.

Against this backdrop it is clear therefore that research-intensive universities have needed to, and will always need to, go to bat for the primacy of research driven by scientific curiosity and a spirit of discovery – in keeping with their fundamental missions. To date, their efforts have been successful partially because institutions with a strong commitment to research have profited from the remarkable growth in well-financed sectors of discovery. We have, in fact, already noted that the derivatives and direct benefits from basic research are increasingly covered by patent applications. While this trend entails its own set of issues and contradictions, it does not contribute to the marginalization of research animated by scientific curiosity and the spirit of discovery.

To forestall an erosion of their research and teaching missions, modern universities, especially research-intensive ones, have had to takes steps to shore up research sectors that receive less support from national science and technology policies. This is the case in the humanities and arts and, to a lesser extent, some branches of the social sciences. In their role as multi-versities in terms of the number and scope of their fields of specialization, this is a commitment that research universities cannot shirk. The university that fails to constantly renew this commitment will risk being unable to meet the challenges – in its own sphere of action and on the basis of its priorities – that are central to the fulfillment of its teaching and research missions today.

In short, it is indisputable that universities in general, and research universities in particular, are more endangered in recent years by government public policies impacting their mission than by privatization trends regarding university-based research. The threat of privatization is thus not nearly as catastrophic as some seem to think. Private research funding, including that provided by business, remains marginal in the overall amounts of monies made available to university-based research. Developing and commercializing research in the university setting is here to stay – as are the science and technology innovation policies that support them, even as they strive to shepherd research activities into the subjects and areas that are national priorities.

However, there is no reason to believe that research universities have been neglecting the commitments inherent in their foundational missions of teaching and research. Despite some failings and in the face of significant challenges we must concede that, in the fundamental sphere of research, universities have not sold out or turned their backs on their founding missions. Of course, tensions, issues, even contradictions, as to the defining role of the research university in today's world remain. We cannot overlook the fact that universities have, overall, addressed these issues more than adequately – drawing on the vibrant exchanges and relationships between their various components and thoroughly overhauled governance practices. This corresponds to Geiger's findings[13] in the case of US research universities, and is also true for their Canadian counterparts.

THE OTHER PRIVATIZATION:
UNIVERSITIES' OPERATING RESOURCES

It is obvious that the question of funding the operations of universities, in particular research universities, is as sensitive as it is complex. The relationship of public resources – in the form of government grants in support of teaching and financial assistance to students – to private resources is at the heart of this issue. Tuition paid by students is foremost among the latter, though other private sources – donations, profits from auxiliary businesses, public fundraising campaigns, etc. – might, on occasion, play a not negligible role in the funding of these institutions.

We have seen that in three-quarters of the university systems examined, tuition levels that are quite high and have risen sharply are a key contributor to funding the operating costs of universities. Does making university students pay tuition reflect some underlying principle? If it does, what share of universities' operating costs can they fairly be expected to assume? Much research has gone into these two questions.[14]

Why charge tuition? In the simplest terms, because the primary beneficiaries of university education are the students themselves. It has been established in Canada that a man with a bachelor's degree will earn 53 per cent more, on average, than a man with a high-school diploma; this differential is 70 per cent in the case of women.[15] University education thus confers indisputable benefits on individuals, so it makes perfect sense that they should bear some of the costs.

We also know that education has a value to society that is supplemental to this private financial yield. Advocates of free or low-tuition university education claim that these benefits, in terms of economic growth and other social benefits of all kinds (reduced crime rates, a more informed electorate, increased civic awareness, improved health, etc.) are so valuable to the community that the general population should assume these costs in their entirety. Many studies have sought to put a value on the magnitude of the benefits other than those accruing directly to the graduate. In a survey of all results of these studies, Castro and Poitevin conclude that the graduate personally receives at least 60 per cent of the aggregate benefits accruing to university education. How can we justify the entire population paying all, or most, of the operating costs of universities when it is the students who personally profit from their degrees?[16]

Tuition fees are not the only cost students enrolled in university must assume. The main cost, in fact, is the earnings they forgo by not working full time, to which we can add the ancillary fees associated with education. Castro and Poitevin estimated the fair share of the costs that tuition should include if all the costs and benefits of university education are considered. They calculate that at approximately 30 per cent. Clearly, if the total cost to students of their education, in conjunction with other constraining socio-cultural factors, limits access to university education for a significant number of individuals with the ability and desire to study, we might encounter a situation in which there is a problematic underinvestment in university education, from a societal perspective, in comparison with the total private and social benefits that would be conferred by a greater stock of human capital.

This is the context in which we must situate potential failings of university systems with shared public–private funding. Among these we can count the progressive financial disengagement of the government from university funding, which can have two consequences. It might entail a compensating hike in tuition fees, bringing them to a level considerably higher than 30 per cent of total costs. Higher tuition fees reduce the private return to university education, and might lead to declining enrolment. This could result in a public underinvestment in higher education, given the unrealized social benefits attributable to a smaller stock of human capital. In the absence of a compensating increase in tuition, the reduction in government funding would result in a decline in the quality of university education itself, in turn undermining the quality of and, ultimately, yield of the stock of human capital. There could also be a generalized, and perhaps disproportionate, inflation of the cost of university education, even if its fundamental quality did not justify this level of investment.

The Case of the United States

For some thirty years, the university system of the United States has been beset by several of these problems, with negative ramifications. First, recall that the share of universities' operating costs financed by tuition rose from 20 per cent in 1980 to over 43 per cent by 2006. This proportion is markedly higher than the 30 per cent advocated by Castro and Poitevin. We have also observed that this trend was accompanied by a severe contraction in government funding of universities. There has not only been a change in government participation in the funding of university education, but also a steep cost of inflation that is reflected in tuition fees. Thus, between 1980 and 2008, in constant dollars, tuition rates in public colleges and universities increased by 235 per cent, whereas real median family income rose by a mere 15 per cent during that same period.[17]

Virtually stable between 1960 and 1980, the relative price of higher education exploded after 1980, with consequences that are becoming ever more evident to analysts of this system. Overall, the balance of public and private funding of the US university system appears to have been overturned – as has the social contract that established the public mission of the university along with bountiful government funding. This is what sustained the remarkable growth of universities in the United States during the period between the Second World War and the 1980s.[18]

Referring again to the principal analytical axes we presented in chapter 8, we might deduce that the institutional self-governance dynamics of US universities are now stymied by the inability of the government to effectively mediate trends toward privatization. Over time, this gradual erosion of both its role as provider of public resources to adequately support the universities and as a regulator of the market effects that condition their access to resources has undermined research universities. It also seriously disrupts the dynamic forces on which they rely and the social missions they have assumed. This has eroded the pillars that once consolidated the contributions made by US research universities and allowed them to dominate the international scene.

Signs of the difficulties that are steering research universities and the entire university system of the United States off course are increasingly in evidence. In a recent paper Geiger noted the clear divide that has appeared between two segments of institutions. The least selective and, generally, least well-performing, which have limited resources, receive the least qualified students and only manage to see half of them through to graduation. A disproportionate share of their student body is from underprivileged socio-economic backgrounds, and these students are typically unable to pay higher tuition fees. Constrained in their tuition policies, these institutions are dependent on the government. Thus, they bear the full brunt of the conditions that push state and federal governments to severely cut back on the resources provided to universities and students and, by extension, undermine the quality of education.

The other segment mainly consists of universities that are more selective and better performers. They rely on more aggressive tuition policies. These high costs, not totally offset by discounts and internal fellowships to mitigate the prohibitive level of official tuition rates, make university more accessible to the wealthiest students, who often have better academic records because they received their entire education from the most endowed and reputed private schools. This second segment also includes high-quality universities, especially private, with undergraduate programs, colleges that specialize in liberal education, and institutions that provide master's degrees. However, it also includes quite a few high-quality public universities with stellar reputations. Both public and private research universities are, in general, a core component of this second segment.[19]

The structural schism between these two segments is deep: Its fallout reaches across institutions and notoriously affects faculty member resources. In recent years, the careers of professors in US universities have been disrupted by major upheavals with unprecedented impacts.[20]

On the one hand, we observe a considerable expansion in the number of full-time academic faculty positions of fixed duration. Not being tenure-track, these positions inflate the number of probationary professorships. In the US system, three out of five full-time positions are now not tenure track. So today there are two streams for careers in academia: Regular full-time professorships parallel part-time or full-time non-tenure-track professorships.

Another change relates to the tasks performed by professors in academia: Even though proficiency in research is a condition for acceptance into US universities, where the curriculum is at least four years, only regular full-time professors are likely to engage in research activities, though there are a handful of exceptions, essentially in the natural and biomedical sciences. It is mostly individuals in the contingent positions who assume the one-dimensional task of teaching.

However, the most consequence-laden aspect is that these changes to the career paths of professors are unequally distributed over the types of institution. This trend deepens the chasm between the two segments of academia. Indeed, the leading US research universities are much less affected by these changes. They are more dependent on a professorial staff that is mostly regular and permanent, even when differences between the public and private sectors are considered.

While the United States is now confronted by the challenge of significantly correcting university attendance rates for the relevant age groups, in particular in university tertiary A studies, the fact that the most selective and best performing universities are out of reach tends to discourage a sizable fraction of potential applicants. According to some seasoned observers, the chasm between the two segments of university education reflects a deeper social inequality in the United States. It is inextricably linked with the shrinking opportunities for socio-economic success of members of the American middle class – stymied by the high cost of education and the resulting debt level (the so-called "middle-class squeeze").[21] The United States is now, as in only a handful of times in its history, confronted by social tensions that are giving the lie to the American dream of intergenerational mobility: that the sons and daughters will be better off than their parents.

More specifically, with regard to US research universities, the economic conditions that have shaken the balance between public and private funding are particularly detrimental to public research universities. As we have seen, notwithstanding their persistence as powerful institutions on the international scene, they have been severely handicapped by the sharp contraction in public funding.

We also know that their financial woes cannot be solved by another round of steep tuition hikes. The room to manoeuvre that they had in that area has been largely used up. This is one of the main findings of the National Research Council's Committee on Research Universities, which advocates a new social contract between these institutions and government authorities – primarily the states, which are responsible for funding the operating costs of universities. In fact, this committee recommends that governments reinstate their participation in the funding of US public research universities to its level before the severe reductions that began in the 1980s.

The Committee thus calls for a return to a more reasonable balance between public and private funding. In other words, it suggests boosting governments' financial intervention. It also expresses a hope for better government regulation of access to resources through the market relationships that public research universities call on to adequately fulfill their missions. As integrated organizational actors, these universities must attain and then manage a better balance between institutional self-governance, government intervention and regulation, and access to resources by means of market relationships.

The Case of Canada

In recent decades the Canadian university system has undergone a sea change in the sourcing of public and private funds for its operations. North of the forty-ninth parallel, the constraints on government finances resulting from economic challenges have also led provincial and federal governments to reassess their priorities. This trend has resulted in higher tuition fees and changes to the financial support provided to students and, by extension, in a certain shift toward the privatization of resources available to universities. Students attending university and, if need be, their families, have had to invest more to obtain a university education. Student debt levels have also risen.

Similarities with the situation south of the border end there, however. The revised division between public and private resources available to universities in Canada has not entailed the kind of disruption that would shatter the equilibrium between public and private financing. The fact that the contribution from tuition fees has risen more than government funding – though the latter have also increased – hás had the effect of bringing the distribution of university financing in line with what the studies recommend, that is, a fair share assumed by tuition at approximately 30 per cent. Furthermore, the absence of strictly speaking private universities in the Canadian system has probably helped to shield it from the excesses of the US system. In the absence of a private component unregulated by the government, the Canadian university system is more or less immune to the risks of excessive cost inflation experienced by its US counterparts.

Indeed, after substantial tuition hikes between the mid-1990s and the mid-2000s, there were systematic interventions by several provincial governments to stabilize the situation and curtail potential excesses. This has allowed participation in university education in Canada to continue to grow despite significant shifts in the balance of university funding. In this regard, Canada is far from the profound crisis that is shaking the US system. It is clear, however, that it would be disastrous to continue to increase the funding of Canadian universities by means of significant tuition hikes. The example of the United States, in this regard, is not reassuring and it would be a serious error to follow in its footsteps. The funding of the Canadian university system has found a good balance, and governments should take heed to ensure that developments in government finances do not carelessly disrupt it.

The refusal of Quebec to adapt to the new balance in the funding of Canada's university system has had the anticipated consequences. The tuition freeze, which has not been compensated by a hike in government funding, has created a severe and chronic state of underfunding in Quebec's university system that has not, incidentally, induced a corresponding real increase in university attendance. This is a serious error that has already had visible repercussions on the quality of Quebec's universities and amounts to a massive mortgage on the future of the province. Equally serious are the systematic assaults on the autonomy of universities that we regularly observe in Quebec. We have repeatedly demonstrated that real self-governance for universities is a key feature of the best performers. In once again succumbing to the temptation to diverge from the characteristics of the most successful universities in North America, Quebec is endangering the remarkable achievements its university system has posted over the past fifty years and seriously undermining the competitive standing of its kernel of research universities.

THE CROWNING DEGREE OF THE RESEARCH UNIVERSITY: THE PHD

It was against the backdrop of the research university that the defining degree of advanced training in research was born: the degree awarded upon completion of doctoral work. In North America it is typically called the PhD, followed by a designation of the field of specialization. Throughout the twentieth century, but especially during its second half, US research universities occupied a privileged position in the area of doctoral education.[22] It is estimated, for example, that between 1975 and 2001, during which the United States accounted for approximately 6 per cent of the world population, US universities conferred over 20 per cent of the global production of PhDs.[23] This output was, of course, part and parcel of the dominant position that the US research university occupied throughout the twentieth century.

The most recent generations of science and technology innovation policies are marked by a certain number of characteristics. Fiscal measures and policies to stimulate innovation by business and services have been retained. But we observe that the emphasis has shifted to men and women who produce new knowledge and shepherd its transfer into multiple spheres of activity. The training of these individuals is thus of paramount importance: They need to be equipped to intervene in several sectors aside from academia only. We expect our top-level specialists in scientific disciplines to also be able to maximize their effectiveness by interacting with other disciplines connected to their own. But most of all, we stipulate that they must have advanced training in research at the doctoral level.

These science and technology innovation policies are on the agenda of member countries of the OECD, which take particular note of the policy options in vogue with the European Union in recent years.[24] They are also consistent with the aforementioned observations by Aghion and Cohen. Nations at the forefront of science and technology innovation exercise leadership in the knowledge-based economies to the extent that they are better able to make use of human capital with advanced training in research at the doctoral level.

OECD member countries have significantly increased their investments in higher education in recent years. In light of the science and technology innovation policies we have been discussing, this trend also extends to advanced training in research, to doctoral education proper. We observe that, in the short span from 1998 to 2006, PhDs awarded by OECD member countries rose by 40 per cent, from 140,000 to over 200,000.[25]

There are, however, great disparities between these countries. For example, US analysts are concerned by the fact that annual growth in PhDs awarded by universities in the United States was only 2 per cent to 3 per cent during that same period. The United States is now ranked seventeenth among the twenty-seven OECD member countries for which this type of data has been calculated. More than half of these countries report growth rates in the number of doctoral degrees awarded that are greater than 5 per cent, and 25 per cent of them post average annual growth greater than 10 per cent.[26] Data published by the OECD on annual rates of graduation from doctoral programs reveal that for at least the past ten years the US rate has hovered around the average for OECD member countries. But if we subtract from that the proportion of degrees awarded to international students by US universities, the performance of the US generally falls below the OECD average.[27]

A rising chorus of voices in the United States is lamenting what they describe as a looming shortfall in the skilled human resources the economy and society desperately need. Of particular concern is the fact that the annual rate of growth in graduates from PhD programs is in freefall. For decades US universities have exerted a great power of attraction for international students, especially at the doctoral level in the case of research universities. In the aftermath of the events of 11 September 2001, and the ensuing tightening of border security in the United States, fears have also been expressed regarding the population of international students currently studying there.[28] Concerns about threats to America's global leadership in this matter are increasingly acute. In 2005, various national scientific academies – through the intermediary of their executive arm, the National Research Council – established a committee mandated to examine the impact of international graduate students and post-doctoral fellows on US science and universities.

This committee was tasked with documenting the consequences of the decisions international students make about whether to remain in the country after graduation and to propose measures to reduce the differences in the work and study conditions available to international and domestic students. It will also identify impediments to the arrival of international doctoral candidates and post-doctoral fellows that result from various existing policies and recommend overall improvements to the global policies that affect these strategic international populations.[29] The game plan is clear: Do whatever it takes to restore the power of attraction of the United States and its research universities for international students in doctoral programs – their hallmark throughout the second half of the twentieth century.

And what of advanced doctoral training in research in Canada? During the period from 1998 to 2006, which we have just discussed for the OECD, Canada's situation was even more problematic than that of the United States. Over this eight-year period, mean annual growth in new PhDs awarded by all Canadian universities was approximately one per cent, which puts Canada in twenty-fourth position among the twenty-seven OECD countries participating in this comparative exercise.[30] What is more, annualized data from the OECD on the rate at which PhDs are awarded generally place Canada below the mean rate of OECD countries. The result is even worse if the contribution made by international students is subtracted. In the awarding of doctoral degrees, Canada is near the bottom of the field of OECD member countries.[31]

Overall, in the past thirty years international student mobility has more than quadrupled (0.8 million in 1975 to 3.7 million in 2009). With a market share of 5.2 per cent of international students attending foreign university tertiary institutions in 2009, Canada does not rank among the champions in this area – the United States, the United Kingdom, Australia, Germany, and France all do better, with market shares between 18 per cent and 6.8 per cent – but it still posts respectable results.[32]

In 2009, the contingent of international students enrolled in university tertiary education in Canada accounted for 6.5 per cent of all students at this level in Canadian universities. This is equivalent to the average for the contingent of international students at the tertiary level in the universities of OECD member countries. We further observe that a minority (8.9 per cent) of international students in Canada's tertiary education sector in 2009 were enrolled in PhD programs. Many other countries, however, are able to funnel approximately 20 per cent of their international students into doctoral programs.

Even though doctoral students are a minority of the international contingent in university tertiary studies in Canada, they constitute a significant share of the enrolment in PhD programs in Canadian universities. In fact, in 2009, one doctoral candidate in five in a Canadian university was an international student. This result places Canada in the lowest ranks of the top third of OECD member countries in terms of the international intensity of their domestic doctoral programs.

Canada has every reason to be concerned about the internationalization of the university education it provides. Quite recently, a committee headed by the president of Western University submitted a report on this issue, which is so important to the future prosperity of the country. It encouraged the various levels of government and the universities to double the number of international students in Canada and to offer them better financial support as well as coordinating and integrating all fellowship programs for international students in graduate and post-doctoral studies. Steps to retain more of these international students after graduation would also be welcome. Finally, integration and immigration policies and measures should be simplified and coordinated to facilitate entry into the country. All of these measures are designed to make Canada a bigger player on the market for attracting and retaining international students.[33]

One conclusion is inescapable: The output of doctoral studies in Canada mirrors that of university tertiary A level studies. It has already been established that, internationally, tertiary A level education in Canada is far from occupying a top position. The trend for PhD programs is roughly similar. We also find that Canada's programs of advanced training in research are somewhat attractive to international students, but they could do better. Other low-population countries, such as Australia, Austria, Belgium, New Zealand, Sweden, and Switzerland, outdo Canada in this regard.[34]

However, we have also seen that Canadian universities stand out on the international scene for their relative contribution to domestic research. No other OECD member country reports such a large share of domestic expenditure on university-based research. Unfortunately, this edge does not seem to translate into a more impressive yield in terms of the rate at which PhDs are awarded by Canadian universities year after year.

In addition, at the turn of the century Canada was the OECD member country with the highest proportion of foreigners with PhDs. It is the only country in which one PhD holder out of two is a foreigner. In fact, the exact value is 54 per cent. Only two or three other countries report a proportion of PhDs that is between 40 per cent and 45 per cent foreign.[35] Moreover, in 2006, of this majority of foreign PhD holders in Canada, approximately two-thirds (64.6 per cent), had arrived in Canada with their degree in pocket.[36]

Thus, it appears that Canada has opted to import a considerable proportion of its most qualified manpower in the area of science and technology innovation. Of course, no country can insulate itself from high-quality international science and technology resources, especially in light of the great mobility of these populations. Any closing off of the opportunities for renewing knowledge and improving the network of researchers and specialists that result from intense international mobility and exchanges could only weaken Canadian universities. Nonetheless, there is a matter of degree here that needs to be mastered.

One could, for example, celebrate a strategy of importing a high-skilled labour force, thus saving Canada the cost of educating PhDs (often among the most expensive), by bringing in this precious resource. But this approach implies a cavalier disregard for the socio-economic costs and the challenges raised by migration, both for the host nation and the migrant. When the volume and intensity of immigration exceeds a certain threshold, the receiving communities and workplaces find themselves swamped and unable to build the bonds of trust with emigrants – beyond purely economic incentives – that are necessary for successful integration in terms of quality of life and collective well-being. According to J. Helliwell, an expert whose perspective is sensitive to the dimensions of social capital and economic well-being, the Canadian community is now becoming more aware of the costs, often too high, associated with immigration and the continuing economic challenges facing the most recent immigrants.[37]

We must also acknowledge that an implicit policy of importing a high proportion of the labour force with advanced training in research to provide a significant share of highly skilled workers would need to be effective in the long term. To do so, it must be adapted to the increasingly competitive environment of knowledge-based societies. We have observed an inescapable trend: Countries at the highest level of industrial development are themselves on the lookout for PhDs. Those that are already banking on the knowledge-based economy, like those that have accumulated the means and resources to work toward this goal, seek to attract the brains that can contribute most to science and technology innovation.

These countries are putting measures in place to educate more PhDs, on the basis of national groups, and repatriate them if they studied abroad. They also seek to attract international students at the highest levels of graduate programs, including PhDs, to contribute to their studies in the hope that they will remain in the country that embraced and educated them. Undue dependence on the international brain pool creates exposure to the fierce competition between countries for this scarce resource – a competition that might drain previously rich international sources of doctoral workers, or significantly restrict access for the nations that continue to use them.

In this environment Canada only has one real option, to bank on a strategy of building – training a highly qualified labour force that notably includes PhDs. This strategy assumes a greater recognition of the role played by tertiary A university education and of the importance of research universities, and a commitment to promoting their success by making all required resources available to them.

There is, thus, an expectation that Canadian universities, especially research universities, will engage in high-intensity scientific discovery activities that are receptive to increasing their contribution to educating and awarding degrees at the doctoral level. Canadian research universities must educate more PhDs, whether native-born or foreign, who will carry the torch for the production of new knowledge and the science and technology innovations the country greatly needs. To attract more students with exceptional potential, these universities must be in a position to vouch for the international quality of their doctoral education. This, in turn, requires transcending the internal benchmarking practices of individual universities by invoking robust quality assessment exercises that systematically compare all doctoral programs in a given discipline nation-wide.

NOTES

FOREWORD

1 The far-reaching debate in the 1960s and '70s on the technology gap
between Europe and the United States was based in part on the apparent
role played by cutting-edge research in universities. We observe that, while
74 per cent of Nobel Prize recipients between 1931 and 1940 were working in Europe and 26 per cent in the United States, by 1961–70 these
numbers were reversed, and this trend has only intensified since then, so
that in 1991–2000, only 23 per cent of Nobel Prize winners were in
Europe, versus 71 per cent in the United States.

CHAPTER ONE

1 Cf. W. Clark 2006.
2 Cf. Ben-David 1984.
3 The Carnegie Foundation applies a classification system with three subgroups to US academic institutions that are active in research and awarding PhDs: 108 RU/VH: Research Universities with Very High research
activity; 99 RU/H: Research Universities with High research activity;
90 DRU: Doctoral Research Universities.
4 Aghion and Cohen 2004.

CHAPTER TWO

1 Cf. Ostriker and Kuh 2003.
2 Cf. http://mup.asu.edu/.
3 Over the course of the past decade several other international rankings, of
varying generality and frequency, have been published. The main ones

include: Leiden World Ranking; Webometrics Ranking of World Universities; Quacquarelli Symonds Limited (QS); SCImago Research Group; Higher Education Evaluation and Accreditation Council of Taiwan. Their content can be found on their respective websites. For a summary of recent developments in these rankings, see Rauhvargers 2013.

4 A good sampling of these criticisms can be found in Liu and Cheng 2005; Billaut, Bouyssou, and Vincke 2010; Lee 2008; Marginson 2007; Rauhvargers 2013.

5 See Holmes 2006; Merisotis and Sadlak 2005; Rauhvargers 2013.

6 Bowman 2010; van Raan 2005; Holmes 2006.

7 Steiner 2007.

8 Information on this ranking can be found at www.timeshighereducation. co.uk/world-university-rankings. Note Quacquarelli Symonds (QS), in charge until 2009 of THES's annual rankings methodology techniques, currently continues its research universities international rankings. An agreement seems to exist between QS and *U.S. News and World Report*, which guarantees a yearly continuity of the international rankings QS had previously launched. Thus, the 2010 edition of a research universities international ranking designed according to QS methodology techniques is posted on the website either of QS or of *U.S. News and World Report*.

9 Clark 2002; Dehon, MecCathie, and Virardi 2009.

10 For more details on the empirical aspect of this chapter, see Lacroix and Maheu 2011.

11 See Hazelkorn 2007 and 2009.

12 Rauhvargers 2013.

CHAPTER THREE

1 The issue of the potential incidence of language on ranking has often been raised. While not wishing to deny that English may play an important role, it is worth noting that if we remove the United States, whose success is attributable to many factors other than language (as we shall see), 48.8 per cent of the remaining universities in the top 400 in table 3.1 are from non-English speaking countries.

CHAPTER FOUR

1 The higher education system in the United States, in particular research universities, stands out for the number of analytical studies of which it has been the subject. These pages, which give the broad outline of its

development, rely largely on the work of J. Ben-David 1977 and 1984; Clark 1995; Geiger 1986, 1993, 2004, and 2010; Touraine 1972; Clark and Neave 1992; Gumport 1993a and 1993b; Altbach, Berdahl, and Gumport 2005.

2 B.R. Clark used the expression "graduate department university" to describe this unique evolution of the US research university, which contributed greatly to its ascendancy throughout the twentieth century in the areas of both doctoral education and research; see Clark 1995 and also Thurgood, Golladay, and Hill 2006.

3 Ben-David 1977, 114, 121, 124.

4 See Thurgood et al. 2006.

5 Ibid.

6 For this section we relied heavily on recent work by Geiger 2004. Data for the latest years are from the report by the National Research Council Committee on Research Universities, 2012.

7 National Research Council Committee on Research Universities, 75–6.

8 Geiger 2004, 134–5; Thurgood et al. 2006; National Research Council Committee on Research Universities 2012, 125–6.

9 Geiger 2004, 135–6.

10 Ibid.

11 Ibid.

12 Kerr 1963.

13 Smelser 2012.

14 Geiger 2004, 140–5.

15 The organization "The Center for Measuring University Performance (MUP)," which was originally associated with the State University of Florida, has been conducting annual reports on the "Top American Research Universities" since 2000, in which they present a variety of statistics on these institutions; see http://mup.asu.edu/research.html.

16 See The Center for Measuring University Performance 2008.

17 Thurgood et al. 2006, 1.

18 Ostriker, Holland, Kuh, and Voyuk, 2010.

19 Geiger 2004, 153–4.

20 National Research Council Committee on Research Universities 2012, 83–5.

21 Clark 1995.

22 Recall that these data do not include income received as grants to research (which we have already accounted for) or fixed asset funds. We have also reduced the universities' revenues by the amounts received from university hospitals, clinics, or health services. Especially in the case of private US

research universities, this last source of income can prove non-negligible
and skew comparisons with competitors in the public sector in the matter
of traditional operating expenditures.

23 In private US universities, net tuition in 1996 was 24 per cent less than
official gross tuition. Private universities give students generous discounts,
in terms of bursaries or other measures, as they compete with other private and public universities. These discounts significantly reduce official
tuition levels, see Geiger 2004, 47–8.

24 National Research Council Committee on Research Universities 2012, 84,
and Geiger 2004, 50.

25 National Research Council Committee on Research Universities 2012, 84,
87.

26 Ibid., 83–4.

27 Geiger 2004, 43–5.

28 Differential tuition levels introduced by public universities end up, in
1996, with states' resident student tuitions, on average, de facto 24 per
cent higher per capita than the official tuition level that should be charged
such state students enrolled in a US public university; see Geiger 2004, 47.

29 On this subject, see Geiger 2011, 61, 64–6.

30 J.P. Ostriker et al. 2010, 88–91.

31 For more details see tables A-4.1 and A-4.2 in the appendix to this
chapter.

32 National Research Council on Research Universities 2012, 88–9.

33 Jencks and Riesman 1968.

34 See also Touraine 1972, 163–70.

35 Ostriker et al. 2010, 88–91.

36 On this matter see the recommendations of the National Research
Council Committee on Research Universities 2012, 90–1.

37 See Goodall 2006, 2009b, 2010.

38 Goodall 2010, 6–7.

39 Ibid., 11–16.

CHAPTER FIVE

1 The UK higher education system includes institutions in all the members,
generally referred to as constituent countries, of the United Kingdom:
England, Scotland, Wales, and Northern Ireland. Some of the subjects we
address in the following pages will lead us to pay special attention to institutions of the higher education system in England, i.e., those under the
aegis of the Higher Education Funding Council for England (HEFCE). It

should be noted that this body, in collaboration with the higher education funding agencies of the other constituent countries (Scottish Funding Council; Higher Education Funding Council for Wales; Department for Employment and Learning, Northern Ireland) assumes functions that affect all the institutions of higher education in the United Kingdom, aside from its special responsibility for those in England. In 2010 England was the country with the largest number of institutions of higher education, at 131; next was Scotland with 19 – the Scottish university system stands out, incidentally, for its long history and outstanding reputation; then Wales with 11; and finally Northern Ireland with 4; see Bruce 2012.

2 B.R. Clark 1995, 57–8.

3 Oxford gave the United Kingdom twenty-five prime ministers, and Cambridge some fifteen; thirteen of the twenty prime ministers of the twentiethth century were from either Oxford or Cambridge. It is estimated that, of the top 500 current leaders in not only government, but also law, journalism, medicine, and business in the United Kingdom, no less than 47 per cent are graduates of Oxford or Cambridge. Despite the fact that only approximately 5 per cent of undergraduates in the United Kingdom attended one of these two institutions in the 1970s and '80s, they contributed to the education of 20 per cent of the elite from 1995 to 2008, according to *Who's Who* current leaders' first listing. On this subject, see Chester and Bekhradnia 2009, 20–1.

4 B.R. Clark 1995, 60–1.

5 Ibid., 60, 65.

6 Committee on Higher Education 1963; Browne 2010.

7 B.R. Clark 1995, 60, 65.

8 Ibid., 61.

9 Ibid., 61–8.

10 For an overview of the issues affecting research in the United Kingdom, in particular in the university setting, see Clark 1993 and 1995; Ben-David 1977 and 1971.

11 Clark 1995, 70.

12 Unsurprisingly, Oxford and Cambridge universities benefit much more from philanthropic donations – an annual average of £120 million in the middle of the first decade of the twenty-first century – than all other universities in the Russell Group combined – approximately £100 million. The difference in this respect between these prestigious UK universities and their US counterparts largely favours the latter: Harvard (nearly US$30 billion) and Yale (nearly US$20 billion) have endowment funds that are much larger than those of Oxford (£3.3 billion) and Cambridge (£4.1 billion). On this subject see Chester and Bekhradnia 2009, 47–8.

13 Observe in passing that certain disciplines – those that lead to professions in medicine and dental surgery – receive specific subsidies for undergraduate teaching, so that students in these programs are not counted for purposes of setting the institutional student quota.

14 A solid majority of universities in England, and specifically those in the Russell Group, have set their tuition levels at the maximum established for 2012–13: £9,000. However, university funding agencies in the other constituent countries have not followed the lead of the HEFCE in this matter. Their respective governments, empowered by the devolution of jurisdiction over higher education, opted for completely different policies. On the basis of their regional strategic plans, they instructed their funding agencies to either make higher education free – the Scottish Funding Council – or to implement hikes that were much less draconian – the Higher Education Funding Council for Wales and, more recently, the Department of Employment and Learning Northern Ireland. See Bruce 2012.

15 Research Assessment Exercises were officially established by the government of the United Kingdom in 1986. They have given rise to periodic operations, in principle every four or five years, of evaluating the research activities of UK universities in support of government funding of research. These will soon be replaced by the Research Excellence Framework (REF), which will primarily differ from the RAE in that it will include new criteria for evaluating university research: its socio-economic impact.

16 In the context of Research Assessment Exercises, quality levels two and one, which are the lowest, apply to units whose research is recognized internationally and recognized nationally, respectively.

17 Note that the data on the Russell Group that will be the subject of the following pages mostly apply to the year 2009–10. At that time this Group contained twenty UK research universities, and all the following tables of data thus represent the situation that prevailed in these twenty research universities at that time.

18 OECD 2010.

19 T. Bruce 2012, 88, 92.

20 J. Chester, B. Bekhradnia 2009, 43–5.

21 United Kingdom Government 2011.

22 See Browne 2010, 22.

23 See Clark 1995, 79–83.

24 See United Kingdom Government 2010.

25 We know that the distinction between master's and doctoral students is not easy to extricate from official statistics in the United States, partly

because the institutions themselves often delay the moment when this distinction is formally made in a graduate student's record.

26 See Clark 1995, 83.

27 See Green and Powell 2007, 90–1 and HEFCE, Commission of Vice-
Chancellors and Principals, Standing Conference of Principals 1996.

28 For more information, see: United Kingdom Government 2010; House
2010; Roberts 2002.

29 See United Kingdom Government 2010, 41; Roberts 2002; and Green and
Powell 2007, 94, 95.

30 See United Kingdom Government 2010, 42.

31 See Chester and Bekhradnia 2009, 29–33.

32 See Clark 1995, 78.

33 See Bruce 2012, 98–100.

34 See Goodall 2006, 2009a, 2009b, and 2010.

35 For all these results, see Goodall 2009, 6–10, 11–16.

CHAPTER SIX

1 *McGill Reporter Special Issue* 2011.

2 The situation began to change during the 1950s with the westward shift
of Canada's economic and financial centre of gravity and the rise of
Toronto as Canada's new hub.

3 Friedland 2002.

4 A comprehensive critical overview of federal intervention in the funding
of universities and university-based research can be found in Cameron
2005.

5 These data are from Harris 1976.

6 Maheu 2007.

7 Thurgood 2006.

8 Macdonald et al. 1969.

9 Maheu 2007, 122.

10 Gingras 1991.

11 Macdonald 1969, 32.

12 Robitaille and Gingras 1999; AUCC 2008.

13 See AUCC 2008, 10.

14 See Macdonald et al. 1969, 48 and 58.

15 Statistics Canada data as reported in CAGS (Canadian Association for
Graduate Studies) *Statistical Report for the years 1980; 1988; 1990–2001
and 1999–2008*; and Maheu 2014.

16 All these numbers from MacDonald et al. 1969, 48 and 58.

17 AUCC 2008, 49.

18 Gingras 1999 (translation by the authors).

19 These data are from the website of the Association of Universities and Colleges of Canada (AUCC).

20 The ten institutions are: University of British Columbia; University of Alberta; University of Toronto; University of Waterloo; McMaster University; Queens University; University of Western Ontario; McGill University; Université de Montréal; and Université Laval.

21 They are the University of Calgary, the University of Ottawa, Dalhousie University.

22 They are the University of Manitoba and the University of Saskatchewan.

23 Lacroix and Maheu 2011.

24 Industry Canada 2010.

25 Notice that this concentration is less pronounced, however, than in the US university system.

26 Comprehensive data on research conducted in these six universities is presented in table A-6.1 in the appendix to this chapter.

27 For more details, see table A-6.1 in the appendix to this chapter.

28 For more details, see table A-6.2 in the appendix to this chapter.

29 On this subject, see Lacroix and Trahan 2007; CRÉPUQ 2011.

30 For more details, see table A-6.3 in the appendix to this chapter.

31 The previously mentioned statistical benchmark for the size of student bodies at the end of the twenty-first century not only refers to a different year, but also covers total student populations. Table 6.7 is strictly full-time equivalent students. The number of part-time students is thus divided by three to obtain full-time equivalence. Intergroup comparisons are more accurate since differences in intensity in the number of part-time students have been normalized across institutions.

32 On this subject, see Maheu 2008.

33 For more details, see table A-6.4 in the appendix to this chapter.

34 For an overview of this subject, see Amaral, Jones, and Karseth 2002.

35 Amaral et al. 2002.

36 Ibid.

CHAPTER SEVEN

1 Liard 1894 (available in French at gallica.bnf.fr); Clark 1995.

2 Musselin 2001, 27–30.

3 Clark 1995, 94.

4 C. Charle 1994.

5 Musselin 2001, 32–3.

6 Ibid., 43–52.

7 Renaut 2002, 78–9 (this citation, and all other citations in this chapter, translated by the authors).

8 Clark 1995, 110.

9 Ibid., 101–2; Musselin 2001, 84.

10 Musselin 2001, 89.

11 Clark 1995, 102.

12 Ibid., 104–5.

13 Ibid., 102–5; Musselin 2001, 90–4.

14 Musselin 2001, 98–102.

15 Neave 1985.

16 Musselin 2001, 96.

17 Ibid., 67–9.

18 For a detailed analysis of the structural impact of contracting operations in French universities, see Musselin 2001, 2nd part.

19 www.nouvelleuniversite.gouv.fr/-pourquoi–la-reforme-de-l-universite.

20 Senate Committee for the Control of Law Enforcement 2013, 65–6.

21 Belloc 2012, 7–8.

22 While in no way wishing to cast doubt on this public assertion by the *Conférence des Grandes Écoles*, we feel it is important to point out that this research is often conducted with the strong involvement of universities and their doctoral schools, making it hard to properly assign credit to one or another type of institutions.

23 In our previous examination of three other university systems, we were able to draw on comprehensive databases that were easily accessible and reliable, and furthermore were disaggregated by establishment. In the case of the French system, finding this level of transparency, accessibility, and even reliability in the data is next to impossible. While we strove to conduct an analysis that was as close as possible to the one we performed for the other systems, in the case of France this proved very difficult and only partially possible. The only data we found disaggregated at the institution level were available for only one year, 2009–10, and their coverage of expenditures on research was very incomplete. This is why, to maintain consistency with the disaggregated data for 2009–10, we used the 2010 edition of the ARWU ranking to generate the subgroup of research-intensive French universities that we subsequently refer to.

24 OECD 2009.

25 Observe that French universities receive research funding from the European Commission, but at the end of the first decade of the

twenty-first century these amounts were relatively modest. They account for less that 2 per cent of their total research funding, and less than 4 per cent of their funding from external sources.

26 Senate Committee for the Control of Law Enforcement 2013, 61–3, 66–7.

27 We note that at the end of the nineteenth century two-thirds of university funding was from the government and the other third from external sources, mostly local authorities, see Musselin 2001, 96.

28 *Rapport d'information* No. 532, French Senate, special session of 2008–09. Observe also that many exemptions to these models were requested by, and granted to, the universities. These exemptions had the net effect of further complicating the centralized administration of the funding of the establishments.

29 The 1999 *Loi sur l'innovation et la recherche* (Innovation and Research Act) gives the universities incentives to diversify their funding sources, Musselin 2001, 96–7.

30 Senate Committee for the Control of Law Enforcement 2013, 98–103.

31 At purchasing power parity. Source: OECD 2008; National Accounts, PPP and exchange rate; Education, Students enrolled by type of institution; Education, Expenditure by funding source and transaction type.

32 We underscore that the data we have used for operating expenditures are fully comparable across the university systems studied. They exclude all expenditures on fixed assets, research, and support for students in the form of fellowships or other subsidies.

33 Website of the Ministry of Higher Education and Research 2010.

34 Musselin 2010, 13–18. Note that accreditation to supervise research, which became mandatory for all disciplines at the beginning of the 1980s, is complemented for some of them by a high-level certification (*l'agrégation du supérieur*), for example in law, economics, management, political science, see Musselin 2001, 14 and 19.

35 Musselin 2010, xii–xiv.

36 Ministry of Higher Education and Research 2011.

37 Musselin 2001, 192, 196. Professors may desire to join an institution because its groups and mixed research units are generously supported by CNRS or other public scientific and technological establishments, but often without revealing this to institutions themselves, see Musselin, ibid.

38 Senate Committee for the Control of Law Enforcement, 90.

39 Ibid., 84–5.

40 Ibid., 92–3.

41 On this subject, ibid., 85.

42 Ibid., 110–11.

43 Ibid., 65.

44 Ibid., 16–17.
45 P. Aghion and É. Cohen 2004, 100.
46 Senate Committee for the Control of Law Enforcement 2013, 11.

CHAPTER EIGHT

1 Clark 2004, 178–80; See also from the same author *Places of Inquiry; Research and Advanced Education in Modern Universities*, 1995; "The Entrepreneurial University: New Foundations for Collegiality, Autonomy, and Achievement," 2001; and *Creating Entrepreneurial Universities: Organizational Pathways of Transformation*, 1998.
2 Aghion and Cohen 2007, 2010.
3 In fact, intramural expenditures for R&D in the higher education sector, which includes external funds and the universities' own funds, amounted to US$172 per capita in the United States, US$178 per capita in the United Kingdom, and US$164 per capita in France. Observe, in this latter case, that these intramural expenditures include funds from the mixed research units that are active in French universities. The amounts mentioned are given at current PPP; see OECD *Main Economic Indicators*, 2009.
4 Fixed asset costs should of course belong to the list of funds that universities access through relationships of a market type but that are also mediated by state regulation. We will not dwell on this aspect since it was rarely discussed in our previous analyses.
5 We have already established that intramural resources for university-based research in the United States were US$172 per capita; they were US$274 in Canada. This represents a total of some US$9 billion invested in university-based research in Canada, or one-sixth of the US$54 billion accessible to US universities. Considering the size of the population and the respective economic weight of the two countries, one would expect this level to be closer to one-tenth.
6 B.R. Clark 2004, 83–5.
7 On this subject, see Salmi 2009. http://portal.unesco.org/education/en/files/55825/12017990845Salmi.pdf/Salmi.pdf and Altbach and Salmi 2011.
8 On this subject, see Krücken 2011 and Krücken and F. Meier 2006.
9 B.R. Clark 2004, 179–80; Lindblom 2001.

CHAPTER NINE

1 At the annual meeting of the presidents of the group of nine Chinese research universities held in Hefei, China in October of 2013, representatives from other national groups of research universities – Association of

American Universities, Australian Group of 8, and the League of
European Research Universities – joined with them to sign a statement on
the ten characteristics of a research university. In so doing, the signatories
undertook to comply with these characteristics and ensure that their member institutions do as well, promoting them as a foundational value of any
policy for the delivery of higher education; see Hefei Statement, 2013.
Other national groups of research universities are currently being solicited
to adhere to this manifesto and sign on to it.

2 On this subject, see Altbach and Salmi eds, 2011; Salmi 2009.

3 These levels are from the International Standard Classification of
   Education (ISCED), developed by UNESCO, which the OECD uses to create its international databases on education. The tertiary level comprises
   ISCED 5 A and B. As we have emphasized, tertiary B corresponds to professional education of shorter duration that does not require a bachelor's
   degree. Tertiary A covers education that is longer, amounting to at least a
   bachelor's degree and also including master's and doctoral education.
   Some of the most recent documents occasionally refer to ISCED levels 6,
   7 and even 8. In this later classification, university education that is
   shorter than a bachelor's degree is classified as ISCED 5, bachelor's degree
   is ISCED 6, master's is ISCED 7, and doctoral is ISCED 8.

4 US Department of Education 2006.

5 On this subject, see the Report of the Spellings Commission and data
   from the OECD 2012, 68, 69, 357.

6 See, for example, Barzun 1968; Kerr 1991; Bok 2006.

7 Brint 2009a and 2009b; Brint, Cantwell, and Hanneman 2008.

8 Brint 2009a, 20–1.

9 Geiger 2004, 275.

10 Canadian Association for Graduate Studies–CAGS 2010, 116.

11 Geiger and Heller 2011, 12.

12 Geiger 2004.

13 Ibid.

14 An excellent review of these studies is found in Castro and Poitevin 2013.

15 Bourdabat, Lemieux, and Riddell 2010.

16 We will not delve into the extensive literature on the link between tuition
   rates and access here. This matter is very well addressed by Castro and
   Poitevin 2013, and Lacroix and Trahan 2007, who show that reasonable
   tuition fees and access are not incompatible provided there is an adequate
   system of loans and fellowships.

17 Geiger and Heller 2011, 4.

18 Reich 2004, 3–5.

19 Geiger 2010, 7–8.

20 On this subject, see Schuster and Finkelstein 2006; Schuster 2007; and Center for the Studies in Higher Education 2007.

21 Geiger 2010, 4–5.

22 Thurgood et al. 2006.

23 The National Academies, Committee on Policy Implications of International Graduate Students and Postdoctoral Scholars in the United States 2005, 88.

24 On this subject, see Maheu, Scholtz, Balan, Graybill, and Strugnell 2013.

25 Auriol 2010, 5–6.

26 Auriol, ibid.

27 OECE 2000, 2006, 2008, 2010.

28 For the years 2003 and 2004 only, a drift of nearly 28 per cent in admission demands, of nearly 20 per cent in officially accepted admissions, and of 6 per cent in effective enrolments in US graduate studies from international students has been documented by the Council of Graduate Schools; see Brown 2004; Brown, Doulis 2005.

29 The National Academies, Committee on Policy Implications of International Graduate Students and Postdoctoral Scholars in the United States 2005.

30 Auriol 2010, 6.

31 OECD 2000, 2006, 2008, 2010.

32 OECD 2011: OECD Indicators, Paris, OECD 2011, 322.

33 Advisory Panel on Canada's International Education Strategy 2012, i–xix.

34 OECD 2011: OECD Indicators.

35 Auriol 2010, 18–19.

36 Data from L. Auriol and the Census of Population 2006, OECD, 2007OECD/UIS/Eurostat Data Collection on Careers of Doctorate Holders; see Maheu 2014.

37 Helliwell 2006, 15–20, 26.

REFERENCES

Advisory Panel on Canada's International Education Strategy. 2012. *International Education: A Key Driver of Canada's Future Prosperity.* Ottawa: Foreign Affairs, Trade and Development Canada.

Aghion, P. 2010. "L'excellence universitaire: leçons des expériences internationales, rapport d'étape de la mission Aghion à Mme Valérie Pécresse, ministre de l'enseignement supérieur et de la recherche." 26 January 2010.

Aghion, P., and É. Cohen. 2004. *Éducation et croissance.* Paris: La documentation française.

Aghion P., G. Cette, É. Cohen, and J. Pisani-Ferry. 2007. *Les leviers de la croissance française.* Paris: La documentation française.

Aguillo, I.F., J. Bar-Ilan, M. Levene, and J.L. Ortega. 2010. "Comparing University Rankings." *Scientometrics* 85: 243–56.

Altbach, G., R.O. Berdahl, and P.J. Gumport. 2005. *American Higher Education in the Twenty-First Century: Social, Political, and Economic Challenges,* 2nd ed. Baltimore: Johns Hopkins Press.

Altbach, P.G., and J. Salmi, eds. 2011. *The Road to Academic Excellence: The Making of World-Class Research Universities.* Washington, DC: The International Bank for Reconstruction and Development/The World Bank.

Amaral, A., J.A. Jones, and B. Karseth. 2002. *Governing Higher Education: National Perspective on Institutional Governance.* The Netherlands: Kluwer.

Angawal, P., M. Said, M. Sehoole, M. Sirozi, and H. de Wit. 2007. "The Dynamics of International Student Circulation in a Global Context." In *Higher Education in the New Century: Global Challenges and Innovative Ideas.* Rotterdam: Sense Publishers and Boston College, Center for International Higher Education.

AUCC. *Momentum: The 2008 Report on University Research and Knowledge Mobilization.* Ottawa: Association of Universities and Colleges of Canada.

Auriol, L. 2010. *Careers of Doctorate Holders: Employment and Mobility Patterns.* STI Working Paper. Paris: OECD. http://www.OECD-ilibrary.org/science-and-technology/careers-of-doctorate-holders_5kmh8phxvvf5-en.

Barzun, J. 1968. *The American University: How It Runs, Where It Is Going.* Chicago: Chicago University Press.

Belloc, B. 2012. "Enjeux de l'enseignement supérieur français et mise en perspective internationale." Unpublished. 14 December.

Ben-David, J. 1971. *The Scientist's Role in Society: A Comparative Study.* Englewood Cliffs, NJ: Prentice-Hall.

– 1977. *Centers of Learning: Britain, France, Germany, United States.* New York: McGraw-Hill.

– 1984. *The Scientist's Role in Society. A Comparative Study.* Chicago: University of Chicago Press, reprinted with a new introduction.

Billaut, J.C., D. Bouyssou, and P. Vincke. 2010. "Should You Believe in the Shanghai Ranking? An MCDM View." *Scientometrics* 84: 237–63.

Bok, D. 2006. *Our Underachieving Colleges.* Princeton: Princeton University Press.

Bourdabat, B., T. Lemieux, and W.C. Riddell. 2010. "The Evolution of the Return to Human Capital in Canada, 1980–2005." *Canadian Public Policy* 36 (1): 63–89.

Bowman, N.A. 2010. "Anchoring Effects in World University Ranking: Exploring Biases in Reputation Scores." *Higher Education,* published online: 1 May.

Brint, S. 2009a. *The Academic Devolution? Movements to Reform Teaching and Learning in US Colleges and Universities, 1985–2010.* Center for Studies in Higher Education, Research and Occasional Paper Series: CSHE.12.09. Berkeley: University of California.

– 2009b. "Student Culture in an Age of Mass Consumerist Higher Education." Unpublished paper presented at Teachers College, Columbia University.

Brint, S., A.M. Cantwell, and R.A. Hanneman. 2008. "The Two Cultures of Undergraduate Academic Engagement." *Research in Higher Education* 49 (5) (August): 383–402.

Brown, H. 2004. *Council of Graduate Schools Finds Decline in New International Graduate Student enrollment for the Third Consecutive Year.* Washington: Council of Graduate Schools.

Brown, H. and M. Doulis. 2005. *Findings from 2005 CGS International Graduate Admission Survey I*. Washington: Council of Graduate Schools.

Browne, J. 2010. *Securing a Sustainable Future for Higher Education: An Independent Review of Higher Education Funding and Student Finance*. London: Government of the United Kingdom, Department for Business, Innovation and Skills.

Bruce, T. 2012. *"Universities and Constitutional Change in the UK: The Impact of Devolution on the Higher Education Sector."* Report, Oxford: Higher Education Policy Institute.

Cameron, D.M. 2005. "Collaborative Federalism and Postsecondary Education: Be Careful What You Wish for." In *Higher Education in Canada*, edited by C.M. Beach, R.W. Boadway, and R.M. McInnis. Montreal & Kingston: McGill-Queen's University Press.

Canadian Association for Graduate Studies. 2009. *38th Statistical Report, 1995–2006*. Ottawa: Canadian Association for Graduate Studies.

Canadian Association for Graduate Studies. 2010. *39th Statistical Report, 1999–2008*. Ottawa: Canadian Association for Graduate Studies.

Castro, R., and M. Poitevin. 2013. *Éducation et frais de scolarité*. CIRANO: Bourgogne report, 2013RB-1 February.

The Center for Measuring University Performance. 2008. *Top 200 Institutions: Federal Research 2008*. http://mup.asu.edu/research_data.html.

Center for Studies in Higher Education. 2007. *On the Brink: Assessing the Status of the American Faculty*. Research and Occasional Paper Series: CSHE.3.07, Berkeley: University of California.

Charle, C. 1994. *La République des Universitaires*. Paris: Seuil.

Chester, J., and B. Bekhradnia. 2009. "Oxford and Cambridge – How Different Are They?" Oxford: Higher Education Policy Institute, Report.

Clark, B.R. 1993. *The Research Foundations of Graduate Education: Germany, Britain, France, United States, Japan*. Berkeley and London: University of California Press.

– 1995. *Places of Inquiry; Research and Advanced Education in Modern Universities*. Berkeley: University of California Press.

– 1998. *Creating Entrepreneurial Universities: Organizational Pathways of Transformation*. Oxford: Pergamon/Elsevier Science.

– 2001. "The Entrepreneurial University: New Foundations for Collegiality, Autonomy, and Achievement." *Higher Education Management* 13 (2).

– 2004. *Sustaining Change in Universities; Continuities in Case Studies and Concepts*. Society for Research into Higher Education and Open University Press, Maidenhead, Berkshire: McGraw-Hill Education.

Clark, M. 2002. "Some Guidelines for Academic Quality Rankings."
  Higher Education in Europe 27 (4).

Clark, W. 2006. *Academic Charisma and the Origins of the Research
  University*. Chicago: The University of Chicago Press.

Committee on Higher Education. 1963. *Higher Education: Report of the
  Committee appointed by the Prime Minister under the Chairmanship
  of Lord Robbins 1961–63*, Cmnd. 2154. London: Her Majesty's
  Stationery Office.

CRÉPUQ. 2011. *Un appel à agir pour permettre aux universités de con-
  tribuer pleinement au développement économique, culturel et social du
  Québec*. Quebec City: CRÉPUQ. January.

Dehon, C., A. MecCathie, and V. Virardi. 2009. *Uncovering Excellence in
  Academic Rankings: A Case Study on the Shanghai Ranking*. Brussels:
  ECARES.

Flexner, A. 1967. *Universities: American, English, German*. New York:
  Teachers College Press.

Friedland, M.L. 2002. *The University of Toronto: A History*. Toronto:
  University of Toronto Press.

Geiger, R.L. 1986. *To Advance Knowledge: The Growth of American
  Research Universities, 1900–1940*. New York: Oxford University Press.

– 1992. "Introduction, Section II: The Institutional Fabric of the Higher
  Education System." In *The Encyclopedia of Higher Education*, Vol. 2:
  Analytical Perspectives, edited by B.R. Clark and G. Neave. Oxford:
  Pergamon Press.

– 1993. *Research and Relevant Knowledge; American Research Universities since World War II*. New York, Oxford: Oxford University Press.

– 2004. *Knowledge and Money: Research Universities and the Paradox of
  the Marketplace*. Stanford: Stanford University Press.

– 2010. *Postmortem for the Current Era: Change in American Higher
  Education, 1980–2010*. Working Paper no. 3. Center for the Study of
  Higher Education: Pennsylvania State University.

– 2011. "The Ten Generations of American Higher Education." In
  *American Higher Education in the Twenty-First Century: Social,
  Political and Economic Challenges*, Vol. 3, edited by P.G. Altbach, P.J.
  Gumport, and R.O. Berdahl. Baltimore: Johns Hopkins University Press.

Geiger, R.L., and D.E. Heller. 2011. *Financial Trends in Higher Education:
  The United States*. Working Paper no. 6. Center for the Study of Higher
  Education, Pennsylvania State University.

Gingras, Y. 1991. *Les origines de la recherche scientifique au Canada*.
  Montréal: Boréal.

– 2009. "Le classement de Shanghai n'est pas scientifique." *Recherche,* May 2009, 430.

Goldberger, M.L., B.A. Maher, and P.E. Flattau. 1995. *Research-Doctorate Programs in the United States: Continuity and Change.* Washington: National Academy Press.

Goodall, A.H. 2006. "Should Research Universities Be Led By Top Researchers, and Are They?" *Journal of Documentation* 62 (3).

– 2009a. "Highly Cited Leaders and the Performance of Research Universities." *Research Policy* 38 (7).

– 2009b. *Socrates in the Boardroom: Why Research Universities Should Be Led by Top Scholars.* Princeton: Princeton University Press.

– 2010. "Why Socrates Should Be in the Boardroom in Research Universities." Center for Studies in Higher Education, Research and Occasional Paper Series: CSHE.3.10. Berkeley: University of California Berkeley, 2010.

Graham, H.D., and N. Diamond. 1997. *The Rise of American Research Universities: Elites and Challengers in the Postwar Era.* Baltimore: Johns Hopkins Press.

Green, H., and S. Powell. 2007. "Doctoral Education in the UK." In *The Doctorate Worldwide,* edited by S. Powell and H. Green. The Society for Research into Higher Education and Open University Press. London: McGraw-Hill.

Grewal, R., J.A. Dearden, and G.L. Lilien. 2006. "The University Rankings Game: Modeling the Competition among Universities Ranking." Discussion paper. Smeal College of Business: Pennsylvania State University.

Gumport, P.J. 1993a. "Graduate Education and Organized Research in the United States." In *The Research Foundation of Graduate Education: Germany, Britain, France, United States, Japan,* edited by B.R. Clark. Berkeley: University of California Press.

– 1993b. "Graduate Education and Research Imperatives: Views from American Campuses." In *The Research Foundation of Graduate Education: Germany, Britain, France, United States, Japan,* edited by B.R. Clark. Berkeley: University of California Press.

Harris, R.S. 1976. *A History of Higher Education in Canada 1663–1960.* Toronto: University of Toronto Press.

Hazelkorn, E. 2007. "The Impact of League Tables and Ranking Systems on Higher Education Decision Making." *Higher Education Management and Policy* 19 (2).

– 2009. Rankings and the Battle for World-Class Excellence: Institutional Strategies and Policy Choices. *Higher Education Management and Policy* 2 (1).

HEFCE, Commission of Vice-Chancellors and Principals, Standing Conference of Principals. 1996. *Review of Postgraduate Education* (M. Harris Report). London: HEFCE.

Hefei Statement. 2013. *The Ten Characteristics of Contemporary University Research.* China, Hefei, AAU, C9, GO8, LERU. http://www. leru.org/index.php/public/news/Hefei-Statement/.

Helliwell, J. 2006. *Highly Skilled Workers: Build, Share, or Buy?* Skills Research Initiative, Working Paper 2006 D-13. Ottawa: Government of Canada.

Holmes, R. 2006. "The THES University Rankings: Are They Really World Class?" *Asian Journal of University Education* 2 (1): 1–14.

House, G. 2010. *Postgraduate Education in the UK.* Oxford: Higher Education Policy Institute.

Jencks, C., and D. Riesman. 1968. *The Academic Revolution.* New York: Doubleday and Company.

Jones, L.V., G. Lindzey, and P.E. Goggeshall. 1982. *An Assessment of Research-Doctorate Programs in the United States.* Washington: National Academy Press.

Kerr, C. 1963. *The Uses of the University.* Cambridge, MA: Harvard University Press.

– "The New Race to Be Harvard or Berkeley or Stanford." *Change* 23 (3) (May/June): 8–15.

Krücken, G. 2011. *A European Perspective on New Modes of University Governance and Actorhood.* Center for Studies in Higher Education, Research and Occasional Paper Series: CSHE.17.1. Berkeley: University of California.

Krücken, G., and F. Meier. 2006. "Turning the University into an Organizational Actor." In *Globalization and Organization: World Society and Organizational Change,* edited by G. Drori, H. Hwang, and J. Meyer. Oxford: Oxford University Press.

Lacroix, R., and L. Maheu. 2011. *L'université de calibre mondial: un acteur incontournable des sociétés fondées sur le savoir.* Project report. Montréal: CIRANO, August.

Lacroix, R., and M. Trahan. 2007. *Le Québec et les droits de scolarité universitaire.* Montréal: CIRANO, Rapport Bourgogne 2007RB-01, February.

Lee, H.E. 2008. Ranking of Higher Education Institutions: A Critical Review. *Quality in Higher Education* 14(3): 187–207.

Liard, L. 1894. *L'enseignement supérieur en France, 1789–1893.* Paris: Armand Colin. gallica.bnf.fr.

Lindblom, C.E. 2001. *The Market System: What It Is, How It Works, and What to Make of It.* New Haven: Yale University Press.

Liu, N.C., and Y. Cheng. 2005. The Academic Ranking of World Universities. *Higher Education in Europe* 30 (2):127–36.

Lombardi, J.V., D.D. Craig, E.D. Capaldi, and D. Gater, 2000. *The Top American Research Universities: An Occasional Paper from the Lombardi Program on Measuring University Performance.* Florida: The Center, University of Florida.

Macdonald, J.B., et al. 1969. *The Federal Government and Research Grants in Canadian Universities.* Science Council of Canada.

Maheu, L. 2007. "Doctoral Education in Canada: A Valued National Product Facing the Challenges of Institutional Differentiation." In *The Doctorate Worldwide,* edited by S. Powell, H. Green. McGraw-Hill: The Society for Research into Higher Education and Open University Press.

– 2008. "Doctoral Education and the Workings of Canadian Graduate Schools: A Differentiated Tier Within Canadian Universities Facing the Challenges of Tension-Driven Functions." *Higher Education in Europe* 33 (1): April.

– 2014. "Canadian PhD: Issues of a 'Building' Strategy." Unpublished.

Maheu, L., B. Scholtz, J. Balan, J. Graybill, and R. Strugnell. 2013. "Doctoral Education and Cultural and Economic Prosperity; Nation-Building in the Era of Globalization." In *Preparing PhDs for a Global Future: Forces and Form in Doctoral Education Worldwide,* edited by M. Nerad. The Hague: Sense Publishers.

Marginson, S. 2007. "Global University Rankings: Where to from Here?" Center for the Study of Higher Education. Australia: University of Melbourne.

McDonough, P.M., A.L. Antonio, M. Walpole, and L.X. Perez. 1998. College Rankings: Democratized College Knowledge for Whom? *Research in Higher Education* 39: 513–37.

McGill Reporter Special Issue. 2011. 14 October.

Merisotis, J., and J. Sadlak. 2005. Higher Education Rankings: Evolution, Acceptance, and Dialogue, *Higher Education in Europe* 30 (2): 97–101.

Ministère de l'enseignement supérieur et de la recherche France. 2011. "Comment devient-on enseignant-chercheur?" May.

– 2010. "Les métiers de l'enseignement supérieur et de la recherche."

Mueller, R.E., and D.W. Rockerbie. 2005. "Do the *Maclean's* Rankings Affect University Choice? Evidence for Ontario." In *Higher Education in Canada,* edited by C.M. Beach, R.W. Boadway, and R.M. McInnis. Montreal & Kingston: McGill-Queen's University Press.

Musselin, C. 2001. *La longue marche des universités françaises*. Paris: Presses Universitaires de France.

– 2010. *The Market for Academics*. New York: Routledge.

The National Academies, Committee on Policy Implications of International Graduate Students and Postdoctoral Scholars in the United States. 2005. *Policy Implication of International Graduate Students and Postdoctoral Scholars in the United States*. Washington: The National Academic Press, 88.

National Research Council Committee on Research Universities. 2012. *Research Universities and the Future of America; Ten Breakthrough Actions Vital to our Nation's Prosperity and Security*. Washington: The National Academies Press.

Neave, G. 1985. "France." In *The School and the University: An International Perspective*, edited by B.R. Clark. Berkeley: University of California Press.

OECD. 2009. [Main Indicators of Science and Technology.] *Principaux indicateurs de la science et de la technologie*.

– 2010. *Principaux indicateurs de la science et de la technologie*.

– 2000, 2006, 2008, 2010, 2011, 2012. *Education at a Glance*.

Ostriker, J.P., and C.V. Kuh, eds. 2003. Committee to Examine the Methodology for the Assessment of Research-Doctorate Programs. *Assessing Research-Doctorate Programs; A Methodology Study*. Washington: The National Academies Press.

Ostriker, J.P., P.W. Holland, C.V. Kuh, J.A. Voytuk, eds. 2010. *A Data-Based Assessment of Research-Doctorate Programs in the United States*, Committee to Assess Research-Doctorate Programs, National Research Council, Washington: National Academy Press.

Rauhvargers, A. 2013. *Global University Rankings and their Impact-Report II*. European University Association.

Reich, R. 2004. *The Destruction of Public Higher Education in America, and How the UK Can Avoid the Same Fate*, 2nd Annual HEPI Lecture. Oxford: Higher Education Policy Institute.

Renaut, A. 2002. *Que faire des universités?* Paris: Bayard Éditions.

Roberts, G. 2002. SET *for Success: The Supply of People with Science, Technology, Engineering and Mathematical Skills*. London: Her Majesty's Treasury.

Robitaille, J.-P., and Y. Gingras. 1999. Le niveau de financement de la recherche universitaire au Canada et aux États-Unis: Étude comparative. *Bulletin de l'enseignement supérieur 4 (2)*, April.

Salmi, J. 2009. *The Challenge of Establishing World-Class Universities: Directions in Development.* Washington: World Bank. http://portal. unesco.org/education/en/files/55825/12017990845Salmi.pdf/Salmi.pdf.

Schuster, J.H., and M.J. Finkelstein. 2006. *The American Faculty: The Restructuring of Academic Work and Careers.* Baltimore: Johns Hopkins University Press.

Science, Technology and Innovation Council, Government of Canada. 2009. *State of the Nation 2008: Canada's Science, Technology and Innovation System.* Ottawa: Government of Canada.

Senate Committee for the Control of Law Enforcement. 2013. *Information report on behalf of the senate commission for the enforcement of laws implementing law no. 2007–1199 10 August 2007 relative to the freedoms and responsibilities of universities.* [Commission sénatoriale pour le contrôle de l'application des lois. 2013. *Rapport d'information sur la mise en œuvre de la loi no 2007–1199 du 10 août 2007 relative aux libertés et responsabilités des universités.* Paris: Sénat no. 446.]

Smelser, N.J. 2012. "Dynamics of American Universities." Center for Studies in Higher Education, Research and Occasional Paper Series: CSHE.1.12. Berkeley: University of California.

Steiner, J.E. 2007. "World University Rankings – A Principal Component Analysis," Instituto de Estudos Avançados, Universidade de Sao Paulo.

Thurgood, L., M.J. Golladay, and S.T. Hill. 2006. *U.S. Doctorates in the 20th Century; Special Report.* Arlington: National Science Foundation, Division of Science Resources Statistics.

Touraine, A. 1972. *Université et société aux États-Unis.* Paris: Seuil.

United Kingdom Government, Department for Business, Innovation and Skills. 2010. *One Step Beyond: Making the Most of Postgraduate Education.* BIS Postgraduate Review: Smith Report.

– 2011. *BIS Economics Paper No. 14.*

U.S. Department of Education. 2006. *A Test of Leadership: Charting the Future of U.S. Higher Education.* A Report of the Commission Appointed by Secretary of Education Margaret Spellings.

Van Raan, A.F.J. 2005. "Challenges in the Ranking of Universities." Center for Sciences and Technology Studies: Leiden University.

INDEX

Note: Page numbers in italics refer to tables.

Academic Ranking of World
    Universities (ARWU), 19, 20–2,
    24–7, 33, 34–5, 36. *See also*
    ranking systems
Agence nationale de la recherche
    (ANR; France), 177
Agence pour l'évaluation de la
    recherche et de l'enseignement
    supérieur (AÉRES; France), 190,
    193
Aghion, Philippe, 194, 197, 204,
    239
American Association for the
    Advancement of Science (AAAS),
    119
Association of American
    Universities (AAU), 60, 124,
    255–6n1
Association of Universities and
    Colleges of Canada (AUCC), 127,
    130
Australia, 41, 42, 43, 45–6, 242
Australian universities: develop-
    ment of high-quality institutions,
    216; Group of 8, 255–6n1;
international rankings, 36, 37,
    46; international students, 18,
    241
Austria, 242

Bayh-Dole Act (US, 1981), 57
Belgium, 242
Ben-David, Joseph, 4, 197, 200
Bologna Agreement, 181
Brazil, 18
Brint, Steven, 224, 225
British North America (BNA) Act
    (1867), 122
British universities, 85–117;
    debates on role of, 5; decision-
    making autonomy, 89–90, 94,
    104, 107, 111–13, 115, 117; fac-
    ulty members, 112–13, 186; gov-
    ernance structure, 86, 113–17;
    government funding, 87, 89–90,
    93–6, 100, 103–4; government
    regulation, 92–7, 115, 117, 206–
    7, 207–9, 217; historical devel-
    opment, 86–8, 91; as integrated
    organizational actors, 217; in

international rankings, 36, 37, 44, 45, 85, 97, 196–7; international students, 17–18, 19, 241; intramural funding for research, 99; market influences and relationships, 87, 93–4, 114, 117, 208–9; as national system, 89, 248–9n1; operating funds, 102–5, 107, 182; "post-92," 89, 115; postgraduate education, 105–6, 108–10, 112; private and charitable financing, 87–8, 93–4, 100, 114; "red-brick," 5, 87; Scottish model for, 86, 87, 92; tuition fees, 94, 95, 101, 103, 104; undergraduate education, 86, 87, 88, 94, 103, 106, 208; US influence on, 91–2, 109. See also HEFCE (Higher Education Funding Council for England); Russell Group; United Kingdom

Browne Review (UK, 2010), 89

Bruce, Tony, 114–15

Bush, Vannevar, 53, 82

business. See industry

Cambridge University: in "golden triangle," 102, 111; international students, 18; organizational structure and values, 86–7; sources of income, 103, 249n12; stamp on British society, 86, 249n3; tradition of research, 92

Canada: education levels and payscales in, 221–2, 233; federal support for research, 124, 126, 132–4, 135, 137, 154–5; federal transfer payments for education, 122–3, 150–1, 210; history, 119–20; immigration to, 243–4;

macroeconomic indicators, 42, 46; provincial funding for research, 133–4, 135, 137, 154–5; provincial responsibility for education, 122–3, 137–8, 143, 148, 210; research intensity, 43, 132, 210; university attendance rates, 126–7, 130, 141, 221–2. See also Canadian universities

Canada Foundation for Innovation, 133

Canada Research Chairs, 133, 134–5

Canadian Institutes of Health Research, 132

Canadian universities, 118–57; anglophone vs. francophone, 121, 128, 129, 135–6; competition from US universities, 129, 209–10; decision-making autonomy, 148–9, 152, 210; faculty members, 127, 132, 145–6, 147–8, 149, 150, 186; foreign influences on, 118, 120–1, 128, 144; funding sources, 122–4, 136–40, 150–1, 182; G-10, G-13 and G-15 groupings, 130–1, 252 nn20–2; governance structure, 148–50; government regulation, 206–7, 208, 209–10; graduate education, 124–5, 126–7, 141, 142–3, 144–5, 181, 226; "Group of Six," 131, 136, 140, 141, 144, 146–7; industry funding, 229; as integrated organizational actors, 216; in international rankings, 36, 37, 44, 46, 197; international students, 130, 241–2; intramural funding for research, 132, 255n5; market influences and relationships, 123, 126, 147, 152, 208, 244; as national system, 130, 150–1, 237–9; in Ontario, 151; tuition fees, 123, 139–40, 237, 238; undergraduate education, 120, 130, 141, 146, 151, 222–3; visionary leadership, 119, 152–3. *See also* McGill University; Quebec universities; University of Toronto

Carnegie Foundation, 8–9, 13–14, 60, 220, 245n3(Ch.1). *See also* ranking systems; research universities

Castro, R., 233, 234

Catholic Church, 121

CEGEP (Collèges d'enseignement général et professionnel), 128, 142

The Center for Measuring University Performance (MUP; University of Florida), 14, 59, 247n15

Centre National de la Recherche Scientifique (CNRS; France), 163, 167–8, 176, 177

Charle, C., 160

China, 18

Clark, Burton R.: on British universities, 105, 108, 208; on markets, 217; three-dimensional model, 197–200, 213, 216; on US universities, 225, 247n2

Clark, William, 3

Cohen, É., 194, 239

Cold War, 126

Columbia University in the City of New York, 84

Commission on the Future of Higher Education (US), 221

Commission sénatoriale d'application des lois (France), 176, 192, 194

Conseil national des universités (CNU; France), 184–5

Cornell University, 84

Council of Graduate Schools (US), 257n28

Dalhousie University, 121, 252n21

Dawson, John William, 119–20, 152

DELNI (Department for Employment and Learning of Northern Ireland), 93, 248–9n1, 250n14

Department of Business, Innovation and Skills (UK), 95, 97

Department of Education (US), 79, 221

Department of Education and Science (UK), 90

Doctoral Training Centres (DTCs; UK), 109

Dutch universities, 33

École centrale de Paris (France), 162

École de génie militaire de Mézières (France), 161

École des mines (France), 161, 162

École des ponts et chaussées (France), 161, 162

École nationale d'administration publique (ENAP; France), 167

École normale supérieure (France), 161

École polytechnique (France), 161, 162

Écoles nationales supérieures d'ingénierie (ENSI; France), 162

Education and Academic Life
Council (France), 170, 188, 193
endowment funds: of British universities, 87, 93, 103; of
Canadian universities, 138;
declining, 56; as funding source
for research universities, 201; for
research infrastructure, 133; of
US universities, 56, 63, 67, 70,
249n12; of US vs. British universities, 249n12
English language, 21, 24, 192,
246n1(Ch.3)
établissement public de coopération scientifique (EPCS; France),
170
établissements publics à caractère
scientifique et technologique
(EPST; France), 176, 183
European Commission (EC),
253n25
European Union (EU), 94, 100,
103, 181, 239
European University Association,
192
Evidence Ltd, 22

faculty members: career paths, 77,
223, 235–6; chair system, 4, 52,
133; as civil servants, 184–5,
188; contractual and supplementary, 186, 227; geographical
mobility, 202, 203; hiring processes, 76–7, 82, 111–12, 145,
147, 184–5, 188; and institutional reputation, 13, 77, 188,
202, 203; international, 23, 30,
186; measures and indicators for,
20, 21, 23–4, 28, 29, 30, 78; procurement of research funds, 61,

64, 77, 100, 102, 110–11, 204;
in ranking systems, 77–8; unionization, 147, 149; value placed
on academic freedom, 229–30;
value placed on teaching vs.
research, 225. See also university
presidents; individual university
systems
faculty-to-student ratios: in British
universities, 86, 87, 88, 105, 113;
in Canadian universities, 127;
in French universities, 164; in
rankings, 17, 23, 28; in US universities, 75
Faure Act (France; 1968), 161,
164–5, 168, 170
Federal Pell Grants (US), 70
Fields Medal recipients, 20, 21
France: colonization of Canada,
119; conduct of research in, 163–
4, 167–8, 170, 172, 175–6, 200,
210–11; education levels in, 43;
funding for higher education,
179–80, 182, 211, 254n27; government intervention in education,
90, 210–13; higher education
system, 161–3, 166, 173, 175;
macroeconomic indicators, 41,
42; research intensity, 174, 175,
210, 255n3; Revolution, 159;
university attendance rates, 164,
172–3. See also French universities; Grandes Écoles
French universities, 158–95;
attempts to reform, 160–1,
164–5, 166–71, 192–3; difficulty
obtaining data on, 174, 253n23;
faculty members, 159–60, 184–8,
212, 254n37; fragmentation of,
165–6, 171; governance structure,

165, 189–92, 217; government
funding for research in, 177; government regulation, 168–9, 178–
9, 184–5, 187–8, 192–3, 210–13;
graduate education, 172, 180–1,
183–4, 190–1; and the Grandes
Écoles, 161–2, 166, 169, 170;
history, 159–66; and Imperial
University Faculties, 159, 160–1,
162, 165, 168; inability to follow
German research model, 162–3;
inability to select students, 164,
166, 167; and institutes of
applied science and engineering,
161–2, 166, 170; as integrated
organizational actors, 171–2,
217; in international rankings,
33, 37, 44, 45, 172, 192; international students, 17–18, 19, 241;
intramural funding for research,
176; lack of decision-making
autonomy, 164–5, 168, 169–70,
176–7, 186–7, 188–93, 212; lack
of market influences and relationships, 177, 179–80, 186, 212–13;
operating funds, 177–80, 182,
211, 254n27; and public research
agencies, 163; tuition fees, 167,
179, 180, 183; undergraduate
education, 164, 166, 180, 192,
213; underperformance, 45, 158,
197. See also Grandes Écoles

Further and Higher Education Act
(UK, 1992), 89, 92

Future Investment Program (PIA;
France), 169

Gaudry, Roger, 152

Geiger, Roger L., 61, 70, 197, 226,
229, 232, 235

German universities: in international rankings, 37, 44–5; international students, 17–18, 19,
241; pioneers of research university model, 3–4, 49, 87, 160

Germany: gymnasium system, 52;
macroeconomic indicators, 42;
proportion of tertiary-educated
population, 43; public research
institutes in, 200; research intensity, 43, 44

GI Bill (US; 1944), 69–70

Gingras, Y., 128

Goodall, Amanda H., 80–1,
116–17

governments: attention to rankings,
17, 31–2, 33; funding of higher
education, 198, 201, 233–4;
funding of research universities,
29, 198, 200, 201, 230, 233–4;
funding of university-based
research, 29, 200, 230; regulation of higher education, 198,
199–200, 205–13; role in knowledge economies, 37. See also
under research funding; individual countries

graduate education: and academic
division of labour, 51, 109, 125,
144–5; costs and tuition levels,
68, 69, 94, 104; funding for, 62,
64, 65, 96, 112, 146, 157; international students, 18–19, 202,
241–2, 244; in knowledge-based
economies, 11; mass, 14, 15,
127; rankings, 16, 28; and
research, 49, 54, 82, 164, 183–4,
226; and research universities, 8,
31, 227; social cost-benefit analysis of, 233. See also PhD

degrees; *individual systems of education*

Graduate Record Examinations (GRE), 73–4

Grandes Écoles: characteristics, 167, 172, 173, 182; impact on French universities, 161; international students, 18; and reform attempts, 167; share of research performed in France, 175. *See also* French universities

Green, H., 108

Haldane, Richard Burdon Haldane, Viscount, 91

Harris Review (UK), 108

Harvard University, 18, *84*, 249n12

Haut Conseil de l'évaluation de la recherche et de l'enseignement supérieur (France), 193

Hazelkorn, Ellen, 32

HEFCE (Higher Education Funding Council for England): assessment and funding of research activities, 96–7, 99, 101–2, 110, 208; introduction of "market" principles, 93, 114; reach over rest of United Kingdom, 248–9n1; student quotas, 95–6; subsidization of scientific training, 95; tuition policies, 94, 95, 250n14

HEFCW (Higher Education Funding Council for Wales), 93, 248–9n1, 250n14

Helliwell, J., 243

HESA (Higher Education Statistics Agency; UK), 98, 114

High Council for the Evaluation of Research and Education (France), 193

Higher Education and Research Act (France; 2013), 192

Higher Education Evaluation and Accreditation Council of Taiwan, 245–6n3

humanities. *See* social sciences and humanities

Humboldt, Alexander von, 3, 160

Imperial College of London, 18, 102

Imperial University of France, 159–60, 165

Independent Review of Higher Education Funding and Student Finance (Browne Review, UK, 2010), 89

India, 18, 33

industry: education in service of, 5, 6; funding of research in Canada, *133, 134, 135, 137, 154–5*, 229; funding of research in the UK, 98, 100; funding of research in the US, 55, 56, 61, 62, 63, 67, 229; and the privatization of research, 228–32; in ranking systems, 23, 30

Institut national de la recherche agronomique (INRA; France), 163

Institut national de la recherche scientifique (INRS; Quebec), 128

Institut national de la santé et de la recherche médicale (INSERM; France), 163, 176, 177

International Standard Classification of Education (ISCED), 256n3

international students: at British universities, 94, 208; at Canadian universities, 130,

241–3; global competition for, 17–19, 244; as ranking indicator, 23, 30; tuition fees, 18, 69, 94, 208; at US universities, 69, 240–1, 257n28

Japan, 42, 43–4
Japanese universities, 37, 43–4
Jencks, Christopher, 77, 223, 225, 226
Jiao Tong University, 19, 20
Johns Hopkins University, 49, 78–9, 84, 120–1

Kerr, Clark, 58
knowledge economies: contribution of universities to, 56–7, 58; development, 5–6, 12; and distribution of research universities, 37–8; and human capital, 10–11, 219–20, 244

Land-Grant Colleges and Universities (US), 5–6
Laval, François de, 119
League of European Research Universities, 255–6n1
Leiden World Ranking, 245–6n3
Liard, Louis, 160
liberal arts colleges, 8, 16
Lindblom, C.E., 217
Loi de l'enseignment supérieur et de la recherche (France; 2013), 192
Loi de programme pour la recherche (France; 2006), 170
Loi relative aux libertés et responsabilités des universités (LRU; France; 2007), 169–70, 171, 178, 187, 191, 192

London School of Economics and Political Science, 18, 80, 102, 111
Loudon, James, 152

Macdonald, William Christopher, 120
Macdonald Commission (Canada), 127
McGill University: founding, 119; funding, 120, 121, 135, 154–5; in G-10 grouping, 252n20; international ranking, 131; leadership role, 128–9; PhD programs, 120–1, 124–5
Maclean's university rankings, 130
McMaster University, 131, 135, 146, 154–5, 252n20
Ministère de l'enseignment supérieur et de la recherche (Ministry of Higher Education and Research; France), 172, 177, 187
Ministère de l'instruction publique (National Ministry of Public Instruction; France), 159
MIT (Massachusetts Institute of Technology), 18, 84
Montreal, 119–20, 121
Musselin, C., 159, 160, 161, 165, 168

National Arts Council (Canada), 125
National Center for Science and Engineering Statistics (US), 60
National Centre for Scientific Research (CNRS; France), 163, 167–8, 176, 177
National Council of Universities (CNU, France), 184–5

National Institute of Scientific Research (INRS; Quebec), 128
National Institutes of Health (US), 53, 57
National Research Agency (ANR; France), 177
National Research Council (Canada), 124, 125
National Research Council (US), 240
National Research Council Committee on Research Universities (US), 56, 60, 64, 69, 73, 205, 237
National Science Foundation (NSF; US), 53, 57, 60, 194
national university systems, 10–11, 34, 98, 189, 197–200, 220–1
Natural Sciences and Engineering Research Council of Canada (NSERC), 132
Nature (journal), 20, 21
Neave, G., 166–7
Netherlands, 33
New Zealand, 242
Nobel Prize recipients, 20, 21, 245n1
Northern Ireland, 93, 115, 209, 248–9n1
Northwestern University, 84

OECD member countries: data on education, 174–5, 256n3; international students in, 242; PhDs awarded in, 240–1; spending on education, 103, 240; spending on R&D, 126, 132; university attendance rates in, 221, 222
Office for Fair Access (OFFA; UK), 95

Office national d'études et de recherches aérospatiales (ONERA; France), 163
Ontario, 122, 129, 151
Opération campus (France), 33, 171, 191
Organized Research Units (ORUs), 57, 58
Oxford University: in "golden triangle," 102, 111; international students, 18; organizational structure and values, 86–7; sources of income, 103, 249n12; stamp on British society, 86, 249n3; tradition of research, 92

Paris-Sorbonne University, 18
Patent and Trademark Law Amendment (Bayh-Dole) Act (US, 1981), 57
patents, 56, 57, 226, 228, 229, 231
peer review process, 8, 57, 59, 61, 99–100, 110
PhD degrees: awarded by OECD countries, 240, 241; granted by Canadian universities, 124, 125, 141, 226, 241, 242–3; granted by US universities, 54, 60, 124, 226, 239–40; importance to research universities, 8, 49, 55; job market for, 51; and program size, 73, 78; in ranking systems, 16, 28; and undergraduate teaching, 52. See also graduate education
Piper, Martha, 152
Plan Campus (France), 33, 171, 191
Poitevin, M., 233, 234
pôles de recherche et d'enseignement (PRES; France), 170, 176–7, 191, 193

Powell, S., 108
presidents. *See* university presidents
Prichard, Robert, 152
Princeton University, 18, *84*
privatization of research and higher
    education, 56, 70, 228–32, 235,
    237
Programme des investissements
    d'avenir (PIA; France), 169

Quacquarelli Symonds (QS), 22,
    23, 33, 245–6n3, 246n8
Quality Assurance Agency (QAA;
    UK), 94–5, 109, 114, 209
Quebec universities: anglophone vs.
    francophone, 121, 128; compar-
    ative disadvantage, 122, 144,
    151; decision-making autonomy,
    238–9; education funding struc-
    ture of, 122–3, 139–40, 144,
    238–9; graduate education,
    142–3, 147; operating costs per
    student, *145*; reorganization,
    128; research expenditures, *146*;
    research funding, 136, *137*, 147;
    tuition, 123, 238. *See also*
    McGill University
Queen's University at Kingston,
    121, 252n20

ranking systems: in Canada, 130;
    classifications of institution
    types, 13–14, 16 (*see also*
    Carnegie Foundation); criticisms
    of, 16–17, 20–2, 22–8, 31; fre-
    quency of repetition, 25, 34;
    influence and use, 19, 31–3;
    international, 19, 36–47,
    245n3(Ch.2); in the mass media,
    14–17; measures and indicators,

13, 16, 20, 22, 28–30; origins in
    the United States, 13–14; reputa-
    tional surveys in, 22–3, 27–8, 30,
    34; stability, 24–7, 30, 34; in the
    United Kingdom, 95
Rauhvargers, A., 33
R&D (research and development):
    in Australia, 42, 43; in Canada,
    98, 99, 126, 132, *133*; in France,
    98, 99, 174–5; in Germany, 44;
    intensity by country, 42, 43,
    98–9, 255n3; in Japan, 42, 43; in
    knowledge economies, 6, 37, 56;
    measurement of, 39, 41; in the
    United Kingdom, 98–9; in the
    United States, 15, 54, 55–6, 58,
    99, 126
rectors. *See* university presidents
Renaut, Alain, 163
research: and academic freedom,
    228, 229; dissociation from
    teaching, 163–4; at expense
    of teaching, 223–6, 227; French
    public agencies for, 163–4, 176;
    integration with undergraduate
    and graduate teaching, 3–4,
    49–50, 51–2, 54, 170, 223;
    measures of, 20, 21–2, 24,
    29–30; peer review and, 57;
    private non-profit support for,
    53–4, 55–6; specialized institutes
    for, 4–5; trend towards privatiza-
    tion, 56, 228–32. *See also* R&D
    (research and development);
    research funding
Research Assessment Exercises
    (RAEs; UK), 96, 99, 101–2, 111,
    116, 208, 250 nn15–16
Research Excellence Framework
    (REF; UK), 250n15

research funding: by British government, 91–2, 93, 96–7, 100–2, 109; by British industry, 98, 100; by Canadian government, 125–6, 132–3, 135, 137, 154–5, 230; by Canadian industry, 133, 134, 135, 137, 154–5, 229; by French government, 174–5, 177; intramural, 55, 58, 99, 132, 176, 255n5; per professor and graduate student, 64, 112, 146; private non-profit, 53–4, 55–6; by US government, 53, 61, 62, 63, 65, 230; by US industry, 55, 56, 61, 62, 63, 229

Research Indirect Costs Program (Canada), 133, 134

Research Planning Act (France; 2006), 170

research universities: challenges, 220–34; Clark's model for understanding, 197–200, 213, 216; definitions and characteristics, 7–9, 220; and demographic factors, 38–9; funding sources, 201–2; government regulation, 198–200, 210–13; with institutional self-governance, 200–5, 214; as integrated organizational actors, 213–18; macro-economic model of international distribution, 36–47, 196; market influences and relationships, 202–10; as part of national systems, 10, 220–3; reputation, 9, 18–19, 104, 203, 214; social benefits, 198–99, 201; structural accretion process, 58, 227

Riesman, D., 77, 223, 225, 226

Robbins Report (Committee on Higher Education, UK, 1963), 89

Royal Commission on the Economic Union and Development Prospects for Canada, 127

Russell Group: endowment funds, 249n12; operating funds, 101; research funds awarded to, 97–8, 100, 102, 111; research spending, 112; student distribution, 106, 107, 108; tuition levels, 250n14

SANREMO model (France), 178

Savary Act (France; 1984), 165, 168, 170

Science (journal), 20, 21

Scientific Council (France), 170, 188, 193

scientific disciplines: biotechnology and biomedical, 56, 57, 64, 134, 229; chair system and, 4, 52; and commercial potential, 228–9; growth of experimental research in, 3–4; importance of English in, 21, 24, 246n1(Ch.3); patents and, 56; and peer review, 57–8; role in economy, 6; UK research councils for, 91–2; in US universities, 50

SCImago Research Group, 245–6n3

Scotland, 86, 93, 115, 209, 248–9n1

Séminaire de Québec, 119

Senate Committee for the Control of Law Enforcement (France), 176, 192, 194

Servicemen's Readjustment Act (GI Bill; US, 1944), 69–70

SFC (Scottish Funding Council), 93, 248–9n1, 250n14

Smelser, N.L., 58, 227
social sciences and humanities:
Canadian funding for, 125;
exclusion from privatization of
research funding trends, 228–9,
231; exclusion from student subsidies in UK, 95; in ranking systems, 20, 21, 24; research council
in UK for, 91
Social Sciences and Humanities
Research Council of Canada
(SSHRC), 132
Sorbonne University, 18
Soviet Union, 17, 54, 126
Spellings Commission (US), 221
Stanford University, 18, 84
Steiner, J.E., 23
Strangway, David, 152
students: admission to US graduate
schools, 73–5; benefits of higher
education to, 39, 233; distribution at British universities, 106–8,
208; distribution at Canadian
universities, 141–3; distribution
at French universities, 180–1; in
early research universities, 3–4;
geographical mobility, 202, 203,
241; government policy and,
69–70, 208; and institutional
reputation, 74, 143–4, 182, 202,
203; and labour market, 224–5;
loans and debts, 70, 94, 237;
opportunity costs to, 233; at private vs. public US universities,
71–3, 75; in ranking systems, 16,
23–4; research funds for, 64, 65;
selection and recruitment, 82,
107–8, 110, 143–4, 166, 206,
213; unionization, 149; as university senate members, 150; use of

rankings, 19, 31. See also international students; tuition fees
student–teacher ratios. See faculty-
to-student ratios
Sweden, 242
Switzerland, 242
SYMPA model (France), 178–9

teacher–student ratios. See faculty-
to-student ratios
Thomson Reuters, 29–30
Thomson Scientific, 20, 21
Thurgood, L., 60
The Times (newspaper), 19, 27–8,
29, 30
Times Higher Education
Supplement (THES) ranking, 19,
22–31, 33, 34–5, 36. See also
ranking systems
Toronto, 120, 251n2
tuition fees: at British universities,
94, 95, 101, 103, 104; at
Canadian universities, 123, 139–
40, 237, 238; at French universities, 179, 180, 183; as funding
source, 201, 232–4; government
regulation, 206; for international
students, 18, 69, 94, 208; at private US universities, 66, 67–8, 70,
210, 234, 248n23; at public US
universities, 66, 69, 234, 248n28;
and social inequality, 235

undergraduate education: in academic division of labour, 51, 75,
144, 215; costs and tuition levels,
65, 68, 69, 94; mass enrolments,
18, 164; measures and indicators, 28; and research, 52, 224,
225, 227; in university systems'

development, 220–3. *See also under individual university systems*

UNESCO, 256n3

United Kingdom: devolution, 92–3, 95, 97, 114–15, 250n14; investment in higher education, 102–3; macroeconomic indicators, 42; research councils, 91–2, 93, 99–100, 101–2; research intensity, 43, 98–9, 255n3; university attendance rates, 88–9, 103, 105–7; university funding councils, 93. *See also* British universities

United States: federal government, 5, 16, 53, 61, 69–70; geographical mobility in, 15; graduation rates, 221; knowledge-based economy, 5, 6, 15, 56, 58, 60; macroeconomic indicators, 42, 48; Obama administration, 221; population, 41, 48; R&D spending in, 54, 55, 255n3; social inequality in, 236; state governments, 61, 66, 68, 74, 80, 206, 207; university attendance rates, 52, 221, 236; War of Independence, 119. *See also* US universities

unités de formation et de recherche (UFR; France), 165

unités d'enseignement et de recherche (UERs; France), 165

Université de France, 159–60, 165

Université de Grenoble, 159

Université de Montpellier, 159

Université de Montréal, 121, 128, 131, 152, 154–5, 252n20

Université de Toulouse, 159

Université Laval, 121, 128, 252n20

Universités du Québec, 128

Universities Funding Council (UFC; UK), 90–1, 93

University and College Employers Association (UCEA; UK), 112

University and Colleges Admissions Service (UCAS; UK), 95–6, 114

University and College Union (UCU; UK), 112

University College of London, 102, 111

University Grants Commission of India, 33

University Grants Committee (UGC; UK), 89–90

University of Alberta, 131, 135, 154–5, 252n20

University of British Columbia (UBC), 131, 152, 154–5, 252n20

University of Calgary, 252n21

University of California, 58

University of Chicago, 18, 84

University of Durham, 86

University of East Anglia, 89

University of Essex, 89

University of Florida, 14

University of London, 86

University of Manitoba, 252n22

University of Ottawa, 252n21

University of Pennsylvania, 84

University of Saskatchewan, 252n22

University of Southern California, 84

University of Sussex, 89

University of Toronto: foreign influences, 128; founding, 119; funding, 134, 135, 136, 140, 146, 154–5; in G-10 grouping, 252n20; international ranking,

131; leadership role, 129; PhD
programs, 120–1, 124–5; size of
student population, 141–2;
visionary leadership, 152
University of Waterloo, 252n20
University of Western Ontario, 242,
252n20
university presidents: in Canada,
119–20, 152–3; in France, 152–
3, 168–9, 170, 187, 188–90,
191–2; role in creating leading
institutions, 216; in the United
Kingdom, 116–17; in the United
States, 80–1
U.S. News and World Report,
15–16, 246n8
US universities, 48–84; decision-
making autonomy, 65, 70, 76–7,
80; division into two segments,
235–6; dominance of international rankings, 36–7, 59, 196;
faculty members, 61, 62–3, 75,
76–8, 82, 186, 204, 223–4;
German influence on, 49; governance structure, 50–2, 57, 58, 75,
78–81, 205; government regulation, 80, 206–7, 221, 237; graduate education, 51, 62, 64, 65, 70,
71–6, 82; impact of financial crisis on, 56, 65, 68–9, 207; institution types, 8, 16; as integrated

organizational actors, 207, 237;
international students, 17–18,
19, 240–1; intramural funding
for research, 55, 58, 255n5; market influences and relationships,
204–5, 224; military research,
53, 126; as national system, 9,
60, 64, 220–1, 234–7; operating
costs and funds, 64–70, 84, 182;
ownership of patents, 57, 229;
private vs. public, 61–4, 65,
66–7, 71–3, 80, 82, 204–5, 207;
research-intensive, 5, 7–8, 9;
trend towards privatization, 70,
229, 235; tuition fees, 66, 67–8,
69, 70, 210, 234, 248 nn23, 28;
undergraduate education, 8, 10,
16, 51, 52, 68, 73, 221

vice-chancellors. See university
presidents
Victoria, Queen of Great Britain, 121

Wales, 93, 115, 209, 248–9n1
Web of Science Database, 29–30
Webometrics Ranking of World
Universities, 245–6n3

Yale University, 18, 84, 249n12
York University (UK), 89